AMERICAN
BANDWIDTH

WEBLOGS AND ESSAYS

MICHAEL E. ROSS

authorHOUSE®

AuthorHouse™
1663 Liberty Drive, Suite 200
Bloomington, IN 47403
www.authorhouse.com
Phone: 1-800-839-8640

First published by AuthorHouse 10/13/2009

ISBN: 978-1-4490-1898-6 (e)
ISBN: 978-1-4490-1899-3 (sc)

Library of Congress Control Number: 2009909859

Printed in the United States of America
Bloomington, Indiana

This book is printed on acid-free paper.

Flagpole Days, a novel

Interesting Times: Essays and Nonfiction

Available through authorhouse.com

TABLE OF CONTENTS

FOR ISHMAEL REED

thinking outside the box
boxing outside the ring

VICTORY OF THE RAPTORS

HAVING done all he could do to moderate the doctrinaire raptors and neocon pterodactyls that have haunted and circled his office for four years, Colin Powell has had enough. Today, Powell, in his customarily succinct, direct and professional style, announced his resignation as Secretary of State, arguably the best since George Marshall. That Powell could submerge for nearly four years his own gut centrist-humanist instincts, to the betterment of a foreign policy devised and practiced by the most ideologically animated president of our time, speaks volumes about the nobility and tragedy that loyalty engenders.

Colin Powell's departure is maybe the clearest, most dramatic indication that the generals have won, at least in the short term, on matters concerning the Iraq war; the pterodactyls are morphing into hawks, and from there into fighters and Hueys destined for either Iraq or Afghanistan. Condoleezza Rice, the hawk perched permanently, it seems, on George Bush's shoulder in his public appearances, is in line to succeed Powell as Secretary of State.

The confirmation hearings are a done deal — bet that. Rice, along with Donald Rumsfeld, Paul Wolfowitz, John Bolton and Douglas Feith, are the architects of the unilateral-action imperative whose primacy at the White House has just been assured.

This would not seem to be a good time to buy real estate in Tehran.

◊ ◊ ◊

Powell's exit is one of several at the White House; previously John Ashcroft and Don Evans made their departures known, and others leaving include Energy Secretary Spencer Abrahams, Agriculture Secretary Ann Veneman, and Education Secretary Rod Paige, who, of the three, was something of an embarrassment to the administration. This happens all the time in the second term of an administration, the literal housecleaning that, we're led to believe, points to

1

fresh thinking for the next four years. But you think about the ideological promises made before the election, and you wonder how many of the new occupants of these musical chairs will be bound up more by partisan inclinations than by their basic competence for the job? Will Ashcroft's replacement be more insensitive to civil liberties than he's been?

And then there is the X factor, the element that squares the equation — the likely, almost certain, imminent retirements from the Supreme Court. William Rehnquist and, possibly, Sandra Day O'Connor, are probable departures, one surely by the recess in June, the other before that first week in October. And Bush's nominee, just as sure as Condi to be confirmed, will complete the payback to the most conservative elements of the Republican Party.

One nominee at a time, George Bush is serving notice that, mostly, the second verse will be the same as the first. In the process of literally rebuilding itself, the administration is reflecting a paradox of modern American government: stasis within change, immobility within transition. Them changes at the top may be no changes at all. And for a president seemingly at odds with the world — and a world at war, at that — no change isn't progress, or even stability. No change is falling behind.

11/16/2004

FALLUJAH

THE battle for Fallujah, long awaited, long dreaded, is underway. U.S. and coalition forces are engaged in a street-by-street, block-by-block ballistic canvass of the holy city of Iraq. The casualties for Americans are mounting; estimates from the U.S. military say 10 Americans were killed Tuesday, the worst single day for American forces in the country in about six months.

What, of course, emerges from the American military spokesman is the boilerplate retreat to the powers of the American armed forces and our resolve to see it through. More than one news report of the day crows that U.S. forces have contained "70 per cent" of Fallujah. Implicit in the statistic is the John Wayne aspect of American might. It suggests a redux of the annihilation of the first Gulf War, an easy dispatch of an enemy whose challenge was the mother of all follies.

But it may be, and probably is, a deception. You can't escape the unsettling fact that the long interregnum between announcement and action has put a lot of people in motion. For weeks the coalition and the interim Prime Minister Ayad Allawi had issued ominous warnings about the then-impending attack. Every day, it seems, there was talk of Allawi losing his patience, threats of the closing of the window of opportunity. And in that time, mercifully, many of the ordinary people of Fallujah got the hell out. But not so mercifully, so did many of the insurgents that American forces are pouring into Fallujah just dying to find in the first place.

The problem with being the world's sole military leviathan is mainly an inability to conceal your intentions. When you're that big, you're not real subtle. You can't be. You are subject to your own mass and power; you can't get out of your own way. So your enemy knows what to do to avoid you, and when to do it. That begins to explain the relative ease with which the U.S.-led coalition has taken so much of the city. Analysts have begun to offer dire scenarios, perfectly plausible, of how the bulk of the insurgents had already made good their escape days, if not weeks, before the United States forces got there. It would be, the reasoning goes, like trying to contain a blob of mercury in a bathroom sink basin on a moving train.

This should be no surprise when you engage in the second longest telegraphed punch in the history of American warfare — the first being the eternity of time between the "axis of evil" State of the Union and the beginning of the shock & awe days. If we'd given the Nazis this much advance warning before the D-Day invasion, we'd never have gotten ashore, or if or when we did, the cost, already horrific, would have increased by orders of magnitude.

That 70 percent containment in Fallujah could be 90 percent by the weekend. The unaddressed question, or at least the underaddressed question, is a good one: Where have all the insurgents gone?

To Samarra, maybe, or Mosul, or Baiji, the site of a major refinery. There's been new violence in all of them, and others, in recent days.

11/11/2004

NEW BOSS, SAME AS THE OLD

IN the Nov. 15 issue of Newsweek, in an essay hopefully titled "A President Who Listens," columnist Anna Quindlen lays out the case for President Bush to make changes in his second term -- mainly, to work hard to be a conciliatory figure, someone who, having achieved the Holy Grail of presidential politics (a second term and a like-minded Congress), might now be inclined to work hard at binding up the nation's wounds, closing the bicolor divide that defines these United States today.

All props to Quindlen (a former denizen of The New York Times who, like your humble narrator, moved on to something better), but even a casual reading of the Bush mindset, and particularly the Bush zeitgeist, will point to how unlikely that sea change is.

"Bush rarely strayed from the reservation of in-house affirmation or cheering crowds," Quindlen writes. "He made up his mind and it stayed made. There was thus no premium and no point in listening to those who had other points of view. ... A second term is terrifying to his opponents, who believe he will use the freedom of incumbency to do everything from loading the [Supreme] court to reinstating the draft ... He could consider how bitter the division in this country are and vow to try to mend them. Lest this sound too altruistic, he might also remember that being a two-term president who leaves behind a nation in which half its citizens can barely tolerate the other half is a surefire way to leave a legacy of colossal failure."

◊ ◊ ◊

Quindlen's noble, hopeful viewpoint, however, runs up against the political realities of the moment. The most pressing of those realities is the national state of war. We're a country at war right now, for better or worse, and that fact alone has been at the root of the Bush administration world-view. Since so much of the Bush world-view stems from that easy, comfortable us-against-them polarity, the available evidence suggests that it's likely to be a waste of time waiting and hoping for any fraction of a wholesale repudiation of his previous identity.

All year long George Bush campaigned with a pit-bull zeal against his immediate opponent, Massachusetts Sen. John Kerry. But in the wider sense Bush was campaigning against a stronger, more problematic opponent. Bush was campaigning against change, against deviating from the course he set this nation on in the wake of the Sept. 11 terrorist attacks. His intransigence, his unwillingness to shift from that course in the slightest, has come to be seen as a strength – maybe the only strength he could most effectively bring to bear against opponents foreign and domestic.

Change is contrary to his world-view, his and that of the proxies and handlers he works with. For George Bush to perform an about-face, for him to morph into Ted Kennedy and make sweeping changes in his policies and initiatives at this point would be to contradict much, if not everything, he stood for throughout his first term. It would amount to an admission of failure -- an admission that, considering his narrow but decisive-enough victory at the polls Nov. 2, would be not only a political blunder but also a repudiation of the 59 million red-state voters who put him over the top.

There's probably no better, more convincing proof of Bush's intention to stay the course than Condoleezza Rice, now the National Security Adviser and soon to be Secretary of State. Rice has always been one of the administration's most resolute hawks, and from her new perch she'll be in an even more solid position to impose her policies and her will on an administration already in lockstep with her thinking.

◊ ◊ ◊

George Bush won't make any wholesale changes in his approach to governing for two more fundamental reasons. First, such changes are beyond his capability. As Quindlen said, we've known since 2000 that Bush set great score by the idea of having an idea and sticking with it, no matter what. Despite his reputation as a Texas governor who was willing to reach across the statehouse aisle to achieve some degree of bipartisan consensus, George Bush as president has consistently defended his own personal focus on a national objective, and how best to achieve it.

That focus was reflected in his steadfast resistance to the Kyoto Accords, his antipathy to the United States being subject to rulings from the International Court in The Hague, his ringing rebuff of the Anti-Ballistic Missile Treaty. Any hope of him offering an olive branch to his opponents here and abroad, of rejecting his own still-emerging conservative stance and becoming the Kum Ba Yah president, went out the window on Sept. 11, 2001. In those terrible moments, George Bush's constitutional conviction of a binary, dualistic, us-vs.-them sense of the world, maybe to that point still subject to persuasion, was vindicated, confirmed and hardened forever. It was ratified again on Nov. 2, 2004.

Why should he throw over such proof of his rightness, his certainty, even if he could?

The second reason, stemming in some ways from the first, is more frightening. George Bush doesn't really care. He stormed back into power on Election Day having made pledges to a base of supporters, and he intends to honor those pledges, and by extension his own sense of mission, no matter what. Opponents be damned. The act of listening presumes that one cares about what somebody else has to say; the Bush doctrine has convincingly shown that is not the case. With no further political horizons to survey, why on earth would he even care about changing now? George Bush can't *see* the divisive course he's set this nation on. With such short-sightedness as a big component of his own identity, there's no real hope of any centrist transformation when this administration has made so many formidable gains by appealing to the starker, grimmer, more ideologically animated aspects of the national identity.

◊ ◊ ◊

Like me, Anna Quindlen is of the era of the baby boomers, those Americans born between 1946 and 1964, that demographic for whom rock & roll was not just diversion but cultural signpost. Quindlen no doubt remembers that Who classic "Won't Get

Fooled Again" -- maybe she (like all of us) copped a buzz in a long-ago dormitory room, shouting the song's signature phrase. *Meet the new boss ... same as the old boss!*"

Pete Townshend was a more astute political thinker than he knew when he wrote it. That phrase expresses what we're likely left with in these edgy days: a president who, emboldened by a political victory narrower than a mandate but broader than a photo finish, will stick to his guns.

"America has spoken ... I gained political capital," he said after the election, "and I intend to spend it." We face a greater danger than before, if that's possible: a president of the United States with nothing to lose.

11/28/2004

THE WAY WE SAY WE LIVE NOW

IN 1999 Jack Nicholson dropped trou. The Oscar-winning actor (who said in "Chinatown" that "I'm not supposed to be the one who's caught with his pants down") mooned the crowd at the Golden Globes Awards ceremony, receiving applause and gales of riotous laughter from the assembled guests, and no punishment whatsoever. In 2005 Minnesota Vikings wide receiver Randy Moss *pretended* to moon the crowd at a pro football game; the National Football League fined him $10,000.

Those two very different reactions to two not dissimilar events underscore the depth of the nation's cultural divide — one recently characterized with color-coding — and an unease in the national mood. There's a disconnect somewhere.

The election in November revealed some of the country's enduring ambivalence; the colors red and blue have come to be a shorthand, a kind of code for differing values and passions.

But that divide's also reflected in a seeming disconnect between outrage and actions — the things Americans say they're angered by and the ways Americans indicate that anger, or fail to for very long. The reactions also show how popular culture, sports and other outlets of the national economy thrive on that outrage, even depend on it for their survival.

Football officials, talk-radio commentators and a range of other Americans, were incensed at an ABC promotional spot aired during the Nov. 15 broadcast of ABC's "Monday Night Football." The promo featured Philadelphia Eagles wide receiver Terrell Owens in a steamy faux locker-room encounter with actress Nicollette Sheridan, a star of ABC's "Desperate Housewives."

Despite the outrage after the incident, or maybe because of it, "Desperate Housewives" continues to enjoy ratings success; the show is regularly one of the top three shows on network TV. Lately it's been the second-most popular show behind "CSI: Crime Scene Investigation," a bonanza for CBS. Since the Monday Night debacle, "Housewives" went on to win two Golden Globe awards, including one for best comedy.

God knows it's not just TV. The popularity of fast foods like Hardee's Monster Thickburger (1,420 calories, 107 grams of fat), has flourished despite prevailing concerns about health and diet, and the outrage of doctors and nutritionists.

The Center for Science in the Public Interest, a Washington-based nutrition and health advocacy organization, has called the Monster "the fast-food equivalent of a snuff film."

That hasn't financially hurt the company; the Monster is part of a high-calorie line of burgers Hardee's introduced in April 2003. Since then, chairman Andy Puzder told the Associated Press, sales for the restaurant chain have risen steadily.

Poker's rising popularity on cable television programs — shows that feature celebrities playing the game for lucrative stakes — is at odds with the parents, educators and state officials opposed to poker playing among high school students.

The clamor for change in professional sports — in the wake of a widening steroid scandal in baseball and the fallout from the Nov. 19 brawl between basketball fans and players for two NBA teams — hasn't yet had a material bottom-line effect on the national obsession with athletes and athletics.

Despite a history of fighting that goes back years, for example, the NBA started the 2004-05 season with strong fan attendance: Seventeen sold-out home-opening games — a record — brought fan attendance to 95 percent capacity for the first week of the season, the AP reported in November.

The record eclipsed the previous sold-out home opener mark of 15, set during the 1997-98 season, The AP reported. The league is on a pace to meet or exceed last season's attendance level of 20.28 million fans, despite the millionaires' brawl on Nov. 19.

◊ ◊ ◊

These dovetailing contradictions point to attitudes at war: America's storied live-and-let-live ethos doing battle with the equally powerful forces of rectitude and social conventions.

For some of those who run afoul of those conventions, the way back to mainstream respectability is all too clear. Reliably, consistently, the path to good graces runs through television. Just ask Pee-wee Herman (Paul Reubens). Or Hugh Grant.

Or Janet Jackson. Maybe nothing illustrates the split between outrage and action like the controversy around her "wardrobe malfunction" at the 2004 Super Bowl.

Jackson bared her right breast for all of five seconds in an animated dance number with the singer Justin Timberlake.

There was a brief but intense backlash in the ensuing weeks and months: Jackson was dropped from some high-visibility projects, endured the scorn of pundits and op-ed writers; and became a target of opportunity for late-night TV. Bad Janet.

Then came the rebound: Jackson took the obligatory All Apologies Tour of some of the same TV talk shows that skewered her. She made an appearance on CBS's "Late Show With David Letterman" and had a guest-host spot on NBC's "Saturday Night Live" — two of the more reliable stops for a major star on the road to much-needed rehabilitation.

"Damita Jo," the Janet Jackson album released just months after the Super Bowl flap, sold more than 3 million copies — a sales figure that's disappointing only when compared to her previous record sales — and the singer got two Grammy Award nominations in December.Feast your eyes on Janet Reborn.

Or consider Martha Stewart, the domestic diva now serving a five-month jail sentence in West Virginia for lying about a stock sale, is set to resume her high-profile life with a one-hour, daily syndicated TV show to be broadcast on NBC starting in the fall. Stewart's resurrection in the public eye started before she's even got out of jail.

◊ ◊ ◊

Gil Reavill, author of "Smut," a book on the growing hypersexualization of popular culture, finds the nation's hot-then-cold reactions to the objects of its ridicule aremostly a matter of an ever-shorter, ever-challenged attention span.

"We're so inured to the constant drumbeat of 'new story, new story, new story' that there's not many stories that hold our attention for that long," Reavill said."It's the nature of the human beast. You lose interest; the novelty of something wears off. It's a tireless search for novelty."

For Robert J. Thompson, director of the Center for the Study of Popular Television at Syracuse University, the seemingly-modern split between what Americans do and what Americans profess has a broader role in history:

"At Plymouth plantation, you had the pilgrims who came here to pursue a religiously-based life with strict parameters," Thompson said. "But if you look at court cases, a lot of those people didn't always adhere to those standards."

"We enjoy the feel of moral outrage at the same time we're guilty of the things we claim to be outraged about. TV is something you consume in the privacy of your home. A lot of people who are outraged are also consuming a lot of the programming they're outraged about," he said.

"In some cases, what's happening is the moral-outrage books have been cooked in a number of ways," Thompson said. "Of course, moral values are important. But Americans have their sanctimonious attitudes on an a la carte basis.

This is both the country that's most obsessed by sex and the country that's most embarrassed by sex. Put those together and you've got a recipe for exactly the situation we have now."

For Thompson, television is symbolic of a wider division. "In some things it's fairly easy to draw the battle lines; the usual suspects line up in the usual places," he said. "TV is obvious because it's everywhere. But in other ways — with high school football in Texas, for example, where the very people arguing against the blasphemy of American media, with its violent images, argue that the sanctity of American football should be preserved in all its glory — it's clear no one set of philosophical principles are applied across the board.

"America's history is one big makeover show," Thompson said. "We've always been a nation that seems perfectly comfortable with contradictions. The ability to navigate those contradictions with a straight face is characteristic of the American identity."

3/7/2005

FEAR AND LOATHING
IN THE NEXT WORLD

HUNTER Stockton Thompson, the kinghell political and cultural journalist who truly stomped terra in a savage career of more than forty years, committed suicide Sunday night at his compound in Aspen. Get your mind around that, folks, and if you haven't bid the 1960's, and its redolent, requisite ambience of personal freedom and out-of-hand laissez-faire goodbye before now, give it a serious sendoff.

Hunter Thompson may have been the last of the true wild men of the modern word, our pharma Hemingway, a writer of wild and outlandish gifts and singular proclivities, part Teddy White and part Charles Bukowski. As it is with all poets, we did not have him for that long -- not in a condition to be at his best, anyway -- but were lucky to have had him at all.

The Associated Press reports that one of Thompson's closest friends said Thompson was in considerable pain after a broken leg and hip surgery. The specifics of the situation aren't really spelled out in news stories yet, though they will iron it all out.

But based what the stories are saying, it's hard to believe that Dr. Thompson, a warrior of the recreational pharmacopeia if there ever was one, couldn't summon whatever was needed to quell the pain from a broken leg. Hell, half the shit he and his attorney had stashed in the trunk of the Red Shark would have numbed that agony down to nothing! In a hurry! *Cazart!*

We will never know the depth of that pain, or the pain that drove him to put a gun to his head and pull the trigger, and how much of it was physical and how much was something else entirely. All we can do is revel in the work.

And the mystique behind the work. A personal recall: I saw Dr. Thompson speak at Denver University in January 1977. I was a green as grass reporter for the Colorado Daily, then the student newspaper at the University of Colorado. I came up with the assignment a few years after reading "Fear and Loathing in Las Vegas," and less than six months after hitchhiking across half the country, from Boulder, Colorado to Los Angeles to San Francisco and back to Boulder, a journey that was my own feverish and inebriate salute to the American Bicentennial in general, and to the vagabond lives of the good doctor and his nominal attorney in particular.

HST arrived at Boettcher Auditorium in his fashion: striped polo shirt, jeans and the trademark cigarette holder clenched in his teeth, on one shoulder was mounted the equally trademark ice chest bearing the doc's chosen recreational defibrillator of the moment, a bottle of Wild Turkey, along with ice and a plastic cup of the convenience-store variety (what I think they call "go cups" in the South).

In the course of discussing a variety of topical events, and answering questions from the audience, Thompson said something that went over people's heads back then, but which now resonates as people try to sort out his reasons for suicide. Looking back on his own life, Thompson observed that night in 1977 that "I didn't expect to live to be 20. I didn't expect to live to be 30. I didn't expect to be 40. I'm 44 now. If this keeps up, I may take matters into my own hands."

Thus, a seemingly suddenly irrational act has a genesis that reaches back decades. Dr. Thompson's bootheels are wandering in some alternate universe, the good doctor now free to put said bootheels in Richard Nixon's ass around the cosmos til the end of time. We're left here in this world, wounded by the loss of a wild and volatile talent, awash in fear & loathing, which is to say, a little more today than usual. Bad craziness.

2/21/2005

'ST. LUKE, REPORT
TO THE NEWSROOM'

FOR a journalist of any standing in the profession, for a wordsmith with at least a shred of self-respect for what he or she does for a living, the results of a recent poll of the American public has to be dispiriting news.

According to the poll by the Annenberg Public Policy Center, Americans make no distinctions, or only the slightest distinctions, between Bob Woodward, mainstay of The Washington Post and one of the reporters whose work during the Watergate scandal helped dismantle the Nixon presidency, and commentator Bill O'Reilly, the Fox News pit-bull apologist for the conservative right running roughshod over America.

Some 40 percent of the 1,500 adults who responded to the poll taken in the spring said they thought O'Reilly was a journalist, while 30 percent said Woodward was one, and (it gets worse) 27 percent said talk show host Rush Limbaugh was a journalist. One in five said they considered newspaper columnist George Will to be a journalist.

Displaying a withering grasp of the obvious, Kathleen Hall Jamieson, director of the policy center, told The Associated Press that the results of the poll suggest the public defines the word "journalist" far differently than those in the press define it. And not surprisingly, O'Reilly leaped into the fray saying that the poll indicated the dawn of a new day in American media, and proclaiming the end of the traditional sources of power and influence in the media (also perfectly obvious to anyone who's watched the network newscasts of the Three Wise Men over the last six months).

Not that we needed another poll to tell us, but the Annenberg survey confirms what we've known for awhile: These are grim times for journalism in America. Setting aside the impact of such confidence destroyers as Jayson Blair, Jack Kelley and other fabulists masquerading as journalists, the press' complicity in reporting the war effort from an administration perspective while insisting it remains independent, skeptical and disinterested has led to the worst kind of disconnect: the press unplugged from the people the press purports to represent.

◊ ◊ ◊

The gravity of the situation was distilled last month with Newsweek's clumsy mea culpa over Iraq-war related reporting in its Periscope section. And an earlier State of the News Media poll, released late in 2004 by the Pew Research Center for the People and the Press, revealed that public perception of the press and the way it performs its mission had fallen to the point where Americans regarded the press as a motley collective of reactionary, self-protective liars and prevaricators one notch above child molesters (an exaggeration, but not by that much).

Between 1985 and 2002, the Pew poll found, the number who thought news organizations were moral fell from 54 percent to 39 percent. Those who felt news organizations tried to conceal their mistakes rose from 13 percent to 67 percent. And the number of Americans who thought news organizations were highly professional declined from 72 percent to 49 percent.

Americans, Pew found, "increasingly think the press as a whole is motivated by money and individual journalists by personal ambition."

How did it get this bad? Can this marriage be saved? The answer is yes, of course; as Watergate illustrates, all it might take is one overarching constitutional crisis from an administration, a situation reported aggressively and accurately by journalists, to return the press to the good graces of the nation. But there is no escaping the fact that, in a big way, the press has no one to blame for the current mess but ... the press. Of all the books to be found and consulted in today's American newsroom, the Bible cries out for a quick reading. Not the whole book, but one passage in particular.

From Luke 4:23: "Physician, heal thyself ... "

◊ ◊ ◊

Enlightened minds can debate when this slide into stasis and public revulsion really began. You can make the case that it started shortly after the Sept. 11 terrorist attacks on the United States. In that time of high vulnerability, or at least the suspicion of Americans being highly vulnerable, the press collectively jumped on the bandwagon to wave the flag and rally round President Bush, the new commander in chief. Some of that reflexive patriotism manifested itself in the graphic cosmetics the media (especially the electronic media) loves to indulge in.

Within a few days of the attacks, American flags popped up anchored to the mastheads of American newspapers, on the lapels of the anchors, on the home pages of newspaper Web sites, and in the on-air Chyron graphics of hundreds of television stations across America. That purely emotional response in a very emotional time was probably warranted, on a short-term basis. But that knee-jerk rush to the colors, which looked to be as much driven by competitive pressures as by any newfound sense of patriotism, set the stage for acquiescing in any number of actions by the Bush administration.

Among the most provocative of those actions would be the efforts by the administration to establish a cause & effect relationship between the events of Sept. 11 and the regime of Iraqi ruler Saddam Hussein. There was no linkage then; no linkage has been proven to this day. But the American media had already largely deserted the high ground of analysis and investigation, content even at that early stage to indulge in flag-draped emotionalism — emotionalism the press couldn't conveniently disconnect itself from as the need for more critical, less patriotically driven responses to White House military initiatives began to emerge.

Look at what happened in March 2003, when the shock-and-awe invasion of Iraq began. When the bombs started falling, you could literally hear otherwise dispassionate journalists being awed by the pyrotechnics loosed on Baghdad. Those same journalists, and their handlers at Media Central in New York, were swept up then in the awesome display of American might, and later were no doubt lulled into thinking (based on projections from their sources at the White House

17

and the Pentagon) that this would be a short war, a cakewalk, a nominal conflict that would end with sweets and ululations from the grateful Iraqi citizens.

The media, not expecting to have to endure the fever pitch of martial patriotism for very long, went along with the White House in ways that are now, in hindsight, an utter embarrassment. It begins with the language used to identify and report the war. From the very beginning, the media — print and electronic — went along with the White House shorthand for the name of the conflict itself. What was marginally a "war on terrorism" became "the War on Terror" in news reports -- bringing to mind a pleasant if improbable scenario: "Just think, folks," the administration seemed to say, "if we win this, that feeling you get on the steepest incline of an amusement-park roller coaster ride will be a thing of the *past!*"

In presumably independent news reports, those people who were captured by U.S. and coalition forces were not "prisoners." They were improbably identified as "detainees." That substitution of a perfectly accurate, idiomatic and serviceable word for a genteel, bullshit descriptor took place almost uniformly in the press (though sometimes, wire services such as The Associated Press engaged in such editorial insincerities as identifying people as "detainees" in one paragraph of a story and calling them "prisoners" a graph or two later, showing nothing so much as a cheap attempt to report the facts and placate the zeitgeist at the same time).

◊ ◊ ◊

Of all the news outlets to gain prominence in the past five years, the Fox News Channel has gained a foothold — some will say "stranglehold" — in the hierarchy of American media. In 2002, the year that the channel overtook CNN for ratings dominance, Fox News' median audience increased by 73 percent, according to the Pew Center. It was roughly at that point when cable television outlets began to sacrifice certain aspects of their editorial integrity and independence in order to hit their numbers on the bottom line. As the war became an unavoidable reality in Americans' lives, the media coverage of that war began to break down along politically partisan lines, with each network doing whatever it could to tack further to the right than its competition. The grim slide had begun in earnest.

It was almost laughable, sometimes. Fox News adopted its "fair and balanced" slogan, the network apparently unable to see just how ridiculous it is, or should have been, for a news network to so loudly trumpet that which should be obvious for a bona fide news organization.

And the MSNBC channel went through any number of changes. In a series of chameleon shifts, MSNBC ("America's Newschannel") brought on (and eventually cashiered) Phil Donahue, talk-show veteran and political moderate; Alan Keyes, erstwhile presidential contender; Michael Savage, rabidly homophobic conservative author, commentator and syndicated radio rottweiler; Pat Buchanan and Bill Press; point-counterpoint hosts and commentators; and others, in a desperate-seeming search to rebrand itself and find the right media mix for a nation that was increasingly restive and, to go by the Republican victories of 2000 and 2004, increasingly conservative.

Former U.S. Rep. Joe Scarborough, a Pensacola attorney, was called to host Scarborough Country" in 2004. And in early 2005, the point-counterpoint approach got a kinder, gentler treatment with the debut of "Connected Coast to Coast," with parallel hosts Monica Crowley from MSNBC's East Coast studios (on the political/geographic right) and Ron Reagan from MSNBC.com studios on the West Coast (on the left).

◊ ◊ ◊

For some the proof of pandering to an audience perceived to be growing in its conservatism was there in a Washington Times article published in early 2003. The article claimed to quote an internal MSNBC memo noting that Donahue was considered "a tired, left-wing liberal" whose antiwar, anti-Bush sentiments represented "a difficult public face for NBC in a time of war." MSNBC brass denied the memo even existed.

For MSNBC, and for other cable networks, data suggested that rebranding made financial, if not journalistic, sense: Some 40 percent of those watching CNN, MSNBC and Fox News identified themselves as conservatives in 2003, according to a Pew Research Center study that year. When such transparently feverish attempts to reinvent oneself are driven more by financial considerations than by journalistic considerations, it shouldn't be a surprise that Americans have less faith in the integrity of their press, and make less of a distinction between one form of the media and another.

There's a statement that's been variously attributed to Thomas Jefferson, Adlai Stevenson and Hunter S. Thompson: "In a democracy, people usually get the kind of government they deserve, and they deserve what they get." It's hard to imagine Jefferson saying that; the phrase bears the edgy, retributive modernity of mid- or late-20th-century thought. Maybe it was Stevenson, in a moment of deep cynicism, or Thompson, in a moment of cynical lucidity.

But whoever said it might have gone a little further. In a climate of furious rebranding to suit the tastes of a politically-partisan audience; in a time of declining financial investment in investigative reporting; in a period of static numbers of minority journalists in newsrooms and faint-hearted industry efforts to boost those numbers; in a time when American journalism seems more prepared to fall for anything rather than stand for something ... the press gets exactly what *it* deserves: the inability of the public it serves to distinguish between reporting and rant.

6/21/2005

AMERICAN TSUNAMI

I T was the imperfect storm of the year, for sure, and maybe the decade: a collision of economic and sociological forces with a meteorological event almost apocalyptic in scale. As it approached the southeastern United States, and the achingly vulnerable Gulf Coast, you saw it in the infrared satellite photos: a white-hot pinwheel of raw energy streaming toward landfall, its motion so regular as to almost resemble breathing.

Katrina.

The storm first made itself felt a week or more before, killing eleven people in Florida as it perambulated around the Gulf of Mexico, seemingly gaining no momentum, destined to be another midlevel noisemaker with more bark than bite. Perhaps it was that complacency, or comfort, or the latent rise of the soul of a riverboat gambler that led many residents of the probable hot zone to stay put. Betsy was bad and they lived through that, they reasoned; Camille was bad, in some ways worse than Betsy, but they got through that too.

Or maybe it was the storied Southern sense of independence and fidelity to the land, so hard come by for many of its citizens. If it was worth dying for to get it, they figured, how can it not be worth dying for to hold it? Many did pull up stakes and leave, gassing up the SUVs, taking the advice of the weather professionals on the networks, the people who were calling Katrina a "catastrophic event" when it was more than a day from landfall. But others went into hunkerdown mode and stayed behind in Mississippi and Alabama.

And they stayed behind in New Orleans, black, thirty-per-cent-poor New Orleans. They lingered often with no choice, or believing they had no choice, no options beyond the government check at the end of the month, no way out of town except in the pine boxes they'd already resigned themselves to. They hunkered down with no alternatives in the birthplace of jazz, a city technically seven feet under water on a dry day, and hoped like hell the levees would deliver them from evil again.

◊ ◊ ◊

Hurricane Katrina managed to combine the biblical force of the Asian tsunami disaster and the riveting human after-spectacle of the Sept. 11 terrorist attacks. For the sheer scope of the disaster, still unfolding at this writing and any writing for months to come; for the forces of chaos and rage unleashed shortly after the energies of the ocean were spent against the land; for the depth of the human suffering revealed; and for the bureaucratic farragos that have snarled even the most basic attempts to feed and water a sudden diaspora, Hurricane Katrina was America's tsunami, as powerful, as wrenching and devastating in the longest terms to this country as the cataclysmic December 26th event was to southeast Asia.

In typical American fashion, the finger-pointing has already begun, with the agencies in charge, however nominally, being readied to take the blame. The Homeland Security Department, the agency previously charged with overseeing domestic security in the wake of the Sept. 11 attacks, has been ham-fistedly retrofitted to resolving a situation largely beyond the scope of its creation.

And FEMA, the Federal Emergency Management Agency now under Homeland Security control, has come under intense scrutiny, with its director, Michael Brown, the former director of the International Arabian Horse Association, a patronage appointee, a woeful incompetent ill-prepared for the still-evolving challenge at hand. Homeland Security Secretary Michael Chertoff more or less formally decapitated Brown at a Sept. 9 press conference, relieving him of overseeing the Katrina relief effort, leaving him -- bet the ranch -- the director of FEMA in name only.

Chertoff's General Patton-in-shirtsleeves act couldn't conceal the way things were coming undone, or appearing to. And administration protestations couldn't hide the rising edge of fear in the eyes of President Bush, the visible flopsweat on the brow of the commander-in-chief a day or two before, the day President Bush got a briefing from the soon-to-be-headless Mr. Brown and said, "Brownie, you're doing a heck of a job," a Beltway valedictory if there ever was one.

For the increasingly ill-at-ease George Bush and his handlers, it's altogether inescapable now and will be more so in the future: Whether they like it or not, the Bush administration has a new agenda, a new mission to parallel the military mission now under way halfway around the world. The drive to achieve democracy in Iraq will be – and must be – accompanied by an initiative to restore democracy in Louisiana.

This new mission will require much of the same expenditure of capital, material, manpower and energy as the war we're fighting in Iraq. And like with the Iraq war, the stakes couldn't be higher: the integrity of the country and its ability to function. Whether he wants to or not, George Bush is compelled to open a new front in the war on terrorism, a domestic front, a tweak of a global mission whose necessity on these shores right now isn't offset at all by the terrorism's climatological origins.

Think about it: Katrina ushered into America vast and impersonal death; untold billions of dollars in insured and uninsured property losses; billions in revenue from the Gulf Coast port infrastructure, now badly compromised; billions in oil revenue from the ten refineries that owned and managed rigs offshore until the hurricane; certainly tens of millions of dollars from vanished casino, gaming and leisure revenue from two of the three affected states; the unfathomable price of an environmental nightmare of human and chemical toxins, a "toxic gumbo" (thank you Aaron Neville) that will require billions of dollars to clean up; and a deep and uneradicated sense of confusion and dread among the region's people.

Was the effect of Sept. 11 any less deeply felt as a defining American experience? Is the devastation of that storm any less powerful than that in an act of human terrorism? Since there is no difference between the depth of the two tragedies, the current situation calls for at least the same intensity of response for this domestic tragedy as that which the nation took to fighting a foreign war -- a war that didn't have to be fought in the first place.

But the intensity of the response to Katrina from this administration is up for debate, and a very uncertain thing. The same intensity of response to the terrors of Hurricane

Katrina as our response to the tinpot tyranny of Saddam Hussein would mean having to repurpose billions and billions of dollars from an international purpose to a domestic one. That purpose would be fighting the effects of Katrina -- effects no less catastrophic, to the Gulf Coast, than the effects of Sept. 11, 2001, four years ago today, were to the City of New York and, by logical extension, the United States of America.

By choice or by demand, this will be George Bush's new gulf war, fought not in the Persian Gulf but in the Gulf of Mexico. The shock and awe for this conflict will come from nature, the original superpower. And there won't be any MISSION ACCOMPLISHED banners flying for many long months to come.

9/11/2005

AMERICAN TSUNAMI II

ON Thursday night, George Bush began the most concerted, most aggressive, most politically necessary exercise in damage control in the five years of his presidency. In full shirtsleeves mode, the president damn near marched across a verdant patch of Jackson Square in the sodden, saddened city of New Orleans and announced the start of as close to a Marshall Plan as we are likely to see in the recovery of the Gulf Coast.

The president spoke in broad strokes and general principles; he was late to take up his role as national clarifier, but by all accounts it was an effective speech, even, in some ways, a departure from the usual scripted blather. A president ill at ease with disciplining others fell on his own sword Thursday night, accepting the responsibility for the disastrously haphazard initial response to the Katrina catastrophe. He went on, drilling down to get to the kernel of grand initiatives about to be unleashed: a Gulf Opportunity Zone spanning the three most affected states: Louisiana, Alabama and Mississippi; and an Urban Homestead Act, by which tracts of federal land would be ceded to the survivors of Katrina free of charge, under condition of their building new homes on the sites.

The president had already committed upwards of $60 billion in immediate relief, with billions more certainly on the way. Somehow, from somewhere, the figure of $200 billion began to make the rounds of the media in the days after Bush's address. John Snow, the treasury secretary, dismissed that amount as errant, presumptuous conjecture in an interview aired Saturday on Bloomberg News. And who could say for sure, with things unfolding on the ground on a daily basis -- and the hurricane season only half over?

But such ambitious ventures have foundered on the rocks of reality before, more often than not about something related to where the money goes and how widely the money gets to where it needs to go. The Sept. 12 Wall Street Journal Online reported that the Bush administration "is importing many of the contracting practices blamed for spending abuses in Iraq" to the Gulf Coast rebuilding effort, likely to be the biggest rebuilding effort in U.S. history.

"The first large-scale contracts related to Hurricane Katrina, as in Iraq, were awarded without competitive bidding, and using so-called cost-plus provisions that guarantee contractors a certain profit regardless of how much they spend," the Journal reported. With heavy hitters like Fluor and Bechtel aboard, can Halliburton be far behind? Probably not.

The administration's response to Hurricane Katrina, and the prospect for more damage if and when Tropical Storm Rita metastasizes into a full-blown hurricane itself, has led to more sharp reaction (read: piling on). The AP reported that Sens. John Kerry and John Edwards, the failed tandem of the 2004 presidential election, weighed in.

Kerry took aim with remarks he delivered at an address at Brown University. He said former FEMA Director and political suicide Michael Brown was to Hurricane Katrina "what Paul Bremer is to peace in Iraq; what George Tenet is to slam dunk intelligence ... what George Bush is to 'Mission Accomplished' and 'Wanted Dead or Alive.' ... The bottom line is simple: The 'we'll do whatever it takes' administration doesn't have what it takes to get the job done."

Edwards said Katrina and its aftermath made it clear that poverty is not a past-tense issue. "If the Great Depression brought forth Hoovervilles, these trailer towns may someday be known as Bushvilles," Edwards told an audience at the Center for American Progress, a liberal D.C. think tank.

Kerry and Edwards' comments can't just be dismissed as the reflexive complaints of the guys who lost the election. At this point, their mistakes during the campaign pale in comparison with the Bushies' errors of judgment. Kerry and Edwards are in the slow process of regaining their bona fides; Sen. Hillary Clinton is in the process of slowly, quietly cultivating her own.

And one of the recovery efforts soon to be fully under way is that for the Republicans, the party with the most political damage to rebound from, and the most to lose in the midterm elections about thirteen-odd months from now.

No amount of effort from the spin merchants on the Potomac is likely to change the popular perception -- present since Sept. 11 and recently confirmed in several opinion polls -- that the Bush administration and its proxies were asleep at the switch, again.

The American tsunami is proving it's got the characteristics of an artichoke, with the situation getting more and more serious, and more complex, as the layers of the initial tragedy fall away to reveal something heavier and scarier underneath. Tropical Storm Rita is brewing just outside the Gulf of Mexico, loitering with intent around the Florida Keys. It's frightening already to think of the worst that could happen: a storm that caught people unawares, and a governmental bureaucracy marginally able to cope with the unexpected.

9/19/2005

AMERICAN TSUNAMI III

WHAT the country and the Gulf Coast have grown to fear over the past three weeks now seems to be less than a day from actually happening. Tropical Storm Rita has completed its transformation into a full-blown hurricane -- it's been wobbling between Category 4 and Category 5 for the last twenty-four hours -- and is now veering toward landfall at some point between the coastlines of eastern Texas and western Louisiana. Within the last few hours, in fact, unlovely Rita has taken a turn to the northeast, and as of now may well be tacking back toward New Orleans, sodden, beleaguered New Orleans. ...

Some are beginning to call the situation in the gulf "the Katrita phenomenon," using a benign portmanteau that's more than just a cute way to describe the impact from two storms three weeks apart. Both Katrina and Rita, likely to be this hurricane season's most cataclysmic one-two punch, will have a huge and resonant impact not just on the region but on the country as a whole.

You have to consider the human tragedy of the first hurricane; it's been all but impossible to come up with a firm body watch from that one, and a second storm maybe just as bad or worse is on its way. The suffering in the Gulf Coast is starting to take on the worst aspects of a new and tragic continuum in American life, a fabric of suffering so total and smothering we can't be sure where the pain of one event ends and another begins.

Then there's the financial cost. The analyst wags on Wall Street are already talking audibly about gas at upwards of $4 a gallon by Halloween – *trick or treat!* – and commodities brokers have gone on the air with dire forecasts about higher costs for everything from orange juice to coffee to any number of goods brought into the port of New Orleans, the city at the mouth of the Mississippi, the national carotid artery for commerce.

The Katrita effect may have created yet another casualty. The National Enquirer, that fount of journalistic integrity, has reported that the President of the United States and heretofore teetotaler-in-chief is said to be drinking again. The Enquirer, citing family sources that are unnamed for a damn good reason, reports that in the wake of the Katrina catastrophe and the still-chaotic situation in Iraq, President Bush recently downed a Texas-sized tumbler of whiskey.

One unnamed insider told the Enquirer it was something of an open secret that Bush had been indulging before he was caught by first lady Laura Bush, who yelled "stop, George!" as the commander-in-chief put one down the hatch. "The sad fact," one source said, "is that he has been sneaking drinks for weeks now. Laura may have only just caught him, but the word is his drinking has been going on for a while in the capital. He's been in a pressure cooker for months."

Another source, ominously, told the Enquirer that a family member "told me they fear George is 'falling apart.'"

◊ ◊ ◊

One hopes the bad-Hamlet history of Richard Nixon doesn't repeat. We want to believe this won't lead to W rattling around the White House a la Tricky, strolling the halls at midnight, sloshing Glenlivet on the carpet, jabbering at the portraits on the walls of the Lincoln Bedroom. But we'll see. At a press conference earlier this week, the president looked a mite green around the gills, unusually unhealthy for a man obsessed with workouts and fitness. There were probably other reasons as well.

This was the week that the fatality count for Americans in Iraq hit another of those numerical milestones. Nineteen hundred killed in uniform. For George Bush, a man said to take every American combat death almost personally, that bloody benchmark of the war was probably bad enough.

We shouldn't wonder at his surrender to temptation in the wake of Katrina; the president may have discovered the ways in which the separate and discrete come together, reveal their interconnectedness, in ways you didn't see coming. It took something the magnitude of an apocalyptic event, and its aftermath, to renew the debate about the war in Iraq and its human and financial cost. In an instant, all the abstract talk about homeland security took on another dimension.

Katrina's impact wasn't terrorism per se, despite the similarity of effect when you watched the news: the flattened landscapes, the military's frantic dispersal of goods and presence; the eyes of locals in three states, vacant of hope.

But the Homeland Security Department, the agency created to at least oversee a reaction to such disasters — having ingested the Federal Emergency Management Agency, that body directly responsible for the federal response -- was slow to react. And people, certainly some in the three states affected so far and more around the country, wondered how much better, how much more uniform and immediate the response to Katrina might have been if such a large percentage of America's citizen soldiers weren't half a world away doing another country's business, but not their own.

9/22/2005

AMERICAN TSUNAMI IV

AFTER Jayson Blair and Jack Kelley, after Memogate and Dan Rather, after any number of missteps over the past three years, the American press came face to face with a new challenge to its primacy and pertinence to the American people. When Hurricane Katrina hit the Gulf Coast one month ago yesterday, it unleashed a tide of young, eager journalists flooding the zone with the best of intentions, or at least the most uniformly competitive of intentions.

What's emerged since then has occasioned a healthy clash of opinions on what worked right and what didn't. As stories of this scale often do, they tell as much or more about the storyteller than they do about the subject of the story.

One of the better debates on how well the media handled the Katrina catastrophe was on the "News Hour With Jim Lehrer" this evening. Two of the participants synthesized both sides of an eager, aggressive press knee-deep in the kind of story that awakens their instinct for the fatalistic, the merciful and the bureaucratic. Their comments also illustrated the maddening Rashomon aspect of the press trying to comprehensively get its arms around a story literally exploding in real time as they reported it, an immediacy that yielded sadly astonishing errors that, again, said more about the teller of the tale than the tale being told.

Keith Woods, an editor with the New Orleans Times-Picayune and director of the Poynter Institute, said the blanket coverage of the Katrina disaster and its inescapable human tragedy revealed "a sense of passion, a sense of empathy, a sense of understanding that they were not telling an ordinary story – any more than the Sept. 11 attacks were an ordinary story.

"I like the fact that journalism understood the size of this story from the very beginning," Woods said.

That was one part of the elephant. Hugh Hewitt, however, would have none of it. Hewitt, the founder of hughhewitt.com, a high-profile Web site of commentary, lit into Woods' argument, and revealed another equally compelling side to the issue.

31

Hewitt lamented big media's seeming inability "to dispel the lurid, the hysterical, the salaciousness of the reporting." And in a smart repudiation of much of the media's self-congratulations, Hewitt said the Katrina mess revealed "a wholesale collapse of the media's own levees. They let in all the rumors, all the innuendo, all the first-person stories because they were caught up in their own emotionalism."

And Hewitt — despite having what feels like the same predisposition toward punitive impulses for the press that's common among conservatives today — made maybe the telling point in the debate: journalists' willingness to suspend the willingness to suspend disbelief.

"They reported panic-inducing, fear-inducing, hysteria-inducing mass-casualty events ... the most squalid journalism you could imagine. ..."

"People have to ask, why was the media so eager and willing to circulate these stories? Is it because [they] were dealing with the urban underclass, largely black, largely a community with which the elite media does not often deal, and as a result they were willing to believe stories about this community that they might not have given credence to, if it were a different situation?"

◊ ◊ ◊

One suspects that the truth lies somewhere in the two not-quite extremes of their positions. It's inescapable that the press, presented in just hours with the story of the year, a vast human drama, tried to hit the ground running on Katrina, saturating the region with reporters covering every vantage point, from the obligatory weather reporter leaning against Category 3 winds to the Gulf Coast embeds who hunkered down for days or weeks to look for the human dimension in depth.

Their zeal for getting the story, though, ran up against the need to get the story *right*. Stories from Katrina survivors took on a life of their own; gossip became exaggerations became rumors became statements from the mayor himself. The tales that emerged from the Superdome in New Orleans in the desperate hours of the evacuation began to sound like the stuff of a Brueghel painting, armies of the dead consuming the living, entrails aflame, blood running in the exits.

That the reality turned out to be far less apocalyptic raises the question of how such a disconnect between journalistic responsibility and journalists' actions could happen. That's the deeper question for reporters and editors going forward: Why report fictional drama, or at least drama you couldn't verify with your own eyes, as the truth? Since when did journalists take anyone's word for anything?

There were challenges to covering the Katrina story, a real-time news extravaganza if there ever was one. At one level American media got it: they understood intuitively that what was unfolding on the Gulf Coast was a national story of rare scale and perhaps unprecedented impact. But the media also overplayed its hand, milking a real drama by adding ninth-circle-of-hell innuendo that was unnecessary, and often a case of sloppy reporting that capitalized on the emotions of the moment.

It's an object lesson for the next time. And there will be a next time.

9/30/2005

AUGUST WILSON'S CENTURY IN BLACKS AND BLUES

WHEN AUGUST Wilson's play "Fences" opened on Broadway in March 1987, in a New York City in the throes of racial conflicts that seemed to permeate every aspect of daily life, the play was hailed as a revelation in American theater. Simply put, the play *reached* people.

Though its characters were African American, the play's central clash — the chafing between a father and son on differing but parallel courses in search of themselves — brought multiracial audiences to tears night after night.

Wilson, who died Sunday at age 60 of inoperable liver cancer, thus enjoyed a wide renown as a playwright unrivaled in the 20th century he documented. And that's not just as a black playwright; assessments of his talent so narrowly defined miss the point of what made his plays work, what made them so eagerly anticipated by theatergoers of every persuasion.

In creating his sweeping 10-play cycle of black American life, Wilson worked in the idiom of black America, but his genius lay both in universalizing that experience for theatergoers largely unaccustomed to black America on stage, and in investing those plays with a deft weave of reality and myth.

Until "Fences," mainstream American theater received black plays with painful infrequency, in indifferently-regarded works that either isolated the black American experience from everything else, or celebrated black life in the trappings of the musical, a theatrical form that fixes narrative and context in a frothier, more dramatically insubstantial framework.

Not that music was alien to Wilson: One of his triumphs of invention was how he used the blues. A music mostly relegated to the national past forms the emotional underpinning for many of his plays. Wilson explained for this reporter in a 1991 interview its importance as soundtrack and spiritual touchstone.

"The music is a specific cultural response of black America to the world, the circumstances and the situation in which they've found themselves," said Wilson, charming and generous of spirit, a man of constant energy whose chain smoking formed a counterpoint to his comments.

"If you didn't know anything about African people and nothing about black people in America, and someone gave you blues records, you could listen and find out what kind of people these were ... their symmetry, this grace ... you'd be able to construct their daily lives."

That he as a playwright found and articulated universal truths is a given; that's the mission of all playwrights. But Wilson's gift was to find the universal within the largely overlooked backdrop of African American life, and to lift that expression of America — subtleties and nuances intact — into view for a wider playgoing audience, one that recognized his name more readily than many other playwrights, black or white.

Wilson crossed over in a way no African American playwright did before or since. Lorraine Hansberry died too young and too soon for her work to have articulated the full dimensions of the civil rights movement, or the role of black Americans in charting their destiny as a result of that movement.

The work of Amiri Baraka (LeRoi Jones) was too often received by theatergoers as angry examples of racial propaganda, mythic exercises long on political education and short on emotional texture. Playwright Ed Bullins began his own naturalistic "Twentieth-Century Cycle" of black life in 1968, years before Wilson's work saw light of day.

But it was Wilson's plays that exploded into wider recognition through his blend of naturalism and poetics, the music of his language, the social forces of his heyday, and that utterly ephemeral aspect of good luck — being in the right place at the right time with the right play.

And in leapfrogging around the black American twentieth century, Wilson made his plays timely for modern audiences with stories that ran counter to the glitzy, mega-scale productions that characterized Broadway for much of the 1980s and early 1990s. Wilson worked in the small scale, found the drama within a smaller circle of intimates: family, friends and acquaintances.

In "Fences," which won the 1987 Pulitzer Prize for drama, the story of conflicts between a bitter, overprotective father and a son intent on accepting a football scholarship assumes wider dimension as the wrenching story of a battle between generations, and the power of sports in American culture.

Ma Rainey's Black Bottom" examines one woman's struggle to nurture her music in the first throes of the mass marketing of communication. "Joe Turner's Come and Gone" looks at black Americans battling to achieve a sense of self-worth in the period of the first generations after the upheaval of the Civil War.

"The Piano Lesson," which won the 1990 Pulitzer for drama, studies the conflicts that arise when a family faces a choice of whether to part with a treasured family heirloom in order to acquire a patch of land in the South.

In "Radio Golf," a wealthy realtor poised to be Pittsburgh's first black mayor dreams of developing a decaying inner city — a dream that confronts the reality of people unwilling to demolish the past.

In these and other plays, the overriding theme of Wilson's work comes through: the African American search for identity and connection, for self-awareness in a world and a country at odds with such discoveries.

In that 1991 interview, Wilson was asked "Is there life after the cycle?" The answer from this charitable, passionate, driven lion of the theater, the most-celebrated American playwright of the past quarter-century, revealed the breadth of his vision as a writer, and the scope of his aspirations for his people and his nation.

"Maybe I'll start over," he said. "I intend to write as least 15 more plays about black folks in America. My biggest problem is to find the time to sit down and do the work. But what is there to do except to write another play?"

10/2/2005
msnbc.com

AMERICAN TSUNAMI V

L IKE we didn't know already: Today, courtesy of memos obtained by the Associated Press, we get a fuller picture of the ineptitude of the Federal Emergency Mismanagement Agency (FEMA) as the magnet for taxpayer dollars struggled to prepare for the arrival of Hurricane Katrina. The memos showed an agency woefully out of touch with the gravity of the situation, an organization that failed to get it before the storm made landfall and didn't fully understand things days after the storm devastated the Gulf Coast.

Among other tragic missteps: FEMA could not find food, ice, water and even the necessary body bags in the days after Katrina hit the city. The agency charged with stockpiling such basic emergency provisions in advance apparently couldn't track them down when the real deal hit.

The AP story recounts running e-mail conversations, policy discussions, bureaucratic infighting and concerns about how the agency would be perceived in the press -- the usual shortcomings of a government agency increased by orders of magnitude by the greatest natural disaster to hit the United States since the Galveston hurricane of 1900.

Of particular note are the shortcomings of Michael Brown, then director of the agency, a man who, on the weight of available evidence, could not find his ass in the Category 5 windstorm that ultimately cost him his job. Five days after the storm hit on Aug. 29, Brown sent an e-mail to an aide saying there had been "no action from us" to evacuate storm victims using planes that airlines had provided.

"This is flat wrong. We have been flying planes all afternoon and evening," said a subordinate, Michael Lowder, in an e-mail sent half an hour later. The question is an obvious one: How can the director of an agency not know whether its planes are in the air or not?

The AP: "A day earlier, a FEMA official in Mississippi received an e-mail asking for Brown's satellite phone number so a senior Pentagon official in the Gulf Coast could call him. 'Not here in MS (Mississippi). Is in LA (Louisiana) as far as I know,' FEMA official William Carwile e-mailed back, seemingly uncertain on the whereabouts of the administration's point man for responding to the disaster."

The late Dr. Laurence J. Peter was the author of "The Peter Principle," a celebrated bible for business management before bibles for business management became the rage. One of the book's core principles is instructive when considering the FEMA debacle: [paraphrasing now] Ineptitude — what Peter describes as "occupational incompetence" — rises to its own level of authority in a given organization.

The curious rise and utterly predictable fall of Michael Brown reveals again how the trajectory of a disaster is something discernible from a long way off — sometimes, even often, from before the disaster even takes place. FEMA's lack of imagination combined with a lack of resources and a lack of willingness to step outside the usual boxes of procedure and routine resulted in a perfect storm within a storm: the hurricane of bureaucratic chaos that doomed hundreds of people as surely as the waters themselves.

10/17/2005

LENNON

IT was Dec. 8, 1980, early in the evening in Boulder, Colorado, and I'm sitting in my bedroom at the foot of my bed with Marjorie, my next-door neighbor and infatuation of the moment. With my roomies sitting in the next room noisily watching ABC's "Monday Night Football," I kissed Marjorie for the first time; we necked and snuggled and considered the possibilities of spending some big percentage of our lives together; and then we heard, with the door not quite closed enough, the unmistakable voice of Howard Cosell telling us, telling the world, that John Lennon was dead.

Things started to turn sour for Marjorie and me from almost that moment on. It took a while to fully play out, but our romantic fortunes went downhill -- which shouldn't have been surprising. One way or another, things went south for all of us from that day on.

Some mile markers in life are unavoidable, like road obstacles that are too big to drive around. There's no escaping them when they happen or even years later. There's behavior that's common to our species — or maybe just particular to our era: we tend to measure the gravity of events in the context of the terminal. We all have our stories of where we were when John F. Kennedy was assassinated, or Malcolm X, or Martin Luther King or Robert Kennedy or Yitzhak Rabin. John Lennon joined that pantheon of eternals, but in a slightly different way.

Lennon always had an *edge* about him. In his life as a Beatle and afterward, there was a sense of the precipitate, the volatile about John Lennon. More than any of the other Beatles -- the often-sullen George, the relentlessly chipper Paul, the phlegmatically loyal Ringo -- John embodied rock and roll's potential for unalloyed danger, that feeling you get in the best rock music of careening headlong into a new and strange place -- and not being frightened by the prospect in the least.

Long before that nightcrawler trapped him in the vestibule of the Dakota, John Lennon wore a target; it's been said that years before the Beatles exploded, when he was still playing with the Quarrymen, blokes in his Liverpool neighborhood wanted him hurt, or worse, for reasons we can only guess at now.

His was rock and roll's first outright assassination. With his killing, legions of fans got the wake-up call they'd been dreading, or avoiding, at least since the Beatles broke up a decade earlier.

And it was hard to let go. It was, and still is, hard to give up that giddy frisson of the Beatles' first performance on the Ed Sullivan Show, when four shaggy knuckleheads in suits landed in a country numb from the loss of Camelot about nine weeks before they arrived. The audience that night, its screams like a flock of crazed birds, was a taste of the future. The screams followed them around the world for six years -- the reaction of fans who lost themselves in a music and a style and a world-view that began the transformation of popular culture.

Not long after the bottom fell out of the Beatles, in 1970, Lennon was warning us. Telling us in his fashion to get ready. Be prepared for anything. Grow up. "I don't believe in Beatles," he told us in the song "God." "The dream is over." Lennon was teaching us to grow up even while, paradoxically, he was growing up himself. There were dalliances for a time when things with Yoko went badly.

He hangs out with Harry Nilsson in L.A. He and Harry get tossed out of the Troubadour for heckling the Smothers Brothers. He goes to another nightclub and gets upbraided by a waitress for wearing a tampon on his head. He learns the process of starting over.

We're lucky that the fruition of that process was something positive. Rather than an obituary of a rock star who passed from the scene with a spike in his arm or a shotgun to his head, we got from John Lennon the evidence of his mellowing, his maturity. You can't listen to "Double Fantasy" without hearing that growth process in the works; like a butterfly fighting its way out of a cocoon, John and Yoko were fighting to regain their own identities — regain, hell! maybe fighting to just *have* identities separate from those foisted on them by the media, the music biz, and always, always, the fans.

We got a taste of that great possible. But only a taste. Now, a quarter century after Lennon died — sounds tree-ring strange saying "quarter century" — we're in some ways more in need of his candor, his wit, his passion, than we ever were before.

John Winston Ono Lennon remains an indelible spirit of our times, a man whose wrestling with demons within and without has made our own caged match with reality a little more bearable. It's a real tribute to someone's life when you find that you miss that person, need that person, feel that person's presence more and more as time goes by, not less.

John Lennon was a rock dropped into the water of our time and our lives, and the ripples from that rock get stronger and stronger all the time, the further and further we get from their source.

Imagine that. Just imagine.

12/8/2005

THE [BRAND NAME HERE] NEWS

IF there was ever any doubt that it's advertising's world and we just live in it, that doubt should have been erased with the announcement, earlier this month, that a radio station in Madison, Wisc., had sold the naming rights to its newsroom to advertisers. Starting Jan. 1, the newsroom for WIBA radio will morph into the Amcore Bank News Center. For journalism, that apocalypse we always talk about being upon us may really, finally be here.

Or has already been here: The Associated Press reports that a Milwaukee station sold its naming rights to another bank, Pyramax, in 2004. Monica Baker, Pyramax's senior vice president of marketing, told The AP that it was just a matter of the bottom line. "This is a way for us to maintain our revenue levels and make the station successful," she said. "The concern about any possible conflict of interest is just ridiculous."

But there's much room for concern among journalists, and there should be with the public as well. The Pyramax and Amcore deals don't just smudge the line between news and advertising, they cross the line with blithe ruthlessness and a reflexive justification on grounds of fiscal responsibility. Such alliances are a problem for anyone hoping for news outlets separate from the corporations that those outlets must sometimes cover.

Company brands on news broadcasts aren't really new. David Klatell, vice dean at Columbia University's Graduate School of Journalism, told The AP that the practice was discontinued in the 1950's, after such broadcasts as the NBC evening news broadcast featured the orange and white Gulf Oil logo on the set.

The problem NBC brass must have figured out then, Klatell noted, is the same issue they'll be forced to wrestle with this time if the trend continues. "They couldn't fairly cover not only Gulf, they couldn't cover anything that was relevant to the oil industry or its competitors."

As more and more American companies engage in the reverse mitosis of mergers and acquisitions, bulking up by consuming their smaller rivals (witness the new AT&T, happily digesting what was once SBC), the inevitability of conflict of interest is obvious. Consider the range of divisions of just some of the country's leading communications companies: from theme parks to magazines, from aircraft engines to the 50-gallon water heater I plan to buy to heat my home.

With a range of interests like that, it's obviously hard enough to maintain some degree of editorial independence when stories even peripherally related to a parent company's bottom line cross the editor's desk. You could imagine, for example, the painful dilemma of regularly reporting on faulty aircraft engines implicated in a series of deadly airline crashes when your network's parent company *makes* the engines in question.

◊ ◊ ◊

That dilemma is that much more transparent when you've branded your news product with the name of your biggest advertiser. Those newsrooms in Madison and Milwaukee can only hope they don't have to deal with any banking scandals tied to anyone working for Amcore or Pyramax banks. But that's the easy call; how will they handle stories on the banking sector in general? Can they be counted on to report news about other banks as aggressively as they'll cover news related to Amcore or Pyramax?

And how do these news departments handle the issue of professional integrity, namely, the matter of not just avoiding conflict of interest but also avoiding the *appearance* of conflict of interest?

That's a matter that two newsrooms, for now, are grappling with. What happens in the future? But with advertisers increasingly challenged to find a way to get into the public mind and stay there, with corporations increasingly challenged to hit their numbers, with news outlets increasingly challenged to inform the public and bludgeon their competition in the process, the Brought To You By News of the past may well be a worrisome development to come.

12/27/2005

THE 'BROKEBACK' EFFECT

TO get a true fix on the battleground where the culture wars are being played out today, you don't have to go any further than your friendly neighborhood multiplex. Ang Lee's deceptively understated but emotionally resonant "Brokeback Mountain" has taken point in what James Dobson, the two Pats (Robertson and Buchanan) and the other presumptive generals of what they would surely call "the culture wars."

But Lee's film has caught them off guard if not flat-out by surprise; there's a sense that as "Brokeback" gathers momentum in the drive toward the Oscars, more than a few of them the usual rock-ribbed conservatives now frantically leafing through their strategy playbooks looking for a way out of a dilemma of identity. Since its release, conservatives have gone out of their way to keep the film, a story of two cowboys and the romantic relationship developing between them – on the margins of respectability and acceptability. The right wing is in full cry right now, for at least two reasons:

The first is because of the film's unexpected penetration into American life. The conservatives had no doubt already conceded some of the cultural high ground to the film's reception in some quarters. They'd forgone the usual suspect audiences for "Brokeback Mountain," the coastal cultural centers like San Francisco, Seattle, Los Angeles, New York and other liberal enclaves the conservatives have already written off as the charnel houses of Satan.

What has to rankle the conservatives is the way in which "Brokeback Mountain" has broken through, trickled down and burrowed into the broader American consciousness, and done so with a deft touch and lightning speed. It's broken out of the isolated audiences of the cognoscenti ¬– generally the film scholars and critics and fans on either coast – and burst into the American heartland, become something that people all over America are talking about, whether they've seen the film or not.

A host of critics from other publications across the country have come up with hosannahs of their own, independent of whatever the major papers thought. And "Brokeback" generated its popular attention by having the towering nerve to successfully assail the celebrated cowboy esthetic, the foundational Marlboro Man archetype that is one of the country's most iconic and deeply-held self-images.

"Brokeback's" success undercuts any right-wing claim that such a film demonstrates fiscal irresponsibility on the part of the studios. The fact that such a successful film has been financed, marketed and distributed by a major studio whose parent is accountable to investors and shareholders is a plain indicator of the studios' willingness to paint outside the usual comfortable creative lines – and to do it to great effect on the bottom line.

"Brokeback's" success sends the clear signal that, contrary to many assumptions, the creative forces that made the film have a better sense of the public mood, a better more accurate track of the American psyche, than the conservatives who rail, profane and fight tooth & nail against both the expression of the life experiences in "Brokeback" and the real-life experiences themselves.

In this little pitched battle for public opinion, at least, the conservatives are thus denied the high grounds of American iconography, populist sentiment, and any hope of winning arguments about a company's fiduciary responsibility by adhering to "American values."

Truth is, "Brokeback Mountain" has blindsided the conservative politicians like it hit the rest of us. The way in which the film has witnessed its steadily increasing audience is problematic to those who would frustrate creation of a national community as indifferent to sexual orientation as it tries to be to race and gender.

Sometimes in the culture, a profound shift happens. And sometimes when that seismic shift happens, it's not because of a Titanic Moment. Sometimes, it's smaller. It's often quieter, less big-sky bombastic than the advertisement campaign mounted to promote it.

It can be the kind of motion picture in which the actors are the best special effects, as great actors usually are. It can be a story of two lonely wounded people striving to survive and thrive in a brittle and indifferent world, people very like us in a world very like our own. And in its understatement, that story can shake the rafters of the national complacency, and rattle the walls of our understanding of what it means to be a human being.

1/23/2006

NOTE TO POTUS:
LAURA TO TAJ MAHAL ASAP

BY all the conventional metrics of politics, President Bush's recent trip to India has been a consummate success. In meetings with Indian Prime Minister Manmohan Singh, the president shored up one of the still-enduring American alliances with Asia, watching out for an emerging powerhouse, a comer if there ever was one.

Bush and Singh agreed on a landmark nuclear energy agreement, a pact that goes a long way to furthering the ties between the world's oldest democracy and the world's biggest. India agreed to open many of its nuclear reactors to international inspection The trip deflected, if only for a Washington minute, the attention to his various other disasters, from the progress of the Iraq war to the equally slow unwinding of the CIA leak investigation and its proximity, or lack of same, to the Oval Office.

President Bush brought along the first lady, Laura, on a trip whose political purpose was obvious but whose emotional potential was apparently unimpressive. The president, you see, has conducted the whole trip -- his entire time spent in India -- without going to the Taj Mahal.

You know the place. That utterly arresting, 17th-century white marble mausoleum, an architectural tribute to love, built by an emperor in the memory of his favorite wife. One of maybe two or three of the most recognizable buildings on earth.

When pressed on why they didn't go there, Bush said it was basically unavoidable.

In an interview with Indian reporters before the trip, recorded by The Associated Press, he blamed his scheduler for the situation.

"Look, if I were the scheduler, perhaps I'd be doing things differently," he said. "But you want me doing one thing. I'll be the president, we've got the scheduler being the scheduler."

Singh didn't let him off the hook. "I am truly sorry the president is not taking you to Taj Mahal this time," the prime minister said. "I hope he will be more chivalrous next time you are here."

Bush had apparently already caught a load of grief about it. "I've been hearing about it from Laura ever since I told her that we weren't going," he told AP.

And rightfully so. Leaving India without touring the Taj Mahal? And blaming his *scheduler?* Sorry, mister sir, but there's just something cheap and hollow and weird about that. You do India, you visit the Taj Mahal. It's that simple. A kid with wanderlust and a credit card near its limit would find a way to do it on the cheap.

And scheduling issues? *What* scheduling issues? When the world dances to your Rolodex, more or less, there *are* no scheduling problems you can't get around. What's the point of being the POTUS — Mover of armies! Swayer of nations! Steward of the public purse! — if you can't tweak your timetable to accommodate your wife, the first lady, the *one person on this planet* willing to put up with you and everything about you for the rest of her life?

And no, coming back in a year or six on a repeat visit doesn't cut it. It's just not the same, having to double back and do what you should have done the first time. Sorry, Mr. President, sir. There's just some things a man's supposed to do for his wife. No excuses, no pressing engagements, no blaming your minions and handlers. When you are within spitting distance of one of the world's signature structures, as exotic and dramatic and *romantic* an object as humans have ever devised ... you're supposed to go.

3/5/2006

CORETTA SCOTT KING
AND THEM CHANGES

CORETTA SCOTT KING passed earlier this week, thirty-eight years after her husband. She had a real good run and she died with family in Mexico. That steady, inexorable arc of decline could belong to any one of us, and no doubt will, give or take details, to all of us. But the life of Coretta Scott King was a life of purpose at a high level, in the service of a cause that animates and resonates in America today and forever. And for African Americans, her passing leaves that which nature can't stand: a vacuum, an absence almost as resonant as the cause she lived for.

With her death the debate has intensified about "the way forward," now that so many of the icons of the African American vanguard are fading with time. Coretta's passing comes on the heels of the death last year of August Wilson, a playwright for the ages; actor playwright, conscience and voice Ossie Davis; and the passing, in January, of preservationist Joyce Maynard, longtime champion of Weeksville, N.Y., a settlement of freedmen and freedwomen that came to produce the state's first black police officer and first black woman doctor.

Some of the comfortable anchors of the past have escaped us for good and we're more adrift now than we were before, if you can imagine that. That potential for drift has alarmed some African Americans; at a time when challenges facing black Americans are more, and more aggressive than before, black America finds itself at a crossroads, with few of the singular personalities we relied on in the 1950's and '60s.

The African American intelligentsia has fragmented, broken off into a number of little pieces, shards of generation and gender, of economic circumstance and even skin color. What's missing, what's been missing for years, is that unifying force with the ability to synthesize disparate elements into something approaching a cohesive whole. Jesse Jackson can't do it; his own personal baggage (child out of wedlock, the lingering memory of "Hymietown") is a problem, one kept largely on the down low but a problem just the same. Some have rightly pointed to Sen. Barack Obama as the kind of inspirational lightning rod black Americans need in the future. Others embrace the homey practicality and growing media savvy of Rev. Al Sharpton.

The 2004 election gave a hint of them changes. That's when African Americans broke with their automatic pulldown of the Democratic lever and actually *increased* their numbers of support for President Bush, dissing Democratic challenger John Kerry for reasons that had as much to do with their sensitivities to "family values" as for Kerry's insubstantial position on the Iraq war.

Whichever way African America goes, it's clear that a major generational shift is happening for black folks. Coretta Scott King's passing only makes clear what's been happening already: the convenience of that single iconic force speaking truth to power on behalf of black Americans has now become, officially, history.

"The old has passed away," Bernice King said as part of the eulogy for her mother at the church in Lithonia, Ga., in the Atlanta suburbs. "There is a new order that is emerging." The shape of that new order, its players and personality, will be the stuff of much debate, probably as soon as this (midterm election) November.

2/2/2006

VIETNAM, THE SEQUEL

THAT'S what one former U.S. official, a man at least passingly familiar with the last national quagmire, suggests about the current conflict in Iraq. Former Reagan Secretary of State Alexander Haig, who after all was once In Control at the White House, said as much on March 11, at a conference in Boston. Victory -- or at least an achievement of some set objective -- requires a commitment to win, a national consensus, that Haig finds absent today.

"Every asset of the nation must be applied to the conflict to bring about a quick and successful outcome, or don't do it," Haig said, according to Associated Press reports. "We're in the midst of another struggle where it appears to me we haven't learned very much."

Haig spoke at a conference at the John F. Kennedy Presidential Library and Museum, an event meant to look at how the Vietnam War and the American presidency were intertwined. It was an occasion to gather some of the best & brightest from previous administrations.

Besides Haig and Vietnam War architect and former Secretary of State Henry Kissinger, there was Jack Valenti, adviser during the Johnson administration and former head of the Motion Picture Association of America.

Valenti observed what the current occupants of 1600 Pennsylvania Avenue seem to have overlooked despite hang-tough pronouncements, that the lessons of Vietnam have been "forgotten or ignored" in Iraq, and that "no president can win a war when public support for that war begins to decline and evaporate."

◊ ◊ ◊

Valenti's assessment is that much more problematic when support for both the president and the war he engineered decline at practically the same time. On this, the third anniversary of the start of the Iraq war, the president faces a restive Congress, an equally querulous electorate and an intractable insurgency that shows every sign of digging in. And as the Republican

51

Haig's comments and the reactions from some in the GOP Congress indicate, the problems for the Bush presidency no longer hew conveniently along party lines. Even presumed allies are finding fault.

It's the kind of situation that makes possible results from the latest poll by Pew Research Center for People and the Press, which put it in perspective: "Bush's overall approval measure stands at 33 [percent], the lowest rating of his presidency." In other data from the same poll, Pew reported that 70 percent of Americans think President Bush "does not have a clear plan for bringing the Iraq conflict to a successful conclusion." Again, it's not a party-line conclusion: Pew reports that "40 [percent] of Republicans share this opinion."

That train wreck of leadership numbers has a nasty parallel in the personality department. "The president's personal image also has weakened noticeably, which is reflected in people's one-word descriptions of the president," stated another part of the Pew report, released March 15. "Honesty had been the single trait most closely associated with Bush, but in the current survey 'incompetent' is the descriptor used most frequently."

It gets worse than that. In a riotous extension of its usual businesslike polling approach, Pew got into the word association game, offering respondents a range of one-word descriptor choices, including "selfish," "ass," "jerk," "idiot," "liar" and other language we can charitably call less than presidential.

I'm forgoing the raw numbers and which words placed highest in respondents' reaction. In some ways the range of words used to describe the commander-in-chief, the highs and lows of such scoring, don't even matter. The very idea that those words could or should be used in juxtaposition with the phrase "President of the United States" is a strong indicator of just how far Bush has fallen in recent months — to say nothing of his decline from just after Sept. 11, 2001, when George Bush the Younger commanded approval ratings in the 80th percentile, the highest such approval ratings for a sitting president since, believe it, Franklin D. Roosevelt.

◊ ◊ ◊

The rise and fall of George Bush as president parallels the rise and fall of a war effort that was problematic from the start. The fact that the administration is staking so much of its reputation and historical standing on the outcome of the war must be a given at this point. The one thing that's in play now, where the latest debate engages, is in the analyses of whether Iraq is or is not now in the midst of a *civil* war.

The administration's perspective is, understandably, in the negative, with various administration talking pointed heads insisting that there *is* no civil war — that the challenges, admittedly serious, are still short of that level of catastrophe. The vested interest in the administration's view of there being no civil war can't be ignored.

But there's also no ignoring the viewpoint of one man in a singular position. Former Iraqi Prime Minister Ayad Allawi said it plain yesterday in an interview with the BBC, calling it "unfortunate that we are in civil war. We are losing each day as an average 50 to 60 people throughout the country, if not more. If this is not civil war, then God knows what civil war is."

There in a succinct, articulate nutshell is the dilemma for the United States: In the face of mounting sectarian depravities, how can the U.S. go on insisting that the same situation Allawi says has already started doesn't yet exist? Allawi's assessment is frightening enough -- with words that have the ruthlessly pragmatic ring of the Truth, and by virtue of their perspective, coming from a man who's certainly in a position to know what he's talking about.

But it gets worse: Allawi told the BBC that if Iraq were to fold, the same ethnic violence that's tearing that country apart would surely metastasize throughout the Middle East, in such a way that Europe and the United States would feel it too.

Various Americans, from Ted Kennedy to gold star mom/ activist Cindy Sheehan, have long been calling the Iraq war a sequel to the debacle of Vietnam. Today, the third anniversary of the start of the Iraq war, the comparisons are that much brighter, clearer, starker and harder to deny -- even for cold warriors like Haig and Valenti. Their grim assessment of the present is based on an intimate knowledge of and participation in the past. Their conclusions deserve to be heard amid the shock and awe of our uncertain future.

3/20/2006

O'CONNOR SPEAKS, NO TAPE AT 11

IN THE FUTURE, a shockingly powerful statement on the prospects for American dictatorship made by retired Supreme Court Justice Sandra Day O'Connor may resonate with an unlikely irony: For generations yet unborn, one reporter's recalled paraphrase of a 400-word precis may be our only indicator of an unsettling assessment of what may be a dangerous American trend.

Irony of ironies: In a time of relentless press coverage of everything under the sun, in the researchable and archivable Internet age, perhaps the most dire, woeful forecast of the nation's possible future ever uttered in public largely managed to fly under the radar of the 24/7 press.

O'Connor's *cri de coeur* (or *cri pour la justice*) took place on March 9, sometime during a speech that morning at Georgetown University. Despite the profile of the speaker, just five weeks removed from being in one of the nine most powerful jobs in American life, it seems that the speech was scarcely covered by the press. From all indications, National Public Radio reporter Nina Totenberg was the only press witness to the event. No recording, no videotape, as yet no official transcript from the speaker herself.

What follows here is a transcript of O'Connor's comments as reported by Totenberg on NPR and published online by RawStory.com:

Totenberg: "In an unusually forceful and forthright speech, O'Connor said that attacks on the judiciary by some Republican leaders pose a direct threat to our constitutional freedoms. O'Connor began by conceding that courts do have the power to make presidents or the Congress or governors, as she put it 'really, really angry.' But, she continued, if we don't make them mad some of the time we probably aren't doing our jobs as judges, and our effectiveness, she said, is premised on the notion that we won't be subject to retaliation for our judicial acts. The nation's founders wrote repeatedly, she said, that without an independent judiciary to protect individual rights from the other branches of government those rights and privileges would amount to nothing. But, said O'Connor, as the founding fathers knew, statutes and constitutions don't protect judicial independence, people do.

"And then she took aim at former House GOP leader Tom DeLay. She didn't name him, but she quoted his attacks on the courts at a meeting of the conservative Christian group Justice Sunday last year when DeLay took out after the courts for rulings on abortions, prayer and the Terri Schiavo case. This, said O'Connor, was after the federal courts had applied Congress' onetime only statute about Schiavo as it was written. Not, said O'Connor, as the congressman might have wished it were written. This response to this flagrant display of judicial restraint, said O'Connor, her voice dripping with sarcasm, was that the congressman blasted the courts.

◊ ◊ ◊

"It gets worse, she said, noting that death threats against judges are increasing. It doesn't help, she said, when a high-profile senator suggests there may be a connection between violence against judges and decisions that the senator disagrees with. She didn't name him, but it was Texas senator John Cornyn who made that statement, after a Georgia judge was murdered in the courtroom and the family of a federal judge in Illinois murdered in the judge's home. O'Connor observed that there have been a lot of suggestions lately for so-called judicial reforms, recommendations for the massive impeachment of judges, stripping the courts of jurisdiction and cutting judicial budgets to punish offending judges. Any of these might be debatable, she said, as long as they are not retaliation for decisions that political leaders disagree with.

"I, said O'Connor, am against judicial reforms driven by nakedly partisan reasoning. Pointing to the experiences of developing countries and former communist countries where interference with an independent judiciary has allowed dictatorship to flourish, O'Connor said we must be ever-vigilant against those who would strong-arm the judiciary into adopting their preferred policies. *It takes a lot of degeneration before a country falls into dictatorship, she said, but we should avoid these ends by avoiding these beginnings.*" [Italics are mine]

RawStory.com, the bloggers and some of the online press, God love 'em all, were on the case almost from the beginning, with transcripts of the statement (or as close to transcripts as secondhand recall would allow). That evening, Keith Olbermann, host of MSNBC's "Countdown," kicked the issue around with Mike Allen of Time Magazine. The Guardian (UK) picked up on the story, with an op-ed piece by Jonathan Raban, followed by Jack Shafer, who weighed in the following Monday in Slate.

But what's clear here is exactly the problem. Almost uniformly, the electronic press at least tried to represent on the issue. The newspapers were way behind the curve. Where were The New York Times, the Los Angeles Times and The Washington Post? Why weren't they at the original event? Georgetown has to be considered the Post's neighborhood -- hell, its very backyard; how'd they get caught asleep at the switch on a story like this?

The story is especially arresting in this election year, in no small part because the comments come from a stalwart of the Republican party speaking — free at last of the need for judicial circumspection — in unflattering terms about the Republican leadership in the Congress. Her comments showed again how fragmented the GOP has become in recent months, from the executive to the legislative branches, and now the judicial.

There may be another side to it. The dead-tree media might make the case that newspapers didn't so much miss the story as they missed the *immediacy* of the story, possibly deciding that by the time they could do anything productive with it in print, they'd have already been outflanked by the bloggers and the electronic mainstream media.

That might be correct; these days it's a given that airborne media gets the jump on everything. But it still doesn't explain why the major dailies, which usually delight in pissing from a great height with such big stories, generally dropped the ball.

The San Francisco Chronicle made the speech the subject of an op-ed five days after NPR aired the Totenberg piece. Raban (writing in The Stranger, an alternative Seattle weekly) reported that the Houston Chronicle and the Salt Lake Tribune also carried op-ed pieces based on Totenberg's reporting. And

The Times finally did show up at the party, trying to bigfoot everybody with a comprehensive story combining O'Connor's comments with those from a similarly-themed speech by Supreme Court Justice Ruth Bader Ginsberg in February.

But frankly, it's day late, dollar short from the branch of the media that can't afford to let itself look complacent or out of touch. O'Connor's statement — in its urgency not unlike Winston Churchill's announcement of "an iron curtain" across Europe, in a March 1946 speech, or President Dwight Eisenhower's warning, in January 1961, of the rise of a "military-industrial complex" — is the kind of lucid, non-ideological, valuable wake-up call Americans often don't even realize *is* a wake-up call, and can't afford to miss. It's a shame that this time, a cross-section of the nation's print media wasn't awake to make it.

4/1/2006

POOH! BABY! MEET ME AT THE IVY

"**O**H BOTHER!" With these words, the characteristically self-effacing Winnie the Pooh got his star on Hollywood's Walk of Fame yesterday, the latest sign of Pooh's steady return to good graces after a long decline in Tinseltown. The recipient of the 2,308th Hollywood star is a survivor in every sense.

Pooh began his Hollywood career late by the usual standards. He was in the public eye since the 1920's, appearing in a successful series of books with longtime companion Christopher Robin. Pooh came to southern California in 1966, working with Disney in its relative infancy as a motion picture company. The fortunes of both increased over the years, with Pooh the star of dozens of films, television specials and cartoons.

Once his generation's version of the King of All Media -- cuddly symbol of an empire of animation, publishing, motion picture and product merchandising -- Pooh fell out of favor in the late 80's, as a childhood public increasingly older than its years, and more and more infatuated with technology and eventually the Internet, ignored Pooh's more juvenile brand of adventure.

A long addiction to honey finally gave way to something worse. With few movie prospects and declining book sales, Pooh began to drink heavily, reportedly downing up to a fifth of scotch every day. In 1992, at the height of the crack epidemic, Pooh was arrested on Sunset Boulevard and charged with possession of crack cocaine.

Old friends, such as Eeyore and Pooh's bosom companion, Christopher Robin, turned away, busy with their own careers in Hollywood. Pooh consumed himself with drink, strippers and parties that got wilder with each passing year. He reached rock bottom in 1995 when, at the Oscar ceremonies -- and witnessed by millions on television -- he staggered into the red-carpet crowd, drunk, raving and disheveled, and vomited on the Oscar statue outside the Dorothy Chandler Pavilion.

After a brief stint in jail, and a highly public probation hearing, Pooh retreated to his estate, Hundred Acre Wood, in the Hollywood Hills. He began the slow process of rehabilitation, chastened in part by the death of his lifelong friend Tigger, killed in a 1996 auto-pedestrian accident in London. Pooh's personal therapy included Zen meditation, a change in diet and six weeks at the Hazelden alcoholism clinic. He was also helped by another lifelong friend, Rabbit, whose move-in intervention in 1997 helped Pooh turn the corner.

Eventually, other old friends began to return. In 2000, Pooh teamed up with Robin for an historic one-time joint appearance on "The Late Show with David Letterman." In 2003 Pooh and Eeyore got together to write a script that's now in development at Fox. Pooh is also now in talks to direct a film starring Mickey Rourke and Paul Reubens.

As Pooh dutifully held back tears, Disney CEO Robert Iger made plain at the Los Angeles ceremony the feelings of millions of readers and moviegoers around the world: "You really are a bother." Here's to Pooh bothering us for generations to come.

4/12/2006

#715

BARRY BONDS hit a line-drive home run off Oakland Athletics pitcher Brad Halsey on May 20 to reach 714 home runs in his career, after a long dry spell finally tying the career home-run record of one George Herman Ruth.

Whenever Bonds digs in and blasts career home run No. 715 into the bleachers of some stadium sometime this year, and bet the mortgage that he will, no one from the stands will be on the field to run the bases with Bonds, as some exuberant souls did on April 8, 1974, when Hank Aaron banged out One Past Ruth. Security will see to that.

And after it happens, you can be just as sure that baseball's numerical hierophants will warm up the asterisk-printing machine, placing what some have called the most significant typographical symbol in baseball right next to Barry Bonds' name.

The reason, of course, will be Bonds' alleged use of steroids in recent seasons, in defiance of federal laws and the hallowed traditions of baseball. But even as the Bonds drama heads toward its conclusion, it's high time to step back from the media and the public's relentless focus on Barry Bonds to take a more comprehensive view of cheating, even a broader sense of how "cheating" itself is defined for a game whose past is as much one that is checkered as it is one to be cherished.

Dictionary definitions aside, in the context of baseball, it's fair to say that to cheat is to compromise the values of the game. By that perfectly reasonable yardstick, you can make the case that Kenesaw Mountain Landis, the monstrously intransigent commissioner of baseball, stained the game in his fashion, by continually barring black players from participating in the National Pastime for the 24 years of his stewardship, with at least some acquiescence of the team owners. Landis' action for none other than purely racial reasons blocked such great players as Josh Gibson, Satchel Paige, Buck O'Neill and others from playing in the major leagues.

Had players like Gibson and others been allowed to play in the majors, had their statistics been weaved into the folklore and nomenclature of the game, we would no doubt have seen a completely different statistical baseline for setting records. The single-season records for Babe Ruth and Roger Maris, for example, might very well never have been the sequoias of achievement they became. Don Larsen's El Perfecto might have taken a back seat to one thrown by Satchel Paige.

That's not to excuse what substance or substances (erythropoietin? human chorionic gonadotropin?) Barry Bonds may have taken to give himself an illegal edge; that's not to say that what Bonds may or may not have done wasn't cheating. It is to say that cheating in baseball needs to be put in a broader historical context than just Barry Bonds 2006. In a game whose history is rife with embroideries of the truth of inches the game lives and dies by, it won't do to pillory Barry Bonds forever.

From the 1919 Black Sox scandal to Mark McGwire's pumped-up single-season record to past (and present?) literal tweaks of the surface of the baseball itself, the game has seen more than its share of cheating. Barry Bonds' tainted achievement, when it comes, will join a pantheon of prevarication that's hand in fielder's glove part of the same game as that which we more loudly celebrate — at Cooperstown.

5/24/2006

MELTDOWN IN L.A.

"HE'S A *nigger!* He's a *nigger!*" a man shouts frantically from the stage, pointing at someone or someones in the audience. It is early in the tirade, one whose intensity eventually clears the room. It's therefore not a speech at a Klan rally or the ravings of people in a neo-Nazi mosh pit. This is the city, Los Angeles, Calif., and on the stage of the Laugh Factory, a comedy club located at 8001 West Sunset Boulevard, the comedian Michael Richards is in the process of apparently losing his mind.

The long-ago star of "Seinfeld," in what appeared to be one step in the career reinvention that is common to Hollywood, had some kind of ... meltdown on Friday, November 17, when he appeared at the club as a stand-up comic.

Richards' folly was captured on grainy, slightly shaky images taken on a cell-phone camera at the club; from there the images have made their way to the TMZ.com Web site, and from there onto the reigning information interstate, YouTube, and from there assuming a permanent place in the idiots' wing of the pop-cultural pantheon.Richards exploded on two black patrons of the club, Kyle Doss and Frank McBride, who were just taking their seats after ordering drinks as part of a group of about twenty other people.

What started with Richards' first salvo became an ugly exchange with the two, and others in the audience. "Shut up!" Richards shouts. "Fifty years ago we'd have you upside down with a fuckin' fork up your ass ... You can talk, you can talk, you're brave now, motherfucker. Throw his ass out. He's a nigger! He's a nigger! He's a nigger! A nigger, look, there's a *nigger!*"

Moderating his outburst at one instance, or perhaps himself realizing he was a man on the verge of a professional breakdown, Richards pulls back a little, telling the audience, "It shocks you, it shocks you" and making some oblique reference to "what lays buried."

◊ ◊ ◊

Watching this professional self-immolation, we considered for a fraction of a fraction of a second: Were we witnessing brilliance? Had Richards retrofit Kramer to make some broader, weightier sociological point about the power of language? It had been done before, most incisively in the legendary N-word monologue by Lenny Bruce, the comedian whose jocular but withering dissection of that word in the volatile '60s made an indelible, lacerating point about tolerance and American society, one that resonates today.

But no. *Hell* naw. Not this time. It's clear after about three seconds of the cell-phone video that's not the case. There was no grand strategy. The absence of context and vision speaks for itself. Richards, manically lashing out at the nearest target of opportunity, overdosing on the power of being the only person in the room with a microphone, just Went Off.

"A nigger! Look, there's a *nigger!*" "They're going to arrest me for calling a black man a nigger!" It goes on and on, a self-destruction playing itself out to an increasingly empty room.

You knew it was, uh, an accident almost immediately, in pop-culcha time, when Richards performed a mea culpa by satellite. Three days later Richards had prevailed on Jerry Seinfeld, friend and fellow "Seinfeld" cast member, to let him issue an apology from a great height: a live satellite transmission broadcast on "The Late Show With David Letterman," where Seinfeld was to be a guest that night.

◊ ◊ ◊

On the broadcast, a clearly beaten-down Richards was effusive with contrition:

"…You know, I'm really busted up over this and I'm very, very sorry to those people in the audience, the blacks, the Hispanics, whites — everyone that was there that took the brunt of that anger and hate and rage and how it came through, and I'm concerned about more hate and more rage and more anger coming through, not just towards me but towards a black/white conflict. There's a great deal of disturbance in this country and how blacks feel about what happened in Katrina, and, you know, many of the comics, many performers are in Las Vegas and New

Orleans trying to raise money for what happened there, and for this to happen, for me to be in a comedy club and flip out and say this crap, you know, I'm deeply, deeply sorry."

◊ ◊ ◊

How could this happen? Letterman asked him. "You know, I'm a performer. I push the envelope, I work in a very uncontrolled manner onstage," Richards said. "I do a lot of free association, it's spontaneous, I go into character. I don't know, in view of the situation and the act going where it was going, I don't know, the rage did go all over the place."

Since the Letterman show Richards has gone on to seek counseling with Revs. Jesse Jackson and Al Sharpton, and other arbiters of African American sensibilities. The Michael Richards All Apologies tour is likely to continue, in other venues, for weeks to come.Jackson, who spoke with Richards, said on MSNBC that "my concern was that this fit of anger and rage went beyond use of the word 'nigger.'

Jackson commented on what Richards told him. "He said, 'I have this inner rage, and maybe it's a feeling of inferiority, maybe I was compensating.'I said, 'you need to see a psychiatrist. This requires you needing to get well.'"

Stepping away from the specifics of the Richards' moment, Jackson spoke of the word's wider use throughout America. And he mentioned how indifference to the suffering from Hurricane Katrina and the political resurrection of Sen. Trent Lott to a position of power after the Strom Thurmond debacle were examples of how you don't have to use the N-word in order to communicate that which the word intends.

But for those who do use the word, some social observers are calling for a uniform moratorium on its word. Even among those who use it more than just about everyone else: black people.

"Words are not value neutral," political analyst Earl Ofari Hutchinson said in his widely-read Political Report blog on Nov. 20. "They express concepts and ideas. Often, words reflect society's standards. If color-phobia is a deep-rooted standard in American life, then a word, as emotionally charged as 'nigger,' will always reinforce and perpetuate stereotypes.

It can't be sanitized, cleansed, inverted, or redeemed as a culturally liberating word. 'Nigger' can't and shouldn't be made acceptable, no matter whose mouth it comes out of or what excuse is tossed out for using it."

Hutchinson thus calls out the hiphop thug crews whose use of the word in the lexicon of the 'hood is a sadly astonishing everyday thing.

◊ ◊ ◊

Doss and McBride, the two objects of Richards' fury, have retained counsel – none other than Gloria Allred, the attorney celebrated for recognizing a lucrative income on the backs of stars of various magnitudes. They want a personal apology and possibly some compensation. They hope to meet with a judge in the near future to negotiate the apology, and to let the judge decide on whether compensation, if any, is warranted.

But you have to wonder, what will they sue for? Slander? Defamation of character? Public embarrassment? Because in that prolonged monster's cry, there's nothing, not one word, that black Americans don't already have to contend with every day, anywhere in this country at any given moment.

Therein lies the central fallacy of the Richards meltdown, and our insistence on that meltdown as an aberration of American conduct: It's not so far off the charts of the way we act, black and white and others, all the time.

We've been here before and before: the action, the vehement and indignant reaction, the big-media contrition, the tendency to forget it all in the wash of a news cycle without end. Until it all happens again. Tongues will wag in the weeks to come about What This Says About America; but the initial hysteria will settle into background chatter, online murmurs increasingly lower on the page-view Richter scale. We'll go back to our comfortable assumptions, our old habits about who we are and who they are. Until it all happens again.

The lesson of the Michael Richards incident is how disinclined we are as a nation to learn lessons from things like the Michael Richards incident.

11/25/2006

THE WAKE-UP BOMB

IT'S ninety-seven pages long; you can read it in a day (hell, you probably will before the president does). It was released to the world on Wednesday, a physically modest report on the American military presence in Iraq, the origins of that presence and the consequences for staying there. While some of it is a narrative, codified form of what people in the United States have been saying for months ((if not years), all of it represents the biggest challenge to the stasis of the current military effort since the war began.

The Iraq Study Report may be the wake-up call for the war effort, a document that, while breaking no new ground on offering solutions, is effective both because of its brevity and its bipartisan genesis. The group, commissioned by Congress in March, was composed of ten bipartisan members and chaired by James Baker III and Lee Hamilton, two former Capitol Hill operatives as known for their clear-eyed intellect and drive as for their political inclinations. Consequently, it won't do for the President to dismiss its findings as the partisan rant of the Democrats looking for payback. The power of the report is the simplicity of its arguments and the variety of voices, from both sides of the aisle, roused to make them.

For some, and despite the sense of fellow feeling the report is meant to convey, criticism of the Republican war effort is implicit in its conclusions. Sen. Barack Obama of Illinois, interviewed Wednesday by CNN's Anderson Cooper, said "it would be hard not to see in this report a rebuke of an ideologically-driven strategy that has been blind to what's [been] happening on the ground for the last several years."

Even before the thing came out, the White House and its proxies were spinning furiously, downplaying the impact of something they hadn't seen yet. Gen. Peter Pace tried to have it both ways when asked to characterize the progress of American forces in Iraq. "We're not winning, but we're not losing," the general said, uttering words that we never thought we'd hear coming from one of the Joint Chiefs of Staff.

Hell, there's not a military man in the last hundred years, from George S. Patton to Beetle Bailey, that doesn't know the fundamental rule of American military might: it is not defined by attrition. Standing still is contrary to the military dynamic – and especially the American military dynamic. With the instincts, power and stealth of a shark, the American military machine is defined by forward action. In the classic zero-sum game scenario, if the U.S. military isn't winning, it *is* losing. And we've come to understand, over the last three years and nine months, that the Iraq war doesn't respond to the convenient polarities of "winning" and "losing" anyway, even if the Cold Warriors still do.

◊ ◊ ◊

For Obama, and no doubt for others, the report is a step toward distilling that kind of verbiage and administration spin into something coherent and accurate. "For the first time, what we're seeing is a bipartisan agreement about facts on the ground," he said.

The big question is what President Bush will do with it. Early signs are not promising. Today a testy Bush did a joint standup with British Prime Minister Tony Blair, himself a lame duck as leader of the UK, and essentially repeated his longstanding contention that staying the course is the only viable strategy.

At the root of the president's persistent calculus is the need to keep American forces in place in Iraq until a viable government can establish rule of law over the entire country. But that reasoning in pursuit of a Middle Eastern democracy that can, in Bush's words, "govern itself, sustain itself and defend itself" may be ultimately self-defeating.

The truest test of a democracy is what happens when you take away the guns needed to start one. Sooner or later, the democratic ideal can't be enforced at gunpoint; a democratic government's got to take root and flourish on its own. Ultimately it stands or falls on nothing more, or less, than the confidence, good will and energies of the people living in it. For that reason, the United States will never know for certain if Iraq is capable of a functional, thriving participatory democracy until we *do* leave.

The Iraq Study Report, therefore, calls out the Bush administration to set a timetable not so much for our troops' withdrawal as for the moment for the Iraqi people to decide -- indigenously, on their own terms -- whether they believe in that form of government or not. At the very least, the report is a forthright cry for reality as well as action. In that respect, it's a valuable document. Let's hope the White House sees that.

12/7/2006

JAMES BROWN: MR. SOUL

SO we limp into Christmas morning fairly sure that, with less than a week left in the year, things *can't* get no worse. We think we've heard from every sad and tragic situation from everywhere on earth and we're mentally ready, at least, to hunker down, burrow in, hibernate in winter's fog until the new year. And then we turn on the TV first thing to find out what went down while we were sleeping. And we find out what went down while we were sleeping.

Early that morning at Emory Crawford Long Hospital in Atlanta, James Brown, JB, Mr. Dynamite, Soul Brother Number One, Godfather of Soul, the Hardest Working Man in Show Business, the Original Disco Man and the King of Funk, gave up the ghost, passing from this world to the next, dying of congestive heart failure complicated by pneumonia, at the age of 73.

When we lose any portion of the double helix of the American songbook – George Gershwin, Frank Sinatra, Ray Charles – whatever's left is diminished, less powerful, less passionate. It goes without saying that we're poorer this Christmas than we were before.

It might go without saying, but some people – those who knew him as friend and confidant – found ways to say it. "He was an innovator, he was an emancipator, he was an originator. Rap music, all that stuff came from James Brown," Little Richard, a longtime friend, told MSNBC.

"James Brown changed music," said Rev. Al Sharpton, another longtime friend and one who toured with him in the 1970s. "He made soul music a world music," said Sharpton, one of the few black men in America with nerve enough to pull off wearing a pompadour today. "What James Brown was to music in terms of soul and hip-hop, rap, all of that, is what Bach was to classical music. This is a guy who literally changed the music industry. He put everybody on a different beat, a different style of music. He pioneered it."

◊ ◊ ◊

Generations were inspired by him; legions of rock & soul's best talents copped his moves and attitude. JB was the template, the wellspring of funk from which everything flowed. From Mick Jagger to Michael Jackson, from Prince to the rappers and hiphop artists who sampled his signature shouts and shrieks – everyone stole from James Brown whether they knew it or not.

Want proof? Get a copy of the 1964 TAMI Show. In that concert, James Brown and the Famous Flames were the evening's penultimate act; the embryonic version of the Rolling Stones was to close the show. But James & crew quite simply tore the stage up, JB doing his best dance moves as he fronted a furiously tight band, the perpetual motion machine bringing the crowd to near frenzy, ankles and hips swiveling at angles we had thought were anatomically impossible.

When Jagger and the Stones took the stage, Mick aped James' best dance moves, doing his earnest 22-year-old best but showing in his way why imitation is the most sincere form of flattery (and that night the most hilarious, too).

Some of James Brown's music dovetailed perfectly with a rising sense of black consciousness. The 1968 song "(Say It Loud) I'm Black and I'm Proud" was embraced by young black America in a time when outwardly assertive black pride was still a nascent phenomenon. James never shied away from his role as a race man, one of the major brothers on the scene no matter when the scene was.

"I clearly remember we were calling ourselves colored, and after the song, we were calling ourselves black," Brown told The Associated Press in 2003. "The song showed even people to that day that lyrics and music and a song can change society."

JB may have been a bit hyperbolic about all that. The move away from "Negro" and "colored" toward "black" was already well underway – had been for almost a year. In 1967 Stokely Carmichael, H. Rap Brown and others on the activist left had started the Black Power movement, coining a phrase that galvanized, though some will say divided, the civil rights movement. But James' song became an anthem, taking the notion of forthright black pride from the college campuses and the grip of the intellectuals, and putting it where it needed to be to really resonate: on the radio. This was social change you could dance to.

◊ ◊ ◊

From the beginning, James Brown was a brother we could understand. James was folks, he was one of us from jump street. Born poor in Barnwell, S.C., in 1933, he was abandoned at the age of four to the care of relatives and friends. James grew up on the streets of Augusta, Ga., getting by every way he could: picking cotton, shining shoes, dancing for dimes in the streets of Augusta, doing the odd armed robbery when the need be.

That's what got him sent up for three years in a juvy camp. After that he tried sports for a while, first as a boxer, then as a baseball pitcher. When injuries kept that from happening, Brown considered music. It was the desperation of the times for a young black man that made trying on so many guises, so many identities, necessary.

"I wanted to be somebody," Brown said years later.

James grew up with Bobby Byrd, a friend whose family took him in. They started a group, the Famous Flames, a distillation of a gospel group they already belonged to. In 1956 some record label – the Associated Press says it was King Records, the Rolling Stone Encyclopedia of Rock & Roll says it was Federal Records -- signed the group, and four months later "Please, Please, Please" was in the R&B Top Ten.

For three decades after that, Brown toured almost nonstop, doing cross-country tours, trying out new songs at concerts and earning the title he gave himself, the Hardest Working Man in Show Business.

Part of that hard work was what he did onstage: raw, spontaneous energy punctuated with over-the-top stagecraft. If you went to a James Brown show in the 60's, you got the full James Brown Experience: the dance moves that others would try at and fail for years, the precise 360-degree spins that found the microphone inches from where James left it when he started the pivot; the heroic splits; the energy of a beat channeled through the funky metronome at the front of the stage.

It went on until James, spent, knelt in exhaustion – and out came the brothers carrying the gold lame cape, covering the weary James and escorting him off the stage.

But then – no: James stops a moment, seemingly shivering under the cape, then he spins, shrugs off the cape and sprints back to the microphone ... there was something he forgot to *tell* y'all. Thus a legend of long and furious encores was born. You can believe it when James said he lost five pounds or more during a show.

◊ ◊ ◊

His group became a training ground for musicians who went on to their own acclaim: Hendrix played briefly with the Flames; so did members of George Clinton's Parliament/Funkadelic hybrid; so did bassist Jack Casady before getting his boarding pass for the Jefferson Airplane.

His "Live at The Apollo, Volume 2" in 1962 is widely considered one of the greatest concert records ever and sold more than a million copies in an era when black records never did that well. James won a Grammy in 1965 for "Papa's Got a Brand New Bag" and for "Living In America" in 1987. He was one of the first artists inducted into the Rock and Roll Hall of Fame in 1986, with Chuck Berry and Elvis Presley.

Throughout his career, and despite the accolades, James burnished his cred as a brother's brother. Songs like "King Heroin" and "Don't Be a Dropout" held undeniable messages for young and restive black America. He sponsored empowerment programs for black kids when it wasn't fashionable; in the flashpoint time after the Rev. Martin Luther King Jr. was assassinated in April 1968, about the time "Say It Loud" was on the charts, James went on television to calm things down, probably preventing a bad situation from getting worse.

◊ ◊ ◊

The man's life had no end of drama. In September 1988, ripped to the tits on PCP and brandishing a shotgun, JB walked into an insurance seminar next to his Augusta office and asked the people there if they were using his private bathroom. After he left the building, police chased him for half an hour from Augusta into South Carolina and back into Georgia in some wild "Dukes of Hazzard" shit that ended when police shot out the tires of his truck. He did two years for that, for aggravated assault and failing to stop for a police officer.

For any other star at the age of 58, that might have been enough to bring on retirement. But James kept working, tweaking his show to pull in a younger generation while bearing true faith and allegiance to the funk, and the audience, that got him where he was. Not long after his release, James hit the stage again at a show you needed to pack a lunch to see: a three-hour, pay-per-view concert at the Wiltern Theatre in Los Angeles with an audience that included millions who watched on cable.

It's sad that, toward the end, James became a parody of himself. In recent years a booking photo from one arrest became part of the pop-cultural photo gallery of stars behaving badly and looking worse (others so honored include Nick Nolte, Wynona Judd, Glenn Campbell and George Clinton).

But that was the minor bullshit, the asterisks and footnotes to a career that, for all practical purposes, continued to the day he checked out. The AP reported that, three days before his death, James joined volunteers at his annual toy giveaway in Augusta, and he planned to perform on New Year's Eve at B.B. King's Times Square blues club in New York.

James was consistent. The flamboyance of forty-some years of entrances and exits on stage was mirrored in his big exit on Christmas at 1:45 in the morning. "Almost a dramatic, poetic moment," the Rev. Jesse Jackson told the AP. "He'll be all over the news all over the world today. He would have it no other way."

In any theoretical Mount Rushmore of musical culture, James, pompadour and all, would have to be chiseled high and large and in stark relief from everyone else.

In all the meaningful ways -- both in his message to a young black America desperate for self-worth and potential, and in his music, which bridged the racial divide like no speech or policy ever could -- the man who wanted to be somebody became The Somebody. And hot damn it, if you're a musician working in rock, hiphop, funk or R&B, no matter how original you *think* you are, you need to hit at least one knee and thank your personal God for James Brown. One way or another, he made what you do possible.

And don't feel bad if you never reach his level of Somebody.

Nobody ever will.

12/26/2006

GERALD FORD, LATELY

"HIS life was filled with love of God, his family and his country," read the statement from the family of Gerald Rudolph Ford, the 38th President of the United States, who died Tuesday evening at his home in Rancho Mirage, Calif., at the age of 93.

He was our first and only accidental president, assuming the position after Richard Nixon resigned in disgrace after Watergate, and for just under nine hundred days he took the reins of power, probably expected by many to be not much more than a caretaker, someone to watch the house until the rightful tenants moved back in, whoever they might have been.

Ford – Eagle Scout, former Michigan football standout, stalwart of the House of Representatives, member of the Warren Commission, Vice President – rose to the unexpected occasion, asserting himself as a leader with a clarity of purpose and sense of duty that are truly clear only now, in retrospect, seen in the rear-view mirror as we drive – hurtle – toward our current uncertain future.

But for all his methodical and decisive aspects as president, Ford governed pursuant to the law of unintended consequences. He doomed his chances to be president in his own right, ironically enough, by suggesting to the American people that he could not be relied on act in his own right. With one Sunday morning statement uttered a month into the accidental presidency, Gerald Ford ended his political career; the wounds wouldn't show for another eight hundred sixty days.

"Our long national nightmare is over," Ford said after being sworn in in August 1974. "Our government is one of laws, and not of men," the new president said, not realizing that a month later he would be accused of acting precisely the same way.

On Sept. 8, 1974, Ford extended to Richard Nixon a "full, free and absolute pardon" for any "crimes he committed or may have committed" during his tenure as President of the United States. This get-out-of-jail card from the gods was meant, Ford said for years afterward, to close the books on the Watergate debacle once and for all.

But by circumventing the procedure of congressional oversight and review, by unilaterally deciding that Nixon would not face charges for high crimes and misdemeanors, Ford effectively assumed the role of the government of a man abrogating unto itself the role of a government of laws. For all its noble intent, his pardon seems especially confusing given Ford's reverence for the deliberative powers of Congress – the constitutionally-guaranteed process of analysis and judgment that would have played itself out, however painfully, in an impeachment trial.

It was a decision that Ford would pay for, in the 1976 election, when the elephant's memory of the American people asserted itself to deny Ford the presidency in his own right.

Ford's pardon of Nixon tarnished his role as conciliator in one respect; less widely reported in the recent postmortems is the fact that, later that month in 1974, Ford issued a clemency plan for those who evaded the draft during the Vietnam War – an act that, while just as potentially divisive as the Nixon pardon, sent the signal that Ford was serious about doing what he could to heal the country.

◊ ◊ ◊

In many recollections of President Ford that have already surfaced on the cable shows, there's a tendency to use the word "decent" to describe Gerald Ford. "Good" and "honorable" are also used as ways to describe the president who sought to "humanize" the presidency.

And this is the source of George Bush's problem. Such generous posthumous assessments of President Ford and his presidency will be, inevitably, contrasted with less generous views for President Bush and his administration. No one will actually mention George Bush's name in apposition to Gerald Ford's in a comparison of personalities. But that's the unspoken takeaway: Gerald Ford was a good and decent man as a leader (unlike – *ahem!* – at least one of his successors). The comparison of the two leaders is nakedly implicit.

Bush doesn't need this, doesn't need anything to take the public eye off the ball of the aggressive, bellicose, largely defensive style of Republicanism that he and his administration have perfected for the last half dozen years.

Something else Bush didn't need is an expression of opinion Ford left behind — a statement not exactly from the grave but one embargoed until he got there.

In July 2004 Gerald Ford had an interview with Bob Woodward of The Washington Post, an interview that, we now know, burnished Ford's reputation as a man who spoke his mind without spin and nuances. By agreement, Woodward withheld publication of the interview until after Ford's death.

When Woodward asked Ford about his feelings about the Iraq war, Ford expressed what could be, uh, conservatively called strong doubts. Some excerpts:

"I don't think if I had been president, on the basis of the facts as I saw them publicly, I don't think I would have ordered the Iraqi war. I would have maximized our effort through sanctions, through restrictions, whatever, to find another answer.

"I've never publicly said I thought they made a mistake, but I felt very strongly it was an error in how they should justify what they were going to do.

"And I just don't think we should go hellfire and damnation around the globe freeing people unless it's directly related to our own national security."

The spinmeisters in the Bush White House will of course try to twist that last statement, saying that, yes, this is one of those missions that *is* related to our national security. But the overall context of Ford's comments will be clear and unmistakable and untweakable. The words "big mistake" speak eloquently for themselves.

And when the ceremonies for President Ford get underway this weekend — ceremonies that President Bush is obligated to lead — they'll take place against a backdrop of anti-war sentiments that get more and more bipartisan all the time. Ford's assessment of the Iraq war is no less acute and insightful because he's dead than it would have been if he'd made the comments available for publication when he was alive.

We can thank Gerald Ford for such honesty, and for other humanizing aspects of his brief time in the White House. Yeah, he fumbled, he stumbled, he was prone to goofs and gaffes and contradictions, one of which cost him an election. But Gerry Ford was president in, well, a kinder, gentler American time. He'll be remembered for closing the chapter on Watergate, biting the bullet on the Vietnam War, dismantling the imperial dimensions of the American presidency, and at least trying to engage in a relatively clear-eyed, pragmatic approach to governing, one that's sorely lacking today.

And after ending one long national nightmare, Ford was candid enough to offer a later generation some needed perspective on another one: the enduring bad dream that persists – 3,000 American lives lost (and counting), 22,000 American lives wounded and damaged (and counting), $400 billion dollars evaporated (and counting) – to this day.

There's been a lot of talk in recent years, not much of it that serious, of adding the visage of Ronald Reagan to the faces on Mount Rushmore. Reagan, the thinking goes, ushered American out of a grim era of self-doubt and division, restoring the nation's confidence in itself.

So did Gerry Ford, and Ford did it first, and Ford did it without the residual stardust of Hollywood on his shoulders, unlike Reagan. Gerald Ford was more like us than we knew, or would admit in public, when he was alive. Maybe Ford's image would be better for Mount Rushmore – an everyman face to represent our humbler, more anonymous American aspect.

NATION TO FORD: THANKS.

12/28/2006

THE LAST MEN STANDING

IF YOU live long enough, it seems, you *will* see everything. On Sunday, Feb. 4, Super Bowl XLI, the forty-first distillation of the great national gladiatorial pastime, the brutal choreography that is American football, will take place amid more history than usual. When the Chicago Bears face off against the Indianapolis Colts, for the first time in both the history of the National Football League and the history of big-money professional team sports in America, the championship game will be played by teams lead by black coaches.

For reasons that go beyond regional partisanship, this will be the first Super Bowl in memory where the whole country wins, no matter which coach or quarterback hoists the Vince Lombardi trophy next month.

It's hard to always make a big deal out of the names of sports teams, but this time the names of the two teams left standing after sixteen weeks are a match for the respective physicalities of the two men leading those teams into the spectacle of the Super Bowl. You can't look at sturdy, methodical Lovie Smith, coach of the Chicago Bears and not come away with a legitimate comparison to an actual bear, big, burly, quietly strong. Likewise, in Indianapolis Colts coach Tony Dungy, there's the lean, wiry, angular countenance of a colt, brash and quick, daring and stronger than it realizes it is.

What they have in common is being brothers at the top of their game, two black men who each defeated teams coached by coaches with Super Bowl rings in their safe-deposit boxes.

It always happens like that: After years of coming up empty, it all comes together in a single day. Smith preceded Dungy to Super Bowl XLI by about four hours, his team beating a game and worthy New Orleans Saints squad, in the National Football Conference championship game, in a 39-14 asswhipping. Then Dungy's Colts had just enough to get past the New England Patriots, 38-34, to win the American Football Conference title game.

And just that fast, history was made. It caught us all unawares. Just look at the Patriots' post-game press conference; coach Bill Belichick and quarterback Tom Brady looked gutshot, not so much speaking as mumbling in the hushed, inaudible fashion of an oration at a funeral.

It didn't stop there.

The same day that Smith and Dungy went to the top of professional football, Mike Tomlin, the defensive coordinator for the Minnesota Vikings, was named the head coach of the Pittsburgh Steelers, an ascension if there ever was one. At the age of 34, Tomlin became the 16th coach in the storied franchise's 74-year history, and its first black head coach, sharing the heady company of Chuck Noll and Bill Cowher.

"I'm still coming to grips with what that means," Tomlin told The AP.

Since this happened — since before it happened, really — there's been largely unintelligent talk among the blognoscenti that it's not really such a big deal as all that, a curious willingness to downplay it as a social achievement. "Why are we so insistent that we go on talking about 'the first black this, the first black that?," goes the thinking.

And such thoughts suggest something hopeful, almost perversely optimistic: the idea that, among some bloggers at least, the factor of race is in and of itself not enough to explain the complexities of modern American life. For some, it seems, there's an exhaustion about the issue of race that's rooted in a kind of existential boredom, rather than connected to the historical emotionalism of arguments on civil rights and discrimination, or even to a basic sense of justice and fair play. There's just too much else going on.

That starts to be the kind of perspective that black Americans, and others in the American mosaic, have had for years: that our differences aren't differences as much as distinctions.

This is the first athletic win-win situation the country's had in some time, and probably ever. Oh, the partisans will be there: yahoos from Indianapolis and yahoos from Chicago will turn up in Miami and make that city a bigger spectacle than it already is. And they'll do what fans from two fiercely loved cities are supposed to do.

But step back, peep the bigger picture. This time, equality wins – not just the idea of equality but the real thing, achieved where everyday people live every day, in the wider culture that defines and explains what we are as a nation.

That's means we all win: because it proves that we all *can* win. And that's grounds for nothing less than hope.

1/22/2007

CAVEMEN 'R' US

NEANDERTHALS walk among us. GEICO, the Maryland-based insurance company known as much for its commercials as for its coverage, has developed for its new ads two cavemen characters, who the company hopes will join its old flack, the gecko, among the most effective brand-associative symbols in advertising. In the shrewdly self-referential spots, the unnamed cavemen try to adapt to the modern world, a rude abrasive place in which they find themselves the object of jokes, ridicule, bias—and advertisements. It's an ad campaign about an ad campaign, and it's very much caught on. "The response to the cavemen has exceeded all of our expectations," says Joe Lawson, copywriter at the Martin Agency, which created the ads. Lawson told *Adweek* his firm was "thrilled to share our version of what it's like to be a caveman in the modern world."

In one of the earliest ads in the series, a GEICO pitchman, by delivering the company slogan ("So easy, even a caveman could do it") runs afoul of the sensibilities of two cavemen in his camera crew. He meekly apologizes to the pair later at an upscale restaurant. "Honestly, we didn't know any of you guys were still around," the GEICO apologist says.

Then, in an ad that first aired in October, one of the two cavemen, a smartly dressed, articulate special pleader for the Neanderthal community, is interviewed on a TV talk show. The caveman has issues with the high-handed tone of the interviewer; the interviewer responds: "Tone aside, historically, you guys have struggled to adapt."

"Right," the caveman sarcastically replies, "walking upright, discovering fire, inventing the wheel, laying the foundation for all mankind. Good point. Sorry we couldn't get that to you sooner." Another guest is asked to respond.

"Sounds like someone woke up on the wrong side of the rock," she says — to the caveman's obvious distress.

Either by coincidence or (more likely) by design, the GEICO caveman campaign takes some of its fish-out-of-water cues from V.T. Hamlin's Alley Oop, a comic strip created in 1933 and still syndicated today, about a caveman who travels

83

in a time machine to the 21st century. But symbolically speaking, GEICO's cavemen join the long history of aggrieved American social classes. Irish, Chinese and Italian immigrants alike were reviled, ostracized and victimized when they came to America, and the tragic history of African Americans run through the fabric of the nation from the beginning.

Today, Latinos face the same obstacles to assimilation. So why mock this universally American struggle in an ad?

To J. Fred MacDonald, author of "Blacks on White TV" and "One Nation Under Television" and a history professor at Northeastern Illinois University, the caveman are "a minority you can attack with impunity. We've seen with 'Borat' what happens when you go after a real country like Kazakhstan," he says, referring to the real-life protests and lawsuits emerging in the wake of the Sasha Baron Cohen film. "But cavemen? No one lobbies for Neanderthals," he said. "You've got a lot of Neanderthals in government, but that's another story."

In MacDonald's view, the need to mock those who are different rests deep in our psyche. "It's the human condition— differences provoke an uneasiness that is not funny but can be exploited with humor." Theoretically, the GEICO ads can dispel some of that. "The tension, the differences between us can be pricked with humor, and that's a positive thing. The cavemen continue the genre of ridiculing the different. It's in the tradition of humor that tweaks our differences. Whether you get it consciously or subconsciously, it's there. Usually those differences are ethnic, linguistic or racial, but it's human, it's cross-cultural."

Robert J. Thompson, director of the Center for the Study of Popular Television at Syracuse University, agrees there's more going on in the GEICO ads than first meets the eye. He sees the GEICO ads as another link in the chain of American humor, from minstrel shows that lampooned blacks to borscht-belt comedy that more recently made Jewish Americans a genial laughingstock. While making no parallels between cavemen and Eastern Europeans, Thompson says society has "made more fun of eastern Europeans—the kind of vague eastern European character—than any other ethnic group," citing Latka Gravas, Andy Kaufman's character from

"Taxi," and the Belky character from "Perfect Strangers" as examples. They're safe targets, ready for ridicule without fear of repercussions because their countries don't seem to exist.

The GEICO ads are an extension of this. "It's very safe territory," he said. "These cavemen are quite articulate. They're really urbane, but with this raging sense of entitlement. They come off as funny; we feel we have permission to laugh about it because it's aimed at people who never existed. Cavemen never spoke in English and ordered in restaurants. But the ads could be perceived as offensive because they're making fun of people who are sensitive about stereotypes." For Thompson, the ads are "the tip of an iceberg of a much larger trend — a backlash against political correctness." Thompson says that while the ads mock a nonexistent group, their real target is those people who take offense at stereotyping, the politically correct who are often the derisive focus of "South Park," a show that pushes the power of free speech in the face of a hypersensitive public. "The show is constantly doing parodies of our sensitivity," Thompson says, "Its treatment of Jews, people in wheelchairs and gay people systematically shocks us and says things that are outrageous."

And that seems to be the gist of GEICO's campaign: Besides their branding value, the GEICO ads represent shock as its own objective, shock for shock's sake. Outwardly, the ads have nothing to do with car insurance. Cars aren't even mentioned or depicted in any way. The ads capitalize on the confrontational style of many recent TV ads. Hummer's recent campaign, with peeved drivers trading in their wimpy old vehicles on a sudden, hyperaggressive whim, is a blatant nod to our more atavistic tendencies and that American appeal for instant gratification. Volkswagen's latest ads, featuring startling corner-of-your-eye accidents, all but literally crash into our living rooms to make a point about safety.

The GEICO ad's mission "is getting you to talk about the ads. It speaks to memorability; you do associate it with GEICO," says Shari Anne Brill, vice president and director of programming at media buyer Carat USA. With the caveman ads and the gecko commercials, Brill says, "you've got brand recall in both of those strategies. In the end, remembering the brand and the product is all that matters when people are seeking car insurance." But what does it say that we find insensitivity more memorable than distasteful?

Maybe the overarching takeaway of the GEICO caveman ads is the way their appeal shows how insensitive we've apparently become to the most sensitive among us. Maybe our fractious, divided, red-and-blue-dominant nation — exhausted by the arguments and complaints of various minorities – has less tolerance for tolerance than it once had. GEICO's cavemen reframe the national debate on political correctness in an advertising campaign that's as much a sign of the times as the cars we drive.

2/2/2007
PopMatters

BARACK OBAMA AND THE E-WORD

AMERICANS are nothing if not creatures of habit. From the choices we make in everything from our personal associations to our politics, we're reluctant to get beyond the comfort zone we keep in the back of our minds, the safe harbors of past experience that keeps us from looking anywhere else for anything else. It's maybe nowhere more obvious than in how we react to the national reflex on race matters.

In earlier, frankly quixotic campaigns for the presidency -- Shirley Chisholm, Jesse Jackson, Alan Keyes -- that reflex was always addressed (mostly by journalists) in that tireless but tiresome question, "Is America ready for a black president?" -- a question that says as much about the timid souls who ask it as it does about the object of their curiosity.

A new report from the Pew Research Center suggests that Americans may be tiring of exercising this reflex. In the face of a nation whose demographic profile is changing ... well, in pretty much the time it takes to read these words, Pew researchers say that Senator Barack Obama of Illinois has perhaps the best chance of being the beneficiary of this powerful dynamic in American life: a willingness of the broad body politic to break with the bitter, cynical, racialist habits of the past.

Whether he read that report or not, Barack Obama today sought to be the embodiment of its findings when he appeared on the steps of the Old State Capitol in Springfield, Illinois, where Abraham Lincoln got his start, and formally announced his candidacy for the presidency of the United States of America.

With an address that aimed for the centerfield fence, a speech that hit the higher themes of Kennedy-era oratory, Obama presented a laundry list of possibles: better schools, full implementation of ethics reform on Capitol Hill, environmental sensitivities, universal health care, improvements in fighting the war on terrorism, building a resurgent image of America around the world, ending American participation in the war in Iraq.

"We've done this before," Obama said. "It is time for our generation to answer that call."

Scott Keeler and Nilanthi Samaranayake, the Pew researchers, say that Obama's solid early showing in the early polls for the 2008 race points to "two significant shifts" on the idea of an African American president.

"The first is that an ever larger majority of the public indeed says that they are willing to vote for an African American for the nation's highest office. The second is that polls conducted in campaigns pitting white and black candidates against each other are doing a better job of accurately predicting the outcome of the election now than in the past, suggesting that hidden biases that confounded polling in biracial elections in the 1980s and early 1990s are no longer a serious problem."

◊ ◊ ◊

Obama's campaign, the researchers find, is no lightning-in-a-thimble effort, the kind of thing that led a surprised Time magazine, in 1988, to put on its cover Jesse Jackson, who'd just won the Michigan primary with carfare for organizational money, behind the words of his name punctuated with exclamation and question marks.

"[R]ecent national polling finds that, although [Obama] trails Hillary Clinton for the Democratic nomination, he does nearly as well as Clinton in general election matchups against the frontrunning Republicans, narrowly leading John McCain and running roughly even with Rudy Giuliani," Pew reported.

Drilling down, the Pew report found that kernel of a willingness to embrace a new idea. "More generally, the vast majority of Americans tell pollsters that they are willing to vote for a qualified African American candidate for president."

"The experience of the 2006 elections indicates that racism may be less of a factor in public judgments about African American candidates than it was 10 or 20 years ago," Pew says.

"[T]his review of exit polls and electoral outcomes in several recent elections suggests that fewer people are making judgments about candidates based solely, or even mostly, on race itself, and that relatively few people are now unwilling to tell pollsters how they honestly feel about particular candidates. In such an environment, the high standing of Barack Obama in presidential polling -- or, for that matter, of Colin Powell prior to the 1996 presidential election -- represents a significant change in American politics."

◊ ◊ ◊

In fact, this shift in American attitudes about race and authority has been underway for years. With Powell and Condoleezza Rice as serial secretaries of state; numerous mayors and congressmen and women in power throughout the country; and as of last November, the choice of Deval Patrick as the first elected black governor of Massachusetts, the ground's been well laid for the acceptance of black Americans in positions of true leverage.

But don't everybody jump up singing "Kum Ba Yah" just yet. The presidency is a different matter entirely. For many of those same presumably egalitarian Americans, the question about Obama is, can this hothouse flower of the moment stand the chill of traveling in Iowa and New Hampshire, and the chilly reception he's likely to receive as he works his way south? Will his platform stand the test of time? For that matter, has he got a platform at all? Do I like him? *Do I trust him?*

In any number of ways, these come down to being applications of the E-word -- electability, that ineffable quality that, in his case, isn't a matter of "would you let your daughter marry one?" as much as "Would you let your son [or daughter] go to war on his say-so?"

The hard sell for Barack Obama will be in countering the corrosive effects of the E-word, a word that, rightly or wrongly, has given the more closed-minded people who skulk among us the license to invoke race without actually doing it.

There were naysayers who held youth and relative inexperience against John F. Kennedy, none of which stopped him from becoming President of the United States at the age of forty-three, very close to the age Obama is today. And while it's true that America loves a war hero – which Jack Kennedy apparently was, in the classic American way – the arc of contemporary global politics today has made Obama another kind of war hero: one with the stones to stand up and say going to war is not always a good idea.

◊ ◊ ◊

Whether people say it or not, whether they tell Pew researchers or not, race plays its shadowy, insidious role in our every interaction, real or imagined. It speaks volumes that Barack Obama has advanced this far having performed his own American brand of levitation, rising (for now, anyway) above the reflex reactions of race and politics as usual.

The senator from Illinois spoke of the things that need changing: "the failure of leadership, the smallness of our politics, the ease with which we're distracted by the petty and the trivial, our chronic avoidance of tough decisions, our preference for scoring cheap political points instead of rolling up our sleeves and building a working consensus to tackle the big problems of America."

"It's time to turn the page, right here and right now."

Whether you thought it was a ground-rule double or a blast safely parked on the apartment roof outside the stadium, Obama's address to the burghers of Springfield, his own state of the union speech, was the kind of political oratory we've had precious little of for the past six years. If Pew is right -- if the American wind's just right – shit, who knows? Maybe the kid fresh out of the farm club has the Roy Hobbs-at-the-plate attitude we need to turn this thing around.

Maybe the country's ready -- finally -- to believe in the unbelievable.

2/10/2007

IMUS IN THE MOURNING

RAGE is a strange and powerful thing. It leads men to temptation, it makes allowances for trespass and brooks no forgiveness for those who trespass against us. It leads us to turbulent waters, clouds the judgment and the heart, and makes people see things that aren't really there. Rage reveals both folly and tragedy in pretty much equal measure; it's fundamental to the national conversation, and if you choose to ignore it, you do so at your own peril.

In the stark Fitzgerald's 3 a.m. of his soul, if he were honest about it, George Bush would tell you this.

So would John Donald Imus.

Imus, the 67-year-old legendary radio personality, noisy scold, tireless social commentator and iconoclastic firebrand, has made a career of outrage and impatience and a certain willingness to take shots at people whether they deserve it or not.

It's all made for a rabidly loyal following of fans -- listeners to his radio shows on WNYC and, more recently, WFAN Radio; public figures at every level, including politicians, authors and musicians; and most recently viewers of "Imus in the Morning," a cable TV-simulcast version of his WFAN radio show broadcast by MSNBC from their studios in Secaucus, N.J.

In a sports segment on April 4, at 6:14 a.m. local time, talk between Imus and his broadcast partners turned to the NCAA women's basketball game between Rutgers University and Tennessee.

"That's some rough girls from Rutgers," Imus cracked. "Man, they've got tattoos and ... " At that point Bernie McGuirk, Imus's longtime friend and producer, jumped in. "Some hard-core hos," he said. Imus, laughing, pressed further. "That's some nappy-headed hos there, I'm going to tell you that now," he said. Belly laughs all around. After a few more ugly jibes, they were on to the next thing.

Unspoken, for the most part, was the fact that April 4 was the 39th anniversary of the assassination of Rev. Martin Luther King Jr. in Memphis.

The shitstorm of protest started early and seriously. The Imus exchange was noted by a sharp-eyed researcher at Media Matters for America, the Washington-based media watchdog group. Then the head of the National Association of Black Journalists called for his ouster. Jesse Jackson and Al Sharpton weighed in (a little automatically but necessarily, too).

And just that fast, the bigger shoes dropped. By April 6, the advertisers began to bail from both CBS Radio and MSNBC. Sprint Nextel, Staples, Ditech, GlaxoSmithKline, General Motors, Procter & Gamble and other deep-pocketed heavy hitters threatened to jump ship; in the minds of many, that prospective desertion by advertisers sounded the death knell for the Imus program as much as any lapse of ethics or social judgment.

In an attempt at damage control, on April 9: Imus said "Want to take a moment to apologize for an insensitive and ill-conceived remark we made the other morning regarding the Rutgers women's basketball team. It was completely inappropriate, and we can understand why people were offended. Our characterization was thoughtless and stupid, and we are sorry."

Note the liberal exercise of the Royal 'We," a transparent attempt, some said, at deflecting the criticism beyond the person responsible: Imus himself.

◊ ◊ ◊

Then came other damage control: MSNBC released a statement the same day: "While simulcast by MSNBC, 'Imus in the Morning' is not a production of the cable network and is produced by WFAN Radio. As Imus makes clear every day, his views are not those of MSNBC. We regret that his remarks were aired on MSNBC and apologize for these offensive comments."

But it was so much weak tea, preceded as it was by previous promises by Imus not to resort to such broad and ruthless castigations. David Carr, the media columnist for The New York Times, wrote that Imus' remark was "the kind of unalloyed racial insult that might not have passed muster on a low-watt AM station in the Jim Crow South."

Imus was put on a two-week suspension by both WFAN/ CBS and MSNBC. That might have been enough if not for something unexpected of Imus' usual targets. The Rutgers team decided to fight back.

The team's coach, Vivian Stringer, spoke eloquently about the impact of Imus' words on the team, and the wider signal it sent about America. Her comments -- long-winded but surely heartfelt -- had the devastating impact of a watershed event. In their own way, Stringer's response and that of the black members of the team were the same kind of *cri du coeur* as those made by Joseph Welch to Sen. Joseph McCarthy at the House Un-American Activities committee hearings in 1953. "At long last, Mr. Imus," Stringer seemed to say, "have you no sense of decency?"

Imus was fired by MSNBC on April 11. CBS Radio cashiered him yesterday.

◊ ◊ ◊

Popular culture, being the debris-strewn superhighway that it is, will move around this little episode. Imus will no doubt turn up somewhere else in the information ether, hopefully a little wiser and circumspect about what he says, more learned in doing one of pop-culture's more enduring dance steps: the Mea Culpa Mea Culpa Kum Ba Yah.

But his comments had an impact beyond the words containing the comments, and an object lesson for anyone who works with words for a living.

For many people, maybe the most galling thing about the Imus comments weren't specific to the comments themselves. Imus' commentary proved, absolutely and undeniably, just how low the behavioral baseline for public discourse has fallen in recent years. With his acutely ridiculous statement, it was no longer enough to be a card-carrying rap artist with gold chains, gold teeth, a gold Glock, ready cash and an appetite for the trademark excesses of the thug life (all of that mental construction as much a fabrication, an imitation of life, as anything remotely resembling reality).

Don Imus reset the mark: Now, and especially if you were African American and young, you were a target if you were ordinary people, hard-working, hard-studying exemplars of middle-class values, people putting one foot in front of the other, trying to survive. Imus' remarks wounded precisely because of the pointless randomness of their intended targets. Everyone, no matter who you are, how undeserving of ridicule, everyone can be a target of the angry cosmology of John Donald Imus.

Words can hurt, words can damage. Anyone who truly respects the power of words understands that. Ten or twenty years later than he should have, Don Imus is learning that now.

4/13/2007

GOD BLESS YOU, MR. VONNEGUT

KURT VONNEGUT, celebrated writer and bipedally-locomotive carbon-based terrestrial life form, fell recently and suffered brain injuries at his home in Manhattan. He died. He was 84. The moral and spiritual impoverishment of our times has increased exponentially. So it goes.

An author whose vision of our world and its people was by turns profoundly pessimistic and profoundly upbeat, Vonnegut brought us a mordant wit wrapped around an irrepressible moral vision. His fascination with science fiction underscored what seemed to be a deeply-held desire for escape from this earthly plane, flight from the charnel house of modern times -- a wish, couched in dark humor, one-liners and philosophical asides, to be anywhere else ... anywhere but here and now.

◊ ◊ ◊

Some of his novels, "Slaughterhouse-Five," "Cat's Cradle" and "God Bless You, Mr. Rosewater" in particular, were personal points of reference for college students in the 1960's and 1970's. For years you were guaranteed to find copies of those works and others at college bookstores and on plywood-and-cinderblock shelves in university dorm rooms across the country — a kind of red badge of undergraduate rebellion.

Vonnegut became something of a literary icon, one adored by students and the left. His very appearance -- bushy hair, tweed jacket, the obligatory Pall Mall cigarettes he favored -- suggesting a renegade college professor straight out of central casting.

Vonnegut came by his pessimism honestly. What may have been the definitive experience of his life was a defining moment for humanity as well. The firebombing of Dresden, Germany by British and American forces in 1945, an event he witnessed firsthand as a prisoner of war. Thousands of civilians were killed in the raids, many of them burned alive or asphyxiated by the firestorm that consumed the oxygen in the air.

"The firebombing of Dresden was a work of art ... a tower of smoke and flame to commemorate the rage and heartbreak of so many who had had their lives warped or ruined by the indescribable greed and vanity and cruelty of Germany," he wrote in "Fates Worse Than Death: An Autobiographical Collage."

"The corpses, most of them in ordinary cellars, were so numerous and represented such a health hazard that they were cremated on huge funeral pyres, or by flamethrowers whose nozzles were thrust into the cellars, without being counted or identified."

◊ ◊ ◊

That experience formed the backdrop of "Slaughterhouse-Five,"published in 1969 during the height of the Vietnam War, an occasion for yet another series of indifferent conflagrations.

In "Kurt Vonnegut's Fantastic Faces," a 1999 essay reprinted on the apparently official Vonnegut Web site, Peter Reed explains the way Vonnegut used sci-fi as a way into our rather more pedestrian world:

"Vonnegut has typically used science fiction to characterize the world and the nature of existence as he experiences them. His chaotic fictional universe abounds in wonder, coincidence, randomness and irrationality. Science fiction helps lend form to the presentation of this world view without imposing a falsifying causality upon it. In his vision, the fantastic offers perception into the quotidian, rather than escape from it."

Tom, a reviewer for Amazon.com, writing from Palatine, Ill., observed that "Vonnegut has a way of combining Orwell's eye with Updike's wit, and the sum is greater still, than the parts."

One of his oft-used visual symbols, what appears to be an asterisk, has done double-duty for years: It could be an anal sphincter. It could be a star in a distant galaxy. In the hands of Vonnegut the graphic artist, it could go either way, a symbol of our highest cosmic aspirations or a symbol of humanity at its most banal.

◊ ◊ ◊

Despite writing celebrated novels that dwelt on the earthiest aspects of humanity, Vonnegut looked up in the night sky of his life and saw more than pinpricks of light. In a brief appearance in a 2002 film, for example, he said that "music is, to me, proof of the existence of God. It is so extraordinarily full of magic and in tough times of my life I can listen to music and it makes such a difference."

That was Vonnegut, all right: the spiritual mixed in with the humorist with a fatalist streak. "I've had a hell of a good time," Vonnegut once wrote. "I tell you, we are here on Earth to fart around, and don't let anybody tell you any different."

In his 1965 novel, "God Bless You, Mr. Rosewater," Vonnegut offered a philosophy strong enough to have been his valedictory if he'd stopped writing then. Written in the language of a greeting to newborns, it's a philosophy that we, today, in a world more fractious and divisive and threatened than ever before, would do well to tell our children, our neighbors, ourselves, from now until the end of time:

"Hello, babies. Welcome to Earth. It's hot in the summer and cold in the winter. It's round and wet and crowded. At the outside, babies, you've got about a hundred years here. There's only one rule that I know of, babies — 'God damn it, you've got to be kind.' "

4/13/2007

97

MURDOCH! MURDOCH! NIGHTAMRE OF MURDOCH!

O N July 31, after months of negotiation and a great wailing and gnashing of teeth in the American media, Keith Rupert Murdoch, legendary boardroom buccaneer and king of tabloid journalism, completed acquisition of The Wall Street Journal, the crown jewel of his News Corporation media empire, for $5 billion – on a per share basis, a handsome runup in the value of the shares of Dow Jones, the Journal's parent company.

The new boss celebrated his latest acquisition with execs and advisers at News Corp. headquarters in Manhattan by breaking out bottles of Australian Shiraz, a fine full-bodied red-wine narcotic. His employees no doubt used something stronger; Oxy-Contin might not even be enough. There's been great trepidation on the part of Journal staff; resumes have reportedly been in circulation for weeks, if not months. But with the deal done, Murdoch has exercised his right to tweak that famous excerpt from the Hindu scripture, the Bhagavad-Gita:

Now I am become Owner, destroyer of standards and reputations."

◊ ◊ ◊

From now until the deal is consummated, probably some time in early October, the mouthpieces of the media will be circling the wagons and calling their bookies to place bets on how this most prestigious American newspaper will be transformed. If past is prologue, and it often is, the signs are not good.

The cognoscenti of the press wasted no time in discussing the issue. On PBS's "Charlie Rose," Ken Auletta, media columnist for The New Yorker, told Rose that the acquisition "gives him enormous power, enormous clout. The Journal will set an agenda the way the [News Corp.-owned] New York Post cannot." Some of that clout will be evident when Murdoch's Fox News Business Channel launches, with the assets and resources of the Journal, in more than 31 million homes, on October 15.

Much of the delay in the acquisition was a result of protracted discussions within the Bancroft family, previously the owners of Dow Jones and a clan Auletta told Rose was "as dysfunctional as Paris Hilton's family." The battlin' Bancrofts dithered and pulled their chins about selling the Journal for months, with some in the family sincerely expressing reluctance to sell based on principles of Journalistic Integrity and Editorial Independence.

But Andrew Ross Sorkin, a brilliant New York Times business reporter, made a telling point on the Charlie Rose program, one that's largely flown under the media radar: That, after all the breast-beating from the Bancrofts about maintaining credibility and upholding the Journal's values and traditions, it all came down to chump change – a relatively small amount of money, given the Bancrofts' already formidable resources.

Sorkin: "On Sunday night the Denver trust [of the Bancroft family], which was the last holdout trust said, 'you know what? We want more than sixty bucks. You gotta give us more than sixty bucks. And Rupert's team said, 'no, we're not giving you anything more, and that's it, and we're gonna walk and that's the game.' And [the Bancrofts] said, 'well … would you think about paying our bankers and advisory fees?' … In the end, that's what put him over the goal line. Forty million dollars!"

The crafty Australian-born magnate was apparently smart to make an offer for Dow Jones north of its market worth right from the start. Murdoch's $5 billion bid valued each Dow Jones share at $60, well above its trading range in the thirties earlier in the year. Thus, Murdoch froze out the competition. For good.

"You'd think everybody and their brother would want to own the Wall Street Journal," Sorkin said. "Well, everybody and their brother *does* want to own the Wall Street Journal, but not at 60 dollars a share. … The idea of not accepting the bid – just think of what would happen: the shares would go down, management would freak out, the staff would be in turmoil and … we would be talking about this for the next two years and Rupert would be back and buying it at half the price.

If you think *this* was a distraction, having said 'no' would be worse."

Meanwhile, concerns about the future of the Journal continue among professional journalists. In today's Boston Phoenix, for example, Adam Reilly recounts how Murdoch and his minions transformed the Boston Herald, which Murdoch acquired in late 1982:

"Step One was changing the layout from four columns to seven -- better for packing the pages with short, easy-to-read stories. Step Two was changing the paper's ethos, from the subdued tabloid style cultivated under Hearst to something more authentically Murdochian -- edgy, sensationalistic, and shameless."

Reilly relates that Les Hinton, an Australian who was assigned to be the Herald's new managing editor, told another editor that "every page should look like it's having a nervous breakdown."

If that's in any way the marching order for the new Journal, we can kiss any enduring sense of its journalistic gravitas goodbye. There's a new sheriff in charge at Wall Street's paper of record. "I may be evil," Rupert Murdoch said, "but I'm not Pol Pot evil." Lord help us all.

8/8/2007

VIETNAM, THE SEQUEL II

AS THE death toll of civilian and Defense Department forces in Iraq sprinted past 3,700, and three scant weeks before the breathlessly awaited report from Gen. David Petraeus, the White House has begun circling the wagons, retrenching to old positions – and reframing old arguments for the war in terms we wouldn't have expected. Its latest rejiggering of old rationales points to just how rudderless this administration has become on how best to resolve its defining debacle.

President Bush spoke Monday at the Montebello meeting of North American leaders in Canada. Expressing a sentiment Americans can sympathize with, Bush admitted to "a certain level of frustration" with the Iraqi government's failure to unify its warring enclaves. His comments came shortly after the top American diplomat in Baghdad, U.S. Ambassador Ryan Crocker, offered a downbeat assessment of the Iraq situation -- a kind of report before the report -- calling political advances there "extremely disappointing."

On Wednesday, in a speech to a Veterans of Foreign Wars convention in Kansas City, Mo., Bush repackaged his standard stick-with-the-plan speech, with fresh urgency:

"Our troops are seeing this progress on the ground. And as they take the initiative from the enemy, they have a question: Will their elected leaders in Washington pull the rug out from under them just as they are gaining momentum and changing the dynamic on the ground in Iraq?"

◊ ◊ ◊

Then the president further tried to make his case by summoning the ghost of the last truly disastrous national military intervention, a specter we would not have thought this White House would dare to arouse.

"Whatever your position in that debate, one unmistakable legacy of Vietnam is that the price of America's withdrawal was paid by millions of innocent citizens whose agonies would add to our vocabulary new terms like 'boat people,' 're-education camps,' and 'killing fields,' " Bush said, alluding to the horrors of Pol Pot and the Khmer Rouge in Cambodia.

But wait. He said the V word! VIETNAM. The images cascade before the national eyes. Choppers landing in blood-soaked LZs to ferry scores of American wounded to a safe place. Frantic firefights. The incineration of innocents. An embassy under siege. The North Vietnamese flag flying over Saigon. American might visually characterized, forever, by the images of empty Huey helicopters pushed from the decks of aircraft carriers into the sea, or crowded Hueys in bugout mode with refugees dangling from the struts.

After seeing an advance draft of the Montebello speech, historian Robert Dallek said in a New York Times interview excerpted on Aug. 21 that the mayhem under the Khmer Rouge "was a consequence of our having gone into Cambodia and destabilized that country."

Dallek's historically-based assertion is surely the right one, and points to another White House misreading of recent American history. But what's more curious, and wholly unexpected, is the administration's relatively sudden embrace of analogies with Vietnam in the voicing of White House policy.

Not so long ago, any phrasal linkage of the war in Iraq with the Vietnam War was anathema to the administration. The connections between the two, so White House reasoning must have gone, were too redolent of historical failure and horrific memories to be of service in establishing the policy language for Operation Iraqi Freedom. Why the switch?

Maybe it was what Alexander Haig said last year. Haig -- a man more or less present at the creation of the Vietnam Experience -- spoke at a March 2006 conference at the John F. Kennedy Presidential Library and Museum in Boston. Haig compared Vietnam to Iraq as an example of America repeating an earlier mistake. "Every asset of the nation must be applied to the conflict to bring about a quick and successful outcome, or don't do it," Haig said, according to the Associated Press. "We're in the midst of another struggle where it appears to me we haven't learned very much."

◊ ◊ ◊

Now, by invoking the Khmer Rouge, the killing fields and other signatures of the Vietnam conflict, the Bush administration seems to have come to terms with the analogies – as well as with validating, whether intending to or not, Sen. Ted Kennedy's long-ago assertion that "Iraq is George Bush's Vietnam."

That would suggest it was intentional. The other possibility is that the administration didn't see the analogy through, that they really don't *realize* how bad the comparison looks. Yeah, the West Wing speechwriters came up with the name of a group of terrorists who slaughtered in wholesale numbers. That's the easy association.

But the dissimilarities between the Khmer Rouge in Cambodia and al-Qaida in Iraq, and the eras in which they grimly prevailed, beg the question of why the Bush White House would use a cold-war symbol to analogize a situation in the current asymmetrical conflict in the first place. Is this just more tone-deafness from the Bush White House? Has Karl Rove left the building yet?

The countdown clock to release of the Petraeus report is off and running, but it would seem the administration is field-testing responses to that report right now. But Bush's Kansas City address summons precisely the historical comparisons the administration used to say were Not Helpful, and points again to a White House at odds with itself. There's a disconnect somewhere, but one not nearly as troubling as the short-circuit of confidence playing out between Washington and Baghdad

The lack of confidence in the Iraqi government the White House has invested blood, treasure and credibility in speaks poorly of the Maliki government, and less well for the U.S. government that made the Maliki government possible.

8/23/2007

TURKEY IN THE STRAW POLL?

CUE the theme from "Rocky": Former Massachusetts governor Mitt Romney had his big moment over the weekend, making like Rocky Balboa running up the steps of the Philadelphia Museum of Art, his arms aloft in triumph. In the Iowa straw poll for Republican presidential hopefuls, an early beauty contest for the GOP candidates, Romney came in first place over his challengers -- *flying hiiiigh now!*

But hold up. Turn the music off. Let's dig a little deeper. Turns out that Romney finished first in a crowded field of exactly three, prevailing in this early test of popularity over former Arkansas governor Mike Huckabee and Kansas Sen. Sam Brownback. The other major challengers for the Republican nomination -- former New York mayor Rudolph Giuliani, Tennessee Sen. Fred Thompson and Arizona Sen. John McCain -- didn't even show up. That fact calls into question just how much traction Romney really has, even using this victory as a springboard to gaining wider gravitas among Americans outside the bustling metropolis of Ames, Iowa.

Leave it to a veteran reporter to put things in perspective. David Yepsen of the Des Moines Register, interviewed yesterday by Tavis Smiley, called this temporary emperor on his wardrobe. Romney, Yepsen said, "got more votes than anybody else, so in that sense he can claim a victory. But I don't think it means a whole lot if you win a fight when the other champions don't get in the ring."

More important to Yepsen, and other pol watchers, was the strong second-place showing of Huckabee, whose folksy, accessible style and serious sense of humor has resulted in a lot of double takes from people once prepared to write him off. Witness the front-page story in yesterday's New York Times, a story whose focus on Huckabee's surprising finish effectively eclipsed Romney, a man the conventional wisdom said was *expected* to win in Iowa.

For Yepsen, Huckabee's strong second was "an indication that [he] is starting to rally some of the social conservatives" looking for a star to hitch to their wagon.

Huck's campaign in Iowa takes on even more significance when you consider the bottom-line factors involved. Romney spent in the mid- to high six figures to win the straw poll, papering the hall with his own paid staffers, there to cheer and wave the placards with the boss's name.

Huckabee spent chump change — about $87,000 by one "Hardball" estimate — to come in a solid second place, making his showing one of the most cost-effective presidential campaign moves since Jesse Jackson won the Michigan primary in 1988 with not much more than what he found in the couch cushions.

It's anyone's guess how Romney would have done against the other contenders. It's questionable whether McCain would have showed up even if he *had* showed up. Fred ("Law & Order") Thompson has been pulling his chin, waiting to officially get into the campaign for so long now, Yepsen said he suspects Thompson will peak the minute he declares. Only Giuliani had any real throw weight among the no-shows.

So really, Romney's yet to be tested. Romney's got the serious deep pockets needed to go the distance; the Boston Globe screamed his net worth, an estimated $250 million, on its front page. But the Book of Mormon still hangs around his neck as a possible political liability, one Romney may have to address in some Major Speech not unlike the one John Kennedy made in defense of his Catholicism back in 1960.

It's early yet, and way too early for anyone to coronate Mitt Romney, or for Mitt Romney to coronate himself. He's not "flying high now" so much as still flying under the radar.

8/14/2007

MSNBC: BLOWIN' WITH THE WIND

IN A STORY published yesterday, The New York Times notes something we've quietly observed for about a year now: that the MSNBC cable channel has shifted in its willingness to take on the Bush administration, with some of its more popular chat hosts going after the administration as reliably and automatically as the Fox News Channel is ready to praise that administration to the skies.

Emboldened by consistently high ratings for "Countdown With Keith Olbermann," a program whose hostchannels Howard Beale, Edward R. Murrow and Bob & Ray in confronting the Bushies on just about everything, MSNBC is now even entertaining the idea of giving unrepentant madcap leftie Rosie O'Donnell her own prime-time show. If it happens, O'Donnell would join Olbermann and Chris Matthews' "Hardball" as on-air champions of the left.

Longtime viewers of MSNBC will note that it wasn't that long ago that Phil Donahue, another chat host with a decidedly left-leaning agenda, was cashiered from the network – ostensibly because of poor ratings, but possibly as a result of reaction by MSNBC brass, who issued an internal memo ordering Donahue's dismissal for being out of step with America's then-mostly hawkish sentiments about the Iraq war.

"He seems to delight in presenting guests who are anti-war, anti-Bush and skeptical of the administration's motives," the memo read in part. The memo, leaked to the All Your TV Web site, warned that Donahue's program could be "a home for the liberal anti-war agenda at the same time that our competitors are waving the flag at every opportunity."

Maybe Donahue was just a victim of bad geopolitical timing. Since his dismissal in February 2003, the U.S.-led war effort has endured a steadily increasing death toll, the Abu Ghraib prison scandal, controversies about cowboy contractors killing unarmed civilians, financial oversights, and growing concerns about the role of Iran in the conflict and political instability in neighboring Pakistan. All strong reasons for a shift in popular sentiment about the war, and for reporting sensitive to that shift.

Whatever the specific reasons, it's been clear for many months – certainly since the midterm elections last year -- that MSNBC feels more confident about taking on the administration, with increasingly confrontational questions for its apologists and excusers. MSNBC is clearly moving with the populist tide.

"[W]hether by design or not, MSNBC is managing to add viewers at a moment when its hosts echo the country's disaffection with President Bush," The Times reported yesterday.

For sure. The Times reported that "Tucker," the early-prime-time program hosted by the tireless GOP apologist Tucker Carlson, is in danger of cancellation, according to an NBC *jefe* who spoke to The Times under cloak of anonymity.

Even Joe Scarborough, the one-time Florida congressman who retooled himself for cable television and was once the host of MSNBC's nakedly conservative "Scarborough Country," has lately had a change of heart, if not of political temperament."I'm just as conservative as I was in 1994, when everyone was calling me a right-wing nut," Scarborough told The Times. "I think the difference is the Republican Party leaders, a lot of them, have run a bloated government, have been corrupt, and have gone a very, very long way from what we were trying to do in 1994. Also, the Republican Party has just been incompetent."

Whether MSNBC's new left-leaning perspective continues is anyone's guess. The network still trails Fox in the ratings, and any military breakthrough stemming from the U.S. troop escalation early this year – if Osama bin Laden is discovered hiding in a spider hole somewhere in the Hindu Kush – might make MSNBC execs rethink the slant of their programming.

For now, though, MSNBC is riding this ninth ninth wave of popular opinion as far as it can. A prime-time show for Cindy Sheehan may not be far behind.

11/7/2007

NORMAN MAILER:
THE LIFE OF OUR TIME

NORMAN MAILER -- the "presumptive general" of American letters, bibulous provocateur, showman, existentialist, misogynist, wannabe mayor, and lover of women, essayist, journalist, novelist, playwright, director, six times a husband and nine times a father, author of more than 30 books and burr under many complacent saddles of American life, died Nov. 10, of renal failure at New York's Mount Sinai Hospital, at the age of 84.

With his passing, American literature has lost perhaps the greatest literary exponent of that "greatest generation" Tom Brokaw has championed – and every generation since. His was the life of our time.

In a career that spanned just short of sixty years, he threw light – often raw and interrogation-brilliant, sometimes refracted through the prism of a formidable ego – into a multitude of America's hidden corners.

The phrase "presumptive general" fit its subject perfectly. All we ever really knew about him was a consequence of conflict. It informed our first understanding of who Mailer was. His debut novel, "The Naked and the Dead," a fictionalization of a patrol experience in the Pacific theater of the war, was published in 1948, and remained No. 1 on The New York Times best-seller list for 11 straight weeks.

He constantly harangued with the press as his prodigious output continued. Works that followed were variously attempts to reveal some deeper, inner precincts of the human experience, including sex, power, and the third-rail issue for our American time, race -- or attempts to extrapolate the turmoil and chaos of his own life to the tumult of his times.

He stabbed his second wife, Adele Morales, with a penknife in 1960. He arm-wrestled with Muhammad Ali in 1965. While filming "Maidstone" in 1968, he bit off part of Rip Torn's ear after Torn reportedly attacked him with a hammer.

Mailer was on point for some of the pivotal protest events of the Vietnam War era, including the 1967 march on the

Pentagon (resulting in "The Armies of the Night" and his first Pulitzer Prize) and the 1968 Republican convention, an assignment for Esquire that led to "Miami and the Siege of Chicago." His style had evolved amid the battles of the day -- the Times' Charles McGrath described it as "bold, poetic, metaphysical, even shamanistic."

If his delivery was evolving, so too were his interests. "Of a Fire on the Moon," initially an assignment for Life magazine, became a book on the 1969 U.S. moon landing. "King of the Hill" was a short but arresting reportage of the second Ali-Joe Frazier fight.

His writings would come over the years to ricochet around history, from "Ancient Evenings," his ambitious novel on ancient Egypt, to "Tough Guys Don't Dance," a hard-boiled detective story, from "Marilyn," a coffeetable appreciation of Marilyn Monroe as pop-culture archetype to the book generally regarded as his best – "The Executioner's Song," his deeply-felt, passionately-drawn study of the life of murderer Gary Gilmore, for which Mailer won his second Pulitzer Prize.

In 1991 the novel "Harlot's Ghost" ventured the Central Intelligence Agency as a kind of postwar government secret society, a clandestine cross of MI6 and the Vatican. A biography of Picasso was issued in 1995; in 1997 he published "The Gospel According to the Son," a first-person novel about Jesus.

There was vast sweep and unquenchable interest. But Michiko Kakutani, a frequent antagonist and writing Nov. 10 in the International Herald Tribune, regretted Mailer's inability to write some hypothetical Big One, doing so in language that let death awaken no sympathy.

"Instead of writing a great Tolstoyan novel about America that would "speak to one's time" and capture the social and political pulse of the nation, he increasingly produced tendentious novels that were scaffolds for his eccentric, sometimes perverse ideas about violence and sex and power, what he once called 'the mysteries of murder, suicide, incest, orgy, orgasm and Time.'"

◊ ◊ ◊

Michael E. Ross

Mailer has been accused of literary prostitution, of cranking out books more motivated by compensation than by inspiration. But the accusations seem mean-spirited and out of character with people who would truly understand the process of literature. Never mind that he needed the money; most writers can relate to that. But Mailer's diversity of topic, of the focus on his creative and emotional lens at any given time, must eventually reflect a diversity of mind, if a thematically scattered one.

To accuse him of enduring hubris and self-importance about his writing and his role in the wider national life is to finally accuse every writer of having nothing more or less than ambition. What major leaguer with any self-respect doesn't want to swing for the fences every time he steps to the plate? What heavyweight champion in mothballs doesn't harbor the dream of one more fight?

Somehow, in his embrace of combat was our own. Charles McGrath, writing in the Times, described him, fairly, it must be said, as "an all-purpose feuder and short-fused brawler, who with the slightest provocation would happily engage in head-butting, arm-wrestling and random punch-throwing. Boxing obsessed him and inspired some of his best writing. Any time he met a critic or a reviewer, even a friendly one, he would put up his fists and drop into a crouch."

In the 1970s it was combat with feminists and proponents of women's liberation. In the celebrated raucous April 1971 debate with "The Female Eunuch" author Germaine Greer, he declared himself an "enemy of birth control."

At times his provocations seemed less based in any serious differences on feminine issues, and more the willful exercise, like the child who pulls the wing off a fly just to see what happens. Sometimes to riotous result:

At the University of Colorado, just after beginning a speaking engagement in 1973, he called on the women in the audience – angry proponents of women's liberation, then in its heyday as a social movement -- to "hiss me resoundingly." When the women complied, Mailer replied with a perfect timing. "Thank you, obedient little bitches," he said.

110

Maybe, Gore Vidal once seemed to suggest, it was showmanship for its own sake. Vidal, one of Mailer's more storied and frequent antagonists, once wrote: "Mailer is forever shouting at us that he is about to tell us something we must know or has just told us something revelatory and we failed to hear him or that he will, God grant his poor abused brain and body just one more chance, get through to us so that we will know. Each time he speaks he must become more bold, more loud, put on brighter motley and shake more foolish bells. Yet of all my contemporaries I retain the greatest affection for Norman as a force and as an artist. He is a man whose faults, though many, add to rather than subtract from the sum of his natural achievements."

◊ ◊ ◊

For all his eccentricities, he seemed to remain hard-wired to shifts not of the public mood, but of the public psyche. In 1984 Mailer was the main force in bringing together writers for a conference, "The Writer's Imagination and the Imagination of the State," perhaps sensing even then (two years into Reagan America) the value in discussing the divergence of imagination in the two vast spheres of public life.

Speaking in an interview with Andrew O'Hagan at the New York Public Library in June 2007 — well into the era of 9/11, this time that has rattled America's sense of its own existence — Mailer expressed what far too many Americans seem to feel these days: a sense of loving but almost fatalistic resignation to the quirks and volatilities of the one you can never leave. "In a certain sense, I've been angry at America most of the years of my life, but I've always been in love with America in the oddest fashion. ... In other words, one's country is one's mate."

And for writers, the practitioners of a solitary craft, one of his valedictory comments, shortly before his passing, is troubling – or damn well should be.

"I think the novel is on the way out," Mailer said. "I also believe, because it's natural to take one's own occupation more seriously than others, that the world may be the less for that."

111

Setting aside the possibility of that comment as his outsize ego's parting shot – "When I'm gone, it's all over" – it's perhaps better to reach for the deeper point he made, one consistent with his philosophy as well as his observations: that in a relentless 24/7 age of instant communication – witness the blogs and message board we speak through at this moment – the novel may call on powers of rumination and reflection that are rapidly dissipating; nuance, shading and personality are flattened to accommodate a growing impatience; the subtleties of the tale are subject to abbreviation based not on its own substance but on our quickly vanishing time in which to absorb it.

Today, the story is too easily storyboarded. For the way we would communicate the texture and nuance of our traditions, our cultures, our values and dreams, there can be no clearer warning than that.

◊ ◊ ◊

He did not go quietly. Mailer was a bitter foe of the Bush White House, condemning the weaponized misnomers of the administration in the furtherance of various Bush initiatives, particularly the war in Iraq.

He took on the Bush administration with the same brio as in his heyday, when he sparred with Johnson and Nixon for the inanities of their respective White House tenures. In 2007 he called George Bush "[t]he worst president in America's history. He's ignorant, he's arrogant, he's stupid in all ways but one, which is he's immensely shrewd about the American people, particularly the less intelligent half of America."

But for the most part, in his later years he was less a brawler than a champion in his winter, weighing in with pronouncements justifiably but reliably more mandarin in sparsity and style with every passing year.

The Times' Charles McGrath captured perfectly the bearded, emeritus Mailer, recalling "something he had said at the National Book Award ceremony in 2005, when he was given a lifetime achievement award: that he felt like an old coachmaker who looks with horror at the turn of the 20th century, watching automobiles roar by with their fumes."

In "The Spooky Art," his 2003 cut-and-paste catalog of mea culpas, and a reckoning of the literal performance of his art and his craft, Mailer offers another telling aspect of his philosophy, a gauntlet throwdown, a valedictory and a summation of his life as durable for a headstone as for history itself.

"[H]e has had the courage to be bold where others might cry insanity."

That our epitaphs should be the same.

So long Norman. *Requiescat in pace*, Nachem Malek.

11/12/2007

BLACK LIKE US

SSAYIST, novelist and cultural hanging judge Stanley
Crouch's indictment-by-origin of Barack Obama in the
Nov. 2 New York Daily News suffers from an obvious
myopia about how history gives way to the present day, how
old ancestral conflicts resurface in the reflexes of the moment,
how a shared historical heritage isn't necessarily as convincing
a determinant of commonality as shared contemporary
experience is.

In one of the most corrosive comments made concerning
Obama's ethnicity, Crouch writes that Obama's bona fides
as a black man are suspect. "After all, Obama's mother is of
white U.S. stock. His father is a black Kenyan. Other than
color, Obama did not — does not — share a heritage with
the majority of black Americans, who are descendants of
plantation slaves."

"So when black Americans refer to Obama as 'one of us,'
I do not know what they are talking about."

What they are talking about is something besides history,
that series of cascading antecedent events you can't do anything
about. Most black Americans aren't engaging with Obama
and his ever-widening presidential campaign at the level of his
personal history – his birth and childhood being events he had
no control over; his heritage, like our own, a fact of life at the
innocent, vulnerable outset of life. African Americans have
been, apparently like Crouch, long plagued with retroactive
vision, an insistence of looking back instead of looking
forward. This tragic misdirection of vision has its legacy in
everything from the rate of incarceration for young black men
to the continued decline of African American health.

◊ ◊ ◊

What Obama proposes, and what many Americans embrace
him for, is taking nothing less than the risk of the courage,
the nerve — yes, the audacity — to look ahead, not because
of our history but in spite of it. The themes of his campaign
call for working past the usual pressure points, intraracial and

interracial, and to see the things we do have in common – both as Americans and, more privately, more personally, as African Americans.

Crouch's focus on the candidate's historical origins is one from a purely academic perspective, an abstract vision of clarity from the world of ivy walls. For Obama's black supporters down on the ground, it's another story. At least once in the campaign, Obama related that he was passed up a cab driver in New York -- an experience once common in the city. Notwithstanding the fact that such snubs don't happen that much there anymore, when Obama was passed up by that cab driver (who may have gone down the street and picked up a white passenger instead) – guess what? That's the level of discrimination too many black Americans still encounter, to varying degrees, every day. In that everyday respect, Barack Obama is very much black like black America.

◊ ◊ ◊

Black Americans still very much still share what Crouch calls "a common body of injustices" with people around the world. Blacks in Mexico and Latin America continue to face discrimination based on skin color, and people of color are routinely targeted for hate crimes in countries from Russia to Germany.

Taken as a whole – from Obama deprived of a taxicab to racially motivated slights and attacks – black Americans have a common cause with black people worldwide, obvious without speaking, as plain as the faces we wear, the ancestry we share, and the popular culture we permanently embody. Palestinian teenagers wear basketball jerseys with Shaquille O'Neal's number. A little boy sprints around the bazaar in Tangier on market day wearing a Michael Jackson T-shirt. Will Smith is a global box-office phenomenon. Years after his last fight, Muhammad Ali is still one of the most recognized, and revered, people on this planet.

Around the world, people want to be black like us. Not black like you, Mr. Crouch. Not even black like Barack Obama. They want to be black like black America.

When that cab driver passed Barack Obama, do you think the driver considered the ancestral origins of the man on the curb before screeching away? No. *Hell* no. He wasn't thinking about ancestry, he was reacting to the color of the man hailing that cab. And that's the world where most black Americans live today – a world that understands, in ways both positive and poisonous, that we have much in common even when we think we have little in common.

To start down the slippery slope of intraracial divisions, to play the old game of blacker-than-thou -- only the slightest variation on the "paper-bag" rule common to some blacks at the turn of the 20th century, that cotillion "Our Crowd" set who used the color of a paper bag to decide who their friends were within the race -- is to jump back into the worst kind of divisiveness, a divide-and-conquer behavior that is truly counterproductive.

Obama's campaign is succeeding precisely because for many Americans it represents the first real, credible, quantifiable opportunity for attitudinal change in American government perhaps since the presidential campaigns of either John or Robert Kennedy, and certainly since the 1992 Clinton campaign. That this groundswell of support should be in the service of an African American candidate is, for his supporters, so much the better. His campaign ratifies the possible truth of the American promise, the American trademark: Everybody gets at least a shot at the brass ring. Even a brother with a last name that's not from the Social Register, or the log books of slaveholders in the American South.

If Obama becomes the Democratic nominee in 2008, it will be a milestone step toward a reframing of America's long and agonizing dance with race and identity. Many hurdles remain, not the least of them being the challenges of telling black Americans that in the everyday world his experience as a black American is similar to their own. Identical would be too much to ask for, Mr. Crouch. There's diversity within singularity.

11/17/2006

MISTY

SEN. HILLARY Rodham Clinton, the tough! tested! experienced! battle-heartened! inside-the-Beltway politico ready to be President of the United States, had a little ... moment today, in front of God, the press and the citizens of New Hampshire. Speculation has already started as to what kind of pivot point in the 2008 campaign it was: the first sign of Hillary revealing a needed human vulnerability in her machine-like drive to the Democratic nomination — or the first evidence of desperation in her so-far fruitless bid to derail the ascendant rival campaign of Sen. Barack Obama.

It happened in the hours before the first actual primary in the 2008 campaign, and just days after Clinton was soundly thumped in the Iowa caucuses.

Clinton was making a twelfth-hour appeal for support as she spoke on the eve of the state's primary, with a plurality of the polls showing her trailing Obama by almost double digits. It was part of the same appeal that, earlier in the day, had her campaign's leadership calling her big-money donors, asking for, well, more big money (calls no doubt fueled by talk in some media outlets that, astonishingly, the Clinton campaign faced the prospect of running out of money before the expected delegate cornucopia of Super Tuesday in February).

Clinton's eyes welled up and her voice broke repeatedly while talking about her campaign with voters at the Cafe Espresso in Portsmouth, N.H. One sympathetic soul asked how she kept going in the relentless, front-loaded campaign. "It's not easy. It's not easy," she said.

"And I couldn't do it if I just didn't, you know, passionately believe it was the right thing to do," she said, voice cracking. "I just don't want to see us fall backward as a nation. ... I mean, this is very personal for me. Not just political. I see what's happening. We have to reverse it."

The moment subsided fairly quickly, in under a minute, and there was no actual waterworks from the former first lady's eyes. But Clinton was clearly near some brief personal precipice.

ABC News got the video ... then Fox ... and the Information Age being what it is, that was that.

The Huffington Post screamed the news on its home page in a splash of verbiage and video that made you wonder how HuffPost will handle the Second Coming. And not surprisingly, the site's bloggers weighed in, indicating some of the different ways voters could look at this spin-proof, misty moment.

Abdiel: Clinton had a mother moment -- and I actually found it refreshing. Up until now, I saw Clinton as a person methodically practicing an academic exercise. Now I'm more inclined to believe that she really DOES care -- that's something new. Didn't see that one coming.

Misterbone: Weird. Did we ever see this emotion even in the darkest days of the Lewinsky scandal? I have no issue with a touch of emotion, especially from a woman, but puh-lease, this is not genuine Hillary at all. She would NEVER let her guard down before the cameras...unless it was premeditated.

Rockyroad: Hillary had better watch out . . . she's becoming a joke. Just as adopting a Southern accent when addressing Southern audiences is cringe-worthy and patronizing, so is manufacturing crocodile tears to engender the empathy of women. As a strong, effective professional woman raised in the South, I find her tactics disingenuous, hypocritical, slimy and just plain offensive. She fails to demonstrate the qualities of leader.

No question about where John Edwards stands. The former senator from North Carolina, and Clinton's other serious nomination rival, wasn't buying it. "I think what we need in a commander-in-chief is strength and resolve, and presidential campaigns are tough business, but being president of the United States is also tough business," he told The Wall Street Journal at a press gaggle in Laconia, N.H.

The Clinton campaign has been having major concerns about Obama since the Iowa debacle. Mike Allen and Ben Smith, of the Politico, noted how a planned negative campaign had been scuttled in the wake of fears of something they couldn't control:

"The senator's aides concluded that negative advertising would not work in the compressed time frame between Iowa and New Hampshire, adding to their worries about their ability to change a media and political environment that is embracing Obama as a historic figure. The campaign also worries that fallout from an all-out attack on Obama could harm Clinton's plans to turn the Democratic race into a grueling marathon."

This is what's facing Hillary Clinton right now: coming up with a campaign strategy that addresses the chance of someone else's inevitability, dealing with a juggernaut that she's not a part of. She said early in the campaign that she'd never even considered the idea that she wouldn't be nominated. Never crossed her mind.

Hillary Clinton may yet prevail. The delegate-rich event of Super Tuesday, Feb. 5, could be expected to boost her delegate count handsomely. And for however well Obama is doing now, some kind of deflation can probably be forecast for his campaign — maybe if no other reason than to cultivate a sense of drama in a campaign robbed of much of that by a ruthlessly abbreviated schedule.

The polling places in New Hampshire open shortly, and the first real quadrennial canvass of the national mood will get under way. Whether Clinton wins or loses, she'll leave the state smarter by one truth, of both life and politics:

The only inevitable thing is disappointment.

1/7/2008

PLAN B (1) (a)

MOMENTUM is a powerful thing. In politics as in physics, momentum can be the irresistible force that makes supposedly immovable objects change their minds. On the basis of early exit polling from voters in New Hampshire, what may be developing is a momentum behind the presidential campaign of Barack Obama. The polls don't close for hours yet, but the media is reporting a raft of new strategies for the Hillary Clinton campaign -- strategic equations that use defeat as a baseline value.

You could call the new Clinton approach "Plan B," except they've already done that. After Iowa.

"With Barack Obama strongly favored -- even within Hillary Clinton's camp -- to win a second straight victory in today's New Hampshire Democratic primary, both rivals are looking to the next battle grounds," Jackie Calmes reports in today's Wall Street Journal. "But his momentum threatens to swamp her in the next two states as well and shows signs of fracturing her support in the party establishment."

"Already," Calmes writes, "some Clinton associates have begun lobbying for her early exit if she loses the primary by a big margin, as polls suggest she could. ...

◊ ◊ ◊

"The road may get harder immediately after New Hampshire," Calmes continues. "The all-important Culinary Workers Union in Nevada, the next state to vote on Jan. 19, is considering backing Sen. Obama a day after a New Hampshire win, say some high-ranking Democrats. The support of the state's largest union by far would virtually hand him a victory in the labor-dominated caucuses there, Democrats say. And the Clinton campaign is considering effectively ceding South Carolina, which votes a week later. Her once-strong support in the state's large black population eroded and Sen. Obama opened a big lead in polls after Iowa's caucus results energized many blacks with the prospect that a man of their race stands a realistic chance of being nominated."

The uphill Clinton climb has some other problems, issues that point to why they're in the difficulty they're in. Even while dealing with fallout from the Portsmouth incident, even while they are presumably in the process of tweaking, rethinking or recalibrating the Clinton message, a senior Clinton adviser -- by accident -- revealed at least one of the faults built-in to the Clinton bid for the White House.

MSNBC's Dan Abrams, back on the air again, interviewed Clinton senior adviser Ann Lewis on Tuesday, asking her, generally, "How'd this happen?"

At first Lewis assumed the obvious reflexive crouch. "Oh, I'm not looking backward today, I'm looking forward." *[Cue the Fleetwood Mac song. You know which one.]*

Then Lewis said, "Looking back at Iowa ... it is clear we didn't do all we could in terms of reaching out to younger voters. We have definitely corrected for that ... "

Thus, with lightning speed four days after Iowa, the Clinton campaign has "corrected" a situation that took months to occur, has suddenly discovered that there are millions of new voters out there that they haven't been reaching -- and now they're *reaching* them! Problem solved, let's move on.

And that's the problem. The Clinton camp suggests they think recognition of a still largely undiscovered bloc of voters — younger, more entrepreneurial, more politically maverick, more likely to communicate by cell phones instead of land lines — is something that's achievable overnight, that it's an event or a milestone rather than what it actually is: a process, something that has to be organic and fundamental to the campaign to really work.

◊ ◊ ◊

One reason for the success of the Obama campaign is his embrace *early on* of the demographic known as the millennials -- voters between 18 and 24 years old -- and the potential those voters represent. Obama got the need for young voters right outta the gate. The newness, the freshness of his insurgent campaign was a natural for a generation in the process of discovering itself and establishing its own priorities. In a very real way, the Obama campaign evolved with the millennials. Obama's reaping the benefits of that now.

The frantic weaves and feints of the Clinton campaign may come to nothing in New Hampshire; returns are due shortly. But Obama strategist David Axelrod, speaking to the Journal, has what might be solid advice for a Clinton post-Plan B: "I would spend more time trying to tell people why Hillary Clinton should be president and spend less of it about why Barack Obama should not."

1/8/2008

SIGN 'O' THE TIMES

T HE specifics of the ever-ascendant Obama campaign have been examined inside and out, six ways to Sunday; journalists and instapundits will go a long way to make sure that microvetting process continues. But there's one aspect of the Obama campaign identity that hasn't gotten much attention, something that works on the campaign's behalf almost subliminally.

In a phrase: "Gimme an 'O.'"

The Obama campaign logo has proven to be an incredibly versatile avatar for the candidate and his message, in ways that aren't immediately apparent.

The logo has a visual appeal that extends beyond the usual tiresome variations on a flag-draped theme we see so often in candidate logos. It's an overdone trope of American politics: the candidate's name side-swiped by a rising star (see John Edwards' logo) or intertwined with a tweak on the colors of the American flag (look at Hillary's logo). All of which makes the Obama logo such a striking departure.

On the Obama campaign Web site blog, one woman, "Obama Mama," took note in a posting from last Feb. 22:

"One huge trend in design right now is the circle. Circles represent infinity, protectiveness (think of encircling arms), and even the Earth. Many women I see wear a diamond circle on a chain around their necks. You see retro circle designs on everything from lithographs to home decor to wrapping paper … This is why I think the graphics people for Senator Obama's campaign are right on the money. Using the O from his name to design his logo is both clever and creative.

"And, as a side note, being a suburban woman, I can safely say that many women I know associate O with Oprah (not to mention the catchphrases "the Big O" and "it's all about the O") ..."

The Obama logo as a subliminal reference to orgasm? We'd rather not go too far in exploring this last point. Some things are best left speculated about — in private.

On the same Web site last Feb. 14, Tower9 explores another side to the logo's possible subconscious appeal. "Instead of a design it's a message. It appeals to the right brain and conveys an [unconscious] message with archetypal images. ... It's the world with a rising sun. It's a row of farmland with a vanishing point going off towards the future. It's America's road to the future, and the circle represents wholeness."

The Obama campaign has also released variations on its own theme, tweaks in the initial design that embrace various groups. One emblazoned with the words "Obama Pride" adopts the rainbow motif of the GLBT community. Another one, headed Kids for Obama, is an apparently hand-drawn variation of the Obama logo, done in what looks like crayon. The symbol for Environmentalists for Obama features the Obama logo rendered in earth tones — green and gold.

"Know your audience," the phrase goes. Whether it's a phrase originally meant for actors, lawyers or authors doesn't really matter. That advice has a new adherent in the world of American politics.

We're waiting on the bumperstrip for Concrete Formsetters for Obama.

1/11/2008

YES HE CAN

A ROUT. A thumping. A buttwhipping. Pick your favorite noun to describe an absolute, inescapable vote of confidence in the idea of change, and an equally inescapable repudiation of business as usual.

If you haven't heard — if you've been under a rock a mile underground somewhere — Sen. Barack Obama of Illinois won the South Carolina Democratic primary on Saturday, defeating Sen. Hillary Clinton by a huge double-digit margin, and sending the clear unmistakable signal that his campaign is well beyond the quixotic, unrealistic images painted by a Billary Clinton campaign more desperate by the day.

In one day the Obama campaign has made good on its initial pledges of being a truly national effort, by reaching black voters (a given in South Carolina), young voters, women voters, older voters and *white male voters* in the first real coalition of Americans — not just Democrats — the country's seen in far too many years.

In one day Barack Obama has done nothing less than recalibrate the Democratic presidential campaign, restating the party agenda with language that soars and inspires, invoking a message that resonates.

In practical terms, it's a whole new race for the White House.

Hillary Clinton, canny pol that she is, didn't even bothering waiting around for the postmortem. "Mrs. Clinton's advisers were minimizing the importance of South Carolina even before polls closed, saying the primaries in Florida on Tuesday and in a swath of states on Feb. 5 were of more importance," Patrick Healy of The New York Times reported. "But she will have to reckon with the rejection of her candidacy by black voters and the mixed support she received from white Democrats and younger voters here — two groups she must have by her side in order to build a cross-section of support in the coming contests."

"The Clintons will now have to deal with a perception of hollowness about her strategy, that she is leaving it to her husband to take care of things and allowing him to overshadow her political message," said Blease Graham, a professor of political science at the University of South Carolina, to The Times.

"We have the most votes, the most delegates ... and the most diverse coalition of Americans that we've seen in a long, long time," Obama told ecstatic supporters at a rally in Columbia, S.C. "You can see it in the faces here tonight. They are young and old; rich and poor. They are black and white; Latino and Asian and Native American."

And before Obama hit the stage, and again as he addressed them later, his supporters chanted something that really symbolized the power of his building coalition — the sort of "gorgeous mosaic" that David Dinkins hailed years ago in his successful drive to be the first black mayor of New York City.

"Race doesn't matter! Race doesn't matter!"

◊ ◊ ◊

"We're looking to fundamentally change the status quo in Washington," Obama said. "And right now, that status quo is fighting back with everything it's got; with the same old tactics that divide and distract us from solving the problems people face."

"We are up against the idea that it's acceptable to say anything and do anything to win an election," Obama said, in a not-quite-obvious shot at divisive comments made against the senator by former president Bill Clinton, who's tried to minimize Obama at every turn — even slyly invoking the race card. "We know that this is exactly what's wrong with our politics," Obama said at the rally. "This is why people don't believe what their leaders say anymore. This is why they tune out. And this election is our chance to give the American people a reason to believe again."

The crowd roared back, "Yes we can!" The way Obama smoked the opposition proved him ready to challenge, in his words, "the assumption that young people are apathetic ... the assumption that African-Americans can't support the white candidate; whites can't support the African-American candidate; blacks and Latinos can't come together."

It got better for the junior senator from Illinois before he even left the stage in Columbia. The talking heads at the networks reported that Caroline Kennedy, daughter of the late President John F. Kennedy, would emerge from a largely private life to make a rare public statement, and an even rarer political endorsement.

"Over the years, I've been deeply moved by the people who've told me they wished they could feel inspired and hopeful about America the way people did when my father was president," she wrote in an op-ed in the Sunday's edition of The Times. "That is why I am supporting a presidential candidate in the Democratic primaries, Barack Obama."

For Obama, that hosannah from the daughter of Camelot must have been especially sweet coming in the pages of The Times, which endorsed Hillary Clinton for president a few days before.

Saturday's mini-landslide — Obama won by 27 percentage points, single-handedly winning more votes on his own than were cast in the entire South Carolina Democratic primary in 2004 — and the Kennedy endorsement puts the Hillary Clinton campaign in a serious box.

Much has been made of Clinton's formidable organization: the war chest, the name recognition, the ties to her husband, the most revered Democratic politician in recent memory. It's these weapons she'll be calling on between now and Super Tuesday, Feb. 5, a day in which more than 1,600 Democratic delegates will be in play across 22 states, the closest thing to a general election we'll have before the real thing, exactly nine months later.

But right now, it's not about fundraising, it's not about organization, it's not about the ground game, it's not about any of the usual, comfortable metrics of American politics. It's about digging down to reach a spiritually exhausted electorate where they live, deep in their hearts, deep in the soil of their aspirations for something more. Something better.

Despite the Clinton campaign's past (and no doubt future) attempt to undercut the groundswell of feeling that's building for Obama, that tidal wave of passion, of emotional connection to a candidate, is building. And there can be no successful drive to the White House without it.

Any attempt by Billary to short-circuit the emotionalism of the Obama campaign will likely fail. The reason why is simple enough: Right now, America wants more than someone to agree with. America wants someone to believe in. With every passing day, with every vote cast, with every nervous pundit, with every new endorsement from unlikely corners, more and more people are starting to believe in Barack Obama.

1/27/2008

LADIES AND GENTLEMEN,
THE SPINNERS

"**H**OW many delegates are in the state of denial?" Newsweek's Howard Fineman asked that last week, discussing another aspect of the campaign, but he could well have been talking the events of Super Tuesday. For those in the media who may have watched the Obama campaign Tuesday with unspoken expectations of the beginning of the end, Tuesday's results can't be spun any other way: the challenger is in it to the *very* end.

Despite the candidate's own understandable reluctance to use the phrase in reference to himself, Obama is nothing other than The Frontrunner — in delegate count, in the number of states he won Tuesday, in the geographic breadth of his victory, in cash available to continue his campaign, and in the increasingly higher expectations he faces from now until the convention in August.

No one, of course, realistically expected Obama's campaign to fall apart after Super Tuesday, but there were nagging questions as to how viable Obama could be without some sizable wins outside states with large minority populations.

Those fears were soundly routed Tuesday. From Alaska to Georgia, Colorado to Connecticut, citizens backed the Obama campaign, convincingly establishing Obama as a viable contender and the beneficiary of what New York Times columnist Bob Herbert called "a huge shift in American culture, a tectonic shift that goes far beyond a presidential race."

The macro story on the Democratic side of Super Tuesday may well have been buried in the slow trickle of returns from one state, the night's biggest delegate prize, California.

The state was called early in the evening — about an hour or so after the polls closed — as a victory for the Clinton campaign. Hillary's mob went to bed secure in that win, a victory by a margin of 22 percentage points. They no doubt expected some contraction but ... no worries.

But that vast double-digit margin didn't hold up. By 6 am today eastern time, Clinton's 22-point spread had gone on a serious diet. With 97 percent of the votes tallied, Clinton's lead had dwindled to just 10 percentage points, one number shy of it being a single-digit win. This in a state where her organization had been laying groundwork for months. This in a state she was expected to win by an overwhelming margin.

Even in the dead of night, with no campaign activity underway at all, with nothing more at work than the rote trickle-in of votes cast hours earlier, the insurgent bid of Barack Obama exhibited the power of momentum, the evidence of an irresistible force that continues to catch polwatchers by surprise.

That momentum has been a trademark of the Obama campaign all season long, and was, not surprisingly, the watchword for much of today's news coverage. But there are some underreported stories that lend weight to the idea that the Obama campaign story deserves, to some degree, to drive the narrative of this campaign.

(1) The media fascination with Clinton winning the "bigger" states — bigger purely on the basis of population — overlooks the more important survey of what matters: the raw delegate count.

Look at the delegate harvest for each candidate in several of the Super Tuesday states:

Idaho: Obama garners 15 delegates, Clinton only 3 (ratio 5:1)
Illinois: Obama gains 87, Clinton gets 44 (almost 2:1)
Kansas: Obama scores 23, Clinton gains 9 (2.5:1)
Minnesota: Obama 48, Clinton 24 (2:1)
South Carolina: Obama 25, Clinton 12 (better than 2:1)
Colorado: Obama 13, Clinton 6 (better than 2:1)

Obama gained well in Utah, Georgia and other states — all of which leads to the delegate total for the day: Obama 838 delegates, Clinton 834. (That's at this writing; those numbers are certain to change, and the tally for New Mexico still isn't in!) The media focus on Clinton winning the bigger states begs the question of what they think was at stake on Super Tuesday. It wasn't the popular vote — that happens in November. It was the delegate tally. By that measure, the night's big winner, *California notwithstanding,* was Barack Obama.

(2) The other still vastly-underreported story is a bottom-line issue: the money that each campaign needs to survive, and the likelihood of getting it.

For months now, with pages from the Howard Dean online playbook firmly in hand, Obama's campaign has been growing money like a virus in a Petri dish and doing it in a highly effective, undeniably populist way, tapping via the Internet the hearts and wallets of everyday people, donors able to pony up $25, $50 or $100 — amounts small enough, at the individual level, not to be painful, but in numbers of contributors large enough to make a huge difference in Obama's drive to forge a truly national campaign.

Contrast that with Hillary Clinton's requests of big-money donors, those people who contributed the $2,300 maximum for individual contributions — those people who, facing down the bills from Christmas, likely can't afford writing any more big checks on her behalf. Her bid for small-dollar donations and her campaign's embrace of the Internet came late, compared to Obama's operation, and remains woefully behind Obama's grassroots fundraising. Result: Hardly broke, Clinton's campaign is a lot less liquid than it could be, should be, right now. She wouldn't lend her own campaign $5 million of her own money if that weren't true.

◊ ◊ ◊

Obama has adopted a fundraising strategy a lot like the pugilistic strategy of Muhammad Ali, whose legendary rope-a-dope approach — conserve energy, be opportunistic, keep the powder dry for the big battles to come — helped him beat a number of opponents in the ring, fighters who didn't see what was coming until it was over.

All of which has led to what's happening today: the art of spinning the results. The media's been spinning Tuesday's events, in the interest of furthering the horse-race drama they've been after since the campaign started. Obama himself today refused to define himself as the underdog, and said it for perfectly justifiable reasons: When you're out in front, you're the biggest target. Obama figures he doesn't need the heat. And the Clinton campaign has satisfied itself with the impact of the California win, making much of the inroads in the Hispanic vote at Obama's expense, downplaying the number of states Obama won, and making more of her victories than a comparative state-by-state count would seem to justify.

Somewhere between the two states of denial lies the truth: Super Tuesday's results show it's a whole new race, a dead heat that suggests another one in the fall. Who's got the stamina to finish strong?

2/6/2008

CALLING THE QUESTION

TODAY, former Massachusetts governor Mitt Romney abandoned his quest for the Republican nomination, and Arizona Sen. John McCain appealed to conservatives to rally around himself as the party's presumptive nominee. This changes *everything*, and not just for the Republicans.

In one day, that intraparty discord within the GOP — something the Democrats have quietly but gleefully counted on (*McCain vs. Romney vs. Mike Huckabee! Yippee!*) — began to end. The coalescing that Republicans are historically known for is happening again, and the only valid counter for the Democrats is to achieve the same kind of intraparty unity, and fast, for exactly the same reasons.

Events unfolded today with a speed that even flummoxed the talking heads. Romney, essentially contradicting statements from the day before indicating his intention to stay in the race, today said "I have to stand aside" for the benefit of the party. He said he was "suspending" his campaign, but for all practical purposes there's a do-not-resuscitate sign at the foot of his campaign's bed.

It's probably been there for weeks, and certainly since the disappointments of Super Tuesday.

The Romney effort has shown how too much money, too little message and too on-message a messenger can doom a political campaign. It stems in some ways from a lack of heart, a failure of some basic conviction -- not the bottom-line determination of a CEO in a quest to make the numbers line up right on a SEC filing, but the organic connection to the people the candidate would hope to lead.

He never quite hooked up with people, especially in the south, where he tried hard. There's always been an airlessness about the Romney campaign, a stilted bigness about its everything (oversize net worth, oversize family, oversize pedigree), and a kind of hermetic perfection about the candidate, a man seemingly pitching the American people a business plan rather than a vision.

James Wolcott, in his blog on the Vanity Fair Web site, pulls no punches: "Is there anyone who gives more uninspired, tone-deaf election night speeches than Romney? — he slides right into his stump speech without realizing his poor wife and staffers are up there on stage, the forced expressions on their faces melting like cakes in the rain the longer he drones on. He's like an actor auditioning for a part that's already been filled and nobody has the heart to tell him."

◊ ◊ ◊

Wednesday was a day of deep reflections at Rancho Romney. The campaign was auguring in, spiraling out of control despite the millions spent, at least $40 million from his own kitty — a burn rate of personal campaign cash that extrapolates to $254,777 for each of the 157 delegates Romney nailed down before he closed up shop.

Even before most of the voting was done Tuesday night, the Romney camp released a statement saying that Wednesday would be a day of "frank discussions" for the campaign, with some announcement later in the day detailing the strategy going forward. The brain trust hunkered down in Boston and sure enough, the campaign said later that they planned to stay in the fight a while longer, despite not getting the results they'd wargamed.

Then came Thursday's change of mind. "Because I love America, in this time of war, I feel I have to stand aside for our party and our country," Romney said at the annual Conservative Political Action Conference in Washington.

Later in the day, after some nasty comments by rightwing-nut author and commentator Laura Ingraham at the conference, McCain spoke (amid catcalls and shouts of "RINO!" [Republican In Name Only]) in his own defense, throwing an olive branch to the wolves before him.

"I am proud, very proud, to have come to public office as a foot soldier in the Reagan revolution," he said. His more controversial views, such as easing immigration restrictions (a logical consequence of his role in a border state) and tweaking campaign finance laws, have kept him under fire with Republicans for years.

"I know I have a responsibility, if I am, as I hope to be, the Republican nominee for president, to unite the party and prepare for the great contest in November," McCain said. "And I am acutely aware that I cannot succeed in that endeavor, nor can our party prevail over the challenge we will face from either Senator Clinton or Senator Obama, without the support of dedicated conservatives.

"It is my sincere hope that even if you believe I have occasionally erred in my reasoning as a fellow conservative, you will still allow that I have, in many ways important to all of us, maintained the record of a conservative," McCain said.

Others are not convinced. "Boy, the narrower this race gets, I'm surprised to find myself wishing Fred Thompson was still in the running," said blogger Skull Dugger, on the New York Times Web site. " 'Go McCain!' I guess (bewildered sigh)."

There's still unfinished business left for the GOP. Some people will be waiting for Ron Paul to pull the plug on the respirator for *his* campaign, a White House bid that, for all the tantalizing PR he got as an insurgent Republican, never got much attention from the beginning. They probably won't wait long. Paul's maverick message — withdrawal from NATO and the UN, ending the federal income tax, troops out of Iraq immediately — never gained traction within the party, and his four delegates don't figure in the outcome of the race. With all due respect for a sincere and principled effort, Paul's fifteen minutes were up ten minutes ago.

◊ ◊ ◊

Of greater concern is the Mike Huckabee factor. Popular with evangelicals, the affable, sharp-witted former Krispy Kreme enthusiast and former governor of Arkansas is the wild electron now, despite ending Super Tuesday with fewer delegates than Romney.

His lock on the indispensable southern states, proven with his five wins, and a personality more voluble, accessible and telegenic than McCain's, make him, among other things, a natural for the Vice President spot. McCain is said not to like him any more than he did Romney —does John McCain like

135

anybody? — but Huckabee may be the hemlock McCain needs to drink to keep himself alive.

The blogosphere is already aflame over the prospect. Even talk-radio Doberman, former recreational pharmaceutical enthusiast and media Prince of Darkness Rush Limbaugh is pushing a McCain-Huckabee ticket. "Here's the thing about McCain: he can't win conservatives in the South by virtue of this primary yesterday," Limbaugh said Wednesday. "These blue states that McCain won last night are places where he has no chance in November."

Such an idea for the GOP ticket presents problems for McCain, whose political temperament is way more moderate than Limbaugh. It might be something he's considering already, but like the man who's asked by his girlfriend to get married, he'd like to think it was his idea.

But Romney's exit and the fallout from it really change the dynamic for the Democrats. In the post "A merger of equals," the idea was floated that, simply put, an Obama-Clinton tie-up (or a Clinton-Obama ticket) concentrates the mind and heart of the American electorate, consolidates party resources, and indicates a willingness to set aside comparatively minor differences for the good of the Democratic party. That fanciful scenario takes on new weight today.

As the Republicans seem to be about to put past differences behind them, it's, shall we say, incumbent on the Democrats to do exactly the same thing. Considering the calculus that's beginning to emerge, a Obama-Clinton/Clinton-Obama ticket isn't an option, it's pretty much a necessity.

◊ ◊ ◊

Consider what each will bring to the other:

Obama's bona fides with younger voters, minority voters and independents, proven on Super Tuesday and before, dovetail nicely with Clinton's strengths among women voters — a significant percentage of the Democratic demographic — and older voters.

A unified bid between the two instantly makes fundraising a far easier exercise, especially for the Clinton camp, whose workers are said to include some asked to work for free (this before the candidate herself ponied up $5 mil to keep things liquid). A joining of fundraising forces over the Internet would turn a very strong Democratic year for political donations into a stellar one.

A Clinton-Obama/Obama-Clinton ticket permanently cements the historic aspects of their mutual candidacies into a single, compelling force of profound historical significance. Intangible? So much the better. People like playing a role in making history. They'll turn out for that.

And in one lightning stroke, the American people, up to now faced with the choice of either Experience or Change, can have both — the two best attributes of contemporary Democratic leadership assembled in a formidable package that would give the Republicans all they can handle in the fall.

The outcome on Super Tuesday should have been an object lesson to the Dems. When the smoke cleared and the votes were counted, the difference in raw popular-vote totals between Obama and Clinton that day amounted to .4 of 1%. There probably hasn't been a narrower national vote of any kind, in the primary season or after the general, since Kennedy-Nixon in 1960.

◊ ◊ ◊

It's of course a matter of timing. The primaries and caucuses between now and June need to run their course. But the gravitational process between both Obama and Clinton, that reach for commonalities instead of conflicts, should be starting very soon and, by the first days of June, should be very public.

For Clinton and Obama to come to terms sooner rather than later saves time, money and energy; unites assets that belong together on the basis of party unity, and heads off the nightmare prospect of a bruising brokered convention in August — something that would evoke for voters exactly the disunity and deadlock the Democrats don't need.

With rancor from within coming to a fever pitch, the Republican party has begun the process of closing ranks and redefining itself, conceding that, despite a constant pursuit of ideological purity, sometimes it's *realpolitik* that gets the job done.

Obama and Clinton need to learn that lesson too. For the Democrats still standing, the time's coming to see the power in the political version of economies of scale. The fact that Barack Obama and Hillary Clinton have each campaigned behind the idea of building a national coalition presents a compelling (if not unavoidable) opportunity: recognizing the need to first build a coalition of their own.

2/7/2008

'THRILLER' RETURNS

WAAAAY back in the day, before things went south, before he turned himself into Skeletor, before the embrace of splendid isolation, before the sordid pedophile allegations and dance moves made on the roof of a car outside a courtroom — before all the trouble ... there was this record by Michael Jackson, this music, this sound that came along and did a drive-by on our expectations, and changed everything.

You could dance to it, and you did. You *know* you did. You danced to it like a young entertainment reporter did at a Colorado nightclub on May 16, 1983, and all eyes in the room were Super Glued to the monitors tuned to the "Motown 25" special airing on NBC, and Michael Jackson came on the screen to the whip-snap-sharp rhythms of "Billie Jean," and in four minutes and change, making moves robotic and fluid, old-school and anatomically from another world, took pop culture and modern music lovingly, provocatively, by storm.

You could dance to "Billie Jean," party to it, make love to it. That spring, "Thriller" seemed to make all things possible in the world of music, which was ready for something new after the onslaught of punk, and a kind of vacuum, a widening gap between the precincts of R&B, funk and rock.

More than just a new album, "Thriller" was the spangled, irresistible dividing line between one incarnation of the music industry and another, between one range of pop culture and the next. A longstanding segregation of black artists from levers of vast exposure in the mainstream media — chief among them MTV — ended with the release of "Thriller."

"Thriller" finally breached that wall of musical segregation with careful, calculated concessions to the rock gods like "Beat It," Dan Charnas observed in The Washington Post. "M.J. achieved nothing less than a reintegration of American music, and he helped pave the way for all who followed, from Prince to Public Enemy."

And what the album didn't do to knock down walls when it was released the previous November was done by Jackson's performance — live on March 25, 1983, taped for air on May

16 by NBC. Both nights were nights for history. It was made first in that TV studio, and then later, with 50 million viewers tuning in from living rooms and bars and nightclubs around the country, where people tried to imitate the "moonwalk" — a move cribbed from James Brown (as anyone who's ever seen his performance at the 1964 TAMI Show will know) and otherwise ascribed to sources from Cab Calloway to the red-capped manakin, a bird indigenous to Central America.

Back then, we all wanted to chase that ice cream truck in the rain. We wanted to be part of what we knew was history. Three songs — "Billie Jean," "Beat It" and the title track — would become the three most recognized songs from what would become the biggest-selling album in history. And the canonization kicked in. What The New York Times said in early 1984 is as true now as it was back then (albeit for different reasons today): "In the world of pop music, there is Michael Jackson and there is everybody else."

◊ ◊ ◊

If you missed it the first time, it's back. Epic has rereleased "Thriller," with a CD of digitally remastered tracks and remixes, a DVD containing the videos and a 48-page booklet, a package befitting the cover-line shout, "The World's Biggest Selling Album of All Time."

Ever the bridge builder between old and new, Jackson has invested the "Thriller 25" compilation with contributors whose presence underlines Jackson's sense of his own history (HIStory?). The original tracks we know & love are reworked and tweaked by artists very much in the pocket of today. The release includes remix contributions from will.i.am, Akon and Kanye West — all of which, ironically, punch up just how singular the original recordings really are, after all these years, after more than 100 million copies sold.

That's why some are still waiting for the rerelease of the man himself — on a stage. "I got no taste for the redux: make with the comeback, already," says Jimi Izrael, blogging on The Root on Feb. 18.

Izrael's old school to his heart; he echoes what a lot of folks have been thinking. "I'm still a fan. He reminds me of an era when you couldn't produce and sell a hit record from your bedroom so easily: You needed talent to get a record deal. Back in the day, you had to show and prove. Now, the radio is over-run with zeros wearing long chains, saggy jeans and sunglasses."

◊ ◊ ◊

Izrael understands: There's a lot to remember, so much that's been so long in the everyday ether, so long a part of pop-culture's armature that you almost forget where it came from. The first velocity of the rhinestone glove and the spangled socks into the culture. The red leather jacket. Fred Astaire's acclaim. The graveyard dance in the "Thriller" video, a cartoon come to dizzyingly electric life. Them all-too-flammable Jheri curls. Lisa Marie Presley. Jordan Chandler.

This year the "Thriller" album is 25 years young. And fans are waiting to see how maturity and time have changed one of the most transcendent artists to hit the scene. Remember, folks, in less than six months from now, on Aug. 29, the thriller known as Michael Joseph Jackson will be 50 years old. That's a good time for a "comeback," in one sense.

But maybe a comeback isn't necessary. In many ways, in the many samples and artists, images and sounds around us every day, Michael Jackson has never left the building.

2/20/2008

THE SUBSTANCE OF SYMBOLISM

MORE than once in this campaign year, Sen. Hillary Clinton has tried to establish a contrast between herself and Sen. Barack Obama, her challenger for the Democratic nomination for the presidency.

With the reflexive use of the word "experience" in her campaign rallies, in reference to herself, she's called into question Obama's time in the national spotlight, his comprehension of the levers of presidential power — in effect, the very essence of his campaign's right to exist.

It's been to now a fruitless attempt to suggest that Obama has no political throw weight — no substance underneath the inspirational surfaces of his public persona. With eight consecutive losses in a row, Hillary's not reaching people with this argument, not necessarily because it's a bad argument, but because people don't believe it.

They are starting to see behind the dull omnipresence of policy. They are starting to see how, with more than policy statements, more than wonkish recitations of data and fact, Barack Obama embodies another necessary reality of a presidential campaign. In addition to wielding the hard facts necessary for a credible run — and there are plenty of his well-articulated positions on everything that matters, if people bother to look — Obama embodies the substance of our symbolism, our peculiarly American way of politics, indeed, our way of life.

◊ ◊ ◊

Consider the U.S. moonshot program. President Kennedy's daring throwdown in 1961, and its successful resolution some eight years later, would come to be couched and justified in scientific terms. It would aid scientists immeasurably in understanding the genesis and composition of the solar system; it would further the field of planetary research, etc., etc. And not to be dismissive: those reasons and more form a scientifically defensible justification for the undertaking.

But for many people, maybe even most people, that doesn't *feel* like the real reason. President Kennedy's cosmic gambit seemed to have something else at its core, something deeper than science, a schoolyard dare on steroids, a nod to the human drama of competition, an unprecedented variation on your own backyard bravado when you challenged the neighbor kid to see who had the better arm, to find out who could throw that stone the farthest unimaginable distance.

That dare didn't originate in Palm Springs with Kennedy sipping martinis with Frank Sinatra, playing his version of "Fly Me to the Moon" on the stereo. It started in the heart, not as a policy but as a possibility. What it said *to* this country *about* this country is no less substantial than facts of its infrastructure or the number of hospital beds available to the poor.

◊ ◊ ◊

Arthur Miller understood the power of symbol. "Democracy is first of all a state of feeling," he observed in "Making Crowds," his 1972 essay on the George McGovern presidential campaign. "A nominee, and later a president, is not a sort of methodical lawyer hired to win a client's claim but an ambiguously symbolic figure upon whom is projected the conflicting desires of an audience."

Barbara Ehrenreich, writing in The Nation on a contrast of Clinton and Obama, glimpsed the distinctions, between 2008's candidates: "While Clinton, the designated valedictorian, reaches out for the ego and super-ego, he supposedly goes for the id. She might as well be promoting choral singing in the face of Beatlemania."

A purely emotional response? For sure, but not to be easily dismissed. Americans have been so oratorically impoverished over the past eight years, maybe it's no wonder that the emotional aspects of the Obama campaign have been so resonant for so many.

◊ ◊ ◊

Consider that factor common to personal technology, from
Internet browsers to portable music players. It's called "look-
and-feel." The look-and-feel factor ultimately can't be assessed
according to metrics or data; it's first and foremost an emotional
response to the operability of a device or a system — its ease
of use, the way it navigates, the way it looks, the way it feels
in your hand.

By all available evidence, then, to this point, the Obama
campaign exhibits the look and feel of an everyday companion
article, portable, comfortable, accessible, information-rich.
Barack Obama is to Hillary Clinton what the iPod is to the
CD player.

"Clinton can put forth all the policy proposals she likes
—and many of them are admirable ones —but anyone can see
that she's of the same generation and even one of the same
families that got us into this checkmate situation in the first
place," Ehrenreich observes. "Whatever she does, the semiotics
of her campaign boils down to two words—'same old.'"

What's shaping up on the Republican side? When former
Massachusetts Gov. Mitt Romney threw his delegates to
Arizona Sen. John McCain, the announcement photo-op —
with McCain standing among the party's old warhorses —
was sadly astonishing in its inability to embrace the emerging
America of 2008.

"Trapped in an archaic black-and-white newsreel, the
G.O.P. looks more like a nostalgic relic than a national political
party in contemporary America," Frank Rich said in the Feb.
17 New York Times. "A cultural sea change has passed it by."

Look-and-feel? Barack Obama is to John McCain what
the iPod is to the phonograph.

◊ ◊ ◊

Barack Obama would go a long way to creating a climate
for atonement, not just (or even necessarily) the narrow and
cynical definition of atonement vis-à-vis the tragedy of the
American racial dynamic. True enough, Obama as our first
biracial president would signal a vast departure from our racial

past, beginning the Sisyphean challenge of freeing blacks and whites alike from the mutual burdens of racial suspicion.

"Can't we all just get along?" Rodney King asked years ago, in the height of Los Angeles' tragic racial drama. Barack Obama is the living, breathing proof that *yes we can* get along, and at the most personal, most intimate levels of human interaction.

"I've got relatives that look like Bernie Mac and I've got relatives that look like Margaret Thatcher," the candidate said once to Oprah Winfrey. "We've got it all."

It's hard to play down symbolism when your opponent is literally a symbol himself.

But Obama as president would also go some distance to healing the global breach with our neighbors, lately alienated and greatly confused by our behavior on the other side of the fence. Domestically and abroad, it's less a matter of making atonement than of reaching accord.

You can make the case that Obama has already taken the first step toward that scale of national and global reconciliation by the very act of running for the presidency.

Setting aside the monumental stones required for *anyone* to seek the presidency in *any* political season, think of the towering sense of self, the self-possession needed to seek the office in this tumultuous year. *Now* add to that the historically outsized daring to run for the American presidency during an era rife with Islamist terrorism or the fear of same — and to do it with an Islamic surname. The outright nerve of such a conceit, the seemingly impossible irony at its very essence, is unmistakably American: the Obama campaign perfectly reflects — distills — our proven national ability to look at the impossible and see the possible within.

Yes, one phrase naturally follows, as full of sarcasm as it is of wonder: Only in America. And there's the deeper truth, one understood by the columnist Andrew Sullivan, writing brilliantly in The Atlantic.com, (and last April, no less): "The simple existence of Obama as a new president in a new century would in itself enhance America's soft power immeasurably, just as a clear decision to leave Iraq would provide much greater leverage for diplomacy and military force in a whole

Michael E. Ross

variety of new ways. Obama would mean the rebranding of America, after a disastrous eight years. His international heritage, his racial journey, his middle name: these are assets for this country, not liabilities.

"This is the reason for his ascendancy. This is what the American people sense and the world await. This is what the Islamists fear. That last alone is reason to feel hope."

◊ ◊ ◊

That hope Sullivan mentions and which Obama has all but trademarked as a campaign basic has many believers. The fact that so many Republicans are coming aboard, publicly or privately, suggests that the base and bedrock of the Republican Party — not the Beltway ideologues and the talk-radio pit bulls, but ordinary Republicans, everyday people who live life down here on the ground — have found in Obama someone who embodied at least some of the very principles they'd been looking for.

"We are the people we've been looking for," Obama said recently to a roomful of Democrats (apparently quoting Maria Shriver quoting a saying from the Hopi Indians). He might well have been saying that to Republicans too. And his reach across that aisle, his pursuit of that kind of political common cause, is less about singing "Kum Ba Yah" and more about practicing the *realpolitik* necessary to position this nation for a torrent of changes to come, whether we're ready or not.

For eight years we've had a CEO, manager, controller, autocrat, tyrant and neighborhood bully in the White House — the descriptors of the Bush brain trust.

Barack Obama, whether his opponents think so or not, has much of the textbook, practical experience to be president: organizer, professor, thinker — all are the macro-word bullet words in his resume. He would be able to wield power and authority like any president; the awesome leverages of the office will see to that. From day one.

But for the first time in far too long, this country will also have a leader — someone for whom the American people will symbolize a spirit instead of a catchphrase; someone for whom

146

conviction is not a matter of convenience but the bedrock that anchors the pilings of his ideas and policies; someone whose life trajectory is an index to the possibilities within our own lives.

Symbols are important in American politics, indeed, American politics couldn't exist without them. They are central to the American ethos; they are the other substance of this nation, and this watershed campaign.

2/17/2008

HILLARY'S COG-DISS PROBLEM

WHERE have you heard these before?:"We arrested our opponent's momentum." "We held our ground in this key battleground state." "Our opponent's margin of victory was smaller than expected."

"We're keeping our powder dry for the big battle to come in *[put state name here]*"

These aren't bullet-point outtakes from the non-campaign campaign of Rudy Giuliani; they are, or have been, the operational boilerplate of the Hillary Clinton campaign for the last two weeks.

Therein lies the problem for a bid for the presidency the Associated Press dared to call "fading," an effort that even her most ardent supporters may be hard-pressed to call anything else.

With Tuesday's double-digit victories in the Hawaii caucuses and the Wisconsin primary, Barack Obama has amassed 10 consecutive election wins in a row. His insurgent challenge is succeeding wildly against the veteran politician thought of as the presumptive nominee since, uh, day one of this presidential campaign.

And in Texas, one of the remaining big-delegate states up for grabs in the primary on March 4th, patterns of early voting (allowed in the state) indicate probable support for Obama. Think of it: Obama's already got votes locked up in a state where the primary is still two weeks away. It's the election-year equivalent of money in the bank (and the Obama campaign has plenty of the real thing too).

As We Speak, the Clinton brain trust is hunkering down with many pots of strong coffee (using Maalox for creamer) in a hotel suite crowded with whiteboards, trying to figure how to cut into the Obama momentum. It will be a merciless job: Clinton lost in Wisconsin by 17 percentage points, in Hawaii by more than 50. By NBC News' estimation, Clinton must win 65 percent of the delegates in the remaining primary and caucus contests to pull ahead of where Obama is now. The AP reported that Clinton must win 57 percent of the remaining delegates in 14 states and two territories to take the lead.

Who's right? Not much difference either way. An uphill battle is an uphill battle.

The situation is such that Newsday went so far as to caption its Wednesday front page with "Fall Preview? Obama vs. McCain" — effectively kicking the Clinton campaign to the curb before the primaries are even done.

◊ ◊ ◊

The problems for the Clinton crew are formidable. Some in the campaign, such as longtime Democratic good-wrench Mandy Grunwald, are calling for an emo charm offensive — an attempt to rebrand Clinton as a compassionate candidate, the better to reinforce her human side. Others, including the candidate herself, seem to be intent on maintaining an attack strategy: focusing on the Deval Patrick speech that Obama borrowed liberally from recently and trying to reframe the Obama mystique as a cult (requiring Clinton as a deprogrammer, of course).

But in all of it, there's more than a whiff of desperation. The Clinton campaign's furious efforts at reframing the debate, dismantling the public perception of Obama and rebranding the public idea of Clinton herself is something like trying to build an aircraft and fly it at the same time.

A degree of failure is baked into their efforts:

There's a basic problem with "holding your ground." That is fundamentally a strategy of attrition. If you are holding your ground, you're not *gaining* ground, you're struggling to maintain the advantage you already have. In this scenario, advancing is basically not an option. That's a problem for a military campaign, and a political one.

When the only upside you can point to is losing by 10 or 12 percentage points instead of 15, you're in trouble. You're running on cognitive dissonance, an old psychological theory that, roughly defined, means putting the best possible spin on the worst possible situation.

Basically, Hillary's cogs got dissed on Tuesday night. Her ground game in Wisconsin was thought to be unstoppable; so, too, it was assumed that a lot of people in Wisconsin were like Hillary herself: a mother with blue-collar affinities (if not income). Wrong. Double-digit wrong. Now it's on Texas, where Obama has already started the process of galvanizing supporters, who have responded with heavy voting in traditionally-Republican strongholds, and pre-emptive protests against voter disenfranchisement.

Back on her home turf in New York today, speaking at Hunter College, Clinton called for a reality check. "Let's get real," she said in an auditorium the New York Observer noted was "packed mostly with the middle-aged women who make up her base." "Let's get real about this election. Let's get real about our future."

Sen. Charles Schumer, Clinton supporter and Democratic Party leader, spoke on her behalf, emphasizing her stature as someone who's already taken the worst mud the Republicans can throw. "When they take out their 2 by 4," he said, assuming a batter's position, "she'll be ready with her 4 by 8 to hit them back."

The baseball analogy is clever enough, and topical enough given Clinton's current troubles: She's still swinging for the fences, but it may be time for the $100-million plus Clinton campaign to consider using some performance-enhancing substances of its own.

2/20/2008

THE McCAIN SCRUTINY

IN a story credited to four reporters, assisted by two researchers and no doubt vetted by numerous copy editors and others higher in its chain of command, The New York Times on Thursday called into question, at least obliquely, the ethics and judgment of John McCain, a presidential candidate who has made ethics and judgment the centerpieces of his campaign.

And ironically (or maybe not too ironically, given the public's near-zero tolerance of the press these days), what's drawn attention from public and press alike has been not the revelations of the story, but the story itself.

The article, written in an expansive feature style, explores the ties between McCain and Vicki Iseman, a lobbyist who had inexplicably "had been turning up with him at fund-raisers, visiting his offices and accompanying him on a client's corporate jet. Convinced the relationship had become romantic, some of his top advisers intervened to protect the candidate from himself — instructing staff members to block the woman's access, privately warning her away and repeatedly confronting him ..."

◊ ◊ ◊

The pundits on the Potomac weighed in almost immediately, calling it a hit job and lamenting what some called a "thinly-sourced" story based strongly on persons speaking "on the condition of anonymity," the anonymous sources that are, often by necessity, the bane of American journalism. With the phrase "protect the candidate from himself" — which conjures up an image of a man out of control, slave to his own appetites — some even flat-out accused The Times of saying that McCain had a romantic relationship with the lobbyist, something the story only peripherally suggests.

Far from being an unprincipled attack on the candidate, though, most of the Times story is a thorough, nuanced recap of McCain's earlier tiptoes up to the line of political propriety, and by extension an examination of his fidelity to the principles

151

that have animated both his campaign and his career. The story, for example, takes special note of McCain's friendship with Charles Keating, he of the savings-and-loan scandal that cost taxpayers more than $3 billion.

"Even as [McCain] has vowed to hold himself to the highest ethical standards, his confidence in his own integrity has sometimes seemed to blind him to potentially embarrassing conflicts of interest," The Times reported.

McCain addressed the issue forthrightly; in a statement released later on Thursday, McCain condemned the Times story as a "hit-and-run smear campaign" and denied its underlying assertions of impropriety.

The Times, assuming the customary defensive crouch, said it stands by its reporting. "On the substance, we think the story speaks for itself," Times Executive Editor Bill Keller said in an initial reply to reader reactions. This sage, impersonal *res ipsa loquitor* response would perhaps have more traction if it came from another august newsgathering body. As a survey of the relatively recent past reveals, the Times' record for unassailable accuracy has not always been the best.

◊ ◊ ◊

One perfectly justifiable reason for the fresh McCain scrutiny is a quote taken from one of his books, an expression of a personal philosophy — straight talk, if you will — that takes on fresh urgency in light of the Times report. "[Q]uestions of honor," McCain wrote, "are raised as much by appearances as by reality in politics, and because they incite public distrust they need to be addressed no less directly than we would address evidence of expressly illegal corruption."

A romantic relationship isn't proven in the Times story; contrary to the wild cries of the chattering class, a romantic relationship isn't even *alleged* in the Times story. What's got readers' knickers in a twist is the sexual angle that's breathing heavily in the second graph. In some respects, it shows a disregard of Journalism 101: The facts at or near the top of a story are central to the story. That's why they're up there.

If the winking tabloid words "romantic" and "relationship" had to be included at all, they should have been positioned in a place directly reflecting their importance to the story's overall assertions. The way the story was published on Thursday, The Times promised something it couldn't possibly deliver.

◊ ◊ ◊

That said, though, The Times offers ample historical grounds for new attention on McCain, the presumptive Republican nominee: His keester in the seats of corporate jets of business executives seeking his support. His hiring a lobbyist to run his Senate office. His role in creating the Reform Institute, a nonprofit group promoting tighter campaign finance rules, followed by his resignation from the group after news reports found the group was getting the very unlimited corporate contributions he opposed.

Even after the potentially damaging impact of the Times story, it seems McCain *still* doesn't get it, still doesn't fully understand how cozy relationships between lawmakers and lobbyists lead to the appearance of questionable honor. On Friday, McCain defended his relationships with lobbyists, some of whom are working on his presidential campaign in senior-level capacities.

''These people have honorable records, and they're honorable people, and I'm proud to have them as part of my team,'' McCain told reporters following a town hall meeting in Indianapolis. The Associated Press reported the meeting with the press on Friday.

The flap over the McCain-Iseman professional relationship — if relationship there ever was — is likely to blow over shortly, pending any follow-up stories from the Times on the matter. The Democratic candidates, Hillary Clinton and Barack Obama, almost certainly won't touch it, taking the high ground on the whole thing. All in all, a tempest in a teapot, if just barely.

But more than anything, the Times story is a warning to McCain — and the other presidential hopefuls — that the press understands how, for a restive and relentlessly informed electorate in the Internet age, past performance can be interpreted, rightly or wrongly, as a possible predictor of future results.

2/22/2008

RALPH REDUX

THERE was no need Sunday to adjust your set or your mental state; it was not a rerun or a flashback: Ralph Nader is indeed again running for president.

The Sunday-morning news interview shows, otherwise known as "the Sabbath gasbag discussions" (thank you Calvin Trillin), are often prime territory for one Major Political Announcement or another. NBC'S "Meet the Press" was the chosen venue for Nader to declare that, for the third straight election cycle, he would pursue the presidency of the United States. "Dissent is the mother of ascent," Nader told "MTP" moderator Tim Russert. "And in that context, I have decided to run for president."

Like the moldy penny you can't seem to get rid of, our hardy quadrennial challenger is again in the mix, this time unattached (at this writing) to any political party.

His rationale seemed detailed and expansive enough. Nader outlined a wide range of issues domestic and international in need of attention, and at least tried to sharply delineate himself from the Democratic and Republican challengers. Besides ending the war, Nader would seek to get an energy bill through Congress, would support single-payer health insurance, repeal the Taft-Hartley Act and "crack down on corporate crime."

"Now, you take that framework of people feeling locked out, shut, shut out, marginalized, disrespected and you go from Iraq to Palestine/Israel, from Enron to Wall Street, from Katrina to the bungling of the Bush administration, to the complicity of the Democrats in not stopping him on the war, stopping him on the tax cuts, getting a decent energy bill through, and you have to ask yourself, as a citizen, should we elaborate the issues that the two [Obama and Clinton] are not talking about?"

"... You know, when you see the paralysis of the government, when you see Washington, D.C., be corporate-occupied territory, every department agency controlled by overwhelming presence of corporate lobbyists, corporate executives in high government positions, turning the government against its own people, you — one feels an obligation, Tim, to try to open the doorways ..."

Nader has of course long been vilified by Democrats by siphoning away votes from Al Gore during the 2000 election, thereby throwing the contest to George Bush — at least that's the popular explanation. Some have said that the 2000 election shouldn't have been such a photo-finish in the first place — that the relative quiet in the country should have made a Democratic victory not just possible but probable.

Whether that's true, we'll never know. But on Sunday Nader defended his right to throw his weatherbeaten hat in the ring: "... Without voter rights, candidate rights don't mean much. And without candidate rights — more voices and choices — voter rights don't mean much."

Russert posited a historical scenario for Nader: that by running again, "when people look back at Ralph Nader, they'll consider him the Wendell Willkie of his generation, someone who kept running and running for president with no chance of winning ..."

In response, Nader was off to the races again, re-litanizing his positions and ending with a pitch to his Web site, described as "a gathering center."

It might be a center to gather at, but it's not likely to be a gathering place *for* the center, the broad cross-section of American voters who have already made their preferences clear. In this bid as in his two previous abortive runs, Nader will no doubt play to the utterly disaffected Americans, those who see no hope of their grievances being aired, and therefore amplify their despair by backing a presidential quest with no hope of victory.

A symbolic move? Without a doubt. But the question becomes one of end results — the practical aspect of symbolism. If Nader's campaign is meant to be a symbolic gesture, what choice, what viable political option does Nader offer that voters didn't have before he got in the race? Conspicuous by their absence at the polls, stay-at-home voters make their sentiments known, too. That's another kind of symbolism.

◊ ◊ ◊

What has angered Democrats about Nader's previous campaigns (and has them and others scratching their heads about this one), what's so infuriating to them is the time, attention, Web traffic and media oxygen to be devoted to covering the political platform of a man seeking a job he doesn't really want.

Ralph Nader doesn't want to be president; he relishes his role as the malcontent, the heckler at the parade, a position less substantive than that which he occupied in Washington as a consumer advocate and activist two generations ago.

And therein lies a problem with third-party bids for the presidency, from Nader's to Ross Perot's and others besides: They seem to rely on a wellspring of American cynicism. They're mounted in hopes that the wide plurality of Americans will vote for them, when most Americans haven't given up hope on the possibility of change within the two parties they already know and respect (or at least tolerate).

Rather than trying to fly before they walk before they crawl, if third parties are serious about being a viable populist alternative to the two-party system, the best place to start is at the level of government most Americans understand: the grassroots level of state, county and city offices, those neighborhood-specific positions that could form the start of a constituency, the infrastructure of a truly meaningful third-party alternative.

Instead, the idea of third-party campaigns is reliably trotted out every four years, with Nader parachuting in for another quixotic presidential try, and every four years it's sent packing. The reason why seems fairly obvious: Third parties aren't taken seriously because they don't seem to take the lives of Americans seriously more than once every presidential election cycle.

That could explain why Nader's vote total in 2000 (2.7 percent) plummeted in 2004, to .4 percent of votes cast. If he were really serious about a third-party quest for the White House, he'd have been laying the groundwork for Sunday's announcement — city council by city council, mayoralty by mayoralty, governorship by governorship — when the election was over in 2004. *That's* how a third party gets street-credible.

◊ ◊ ◊

Ironically, the populism his insurgent White House bid would generate has already been well underway without him; turnout in the primary season has exceeded previous levels to this point in the campaign, and it's likely to continue for the general election. Considering the wide cross-section of the country that's already voted for either Obama, Clinton or John McCain — a span of race, ethnicity, age, gender, sexual preference and income — there's less reason for Nader's campaign now than there was before. People are already asking if it even matters.

Nader's reset the hourglass on his fifteen minutes, again. We'll see if what he brings to the campaign party has any substance — if he can offer a Bushed nation more than his own frustrated self-importance before the clock runs out.

2/25/2008

HILLARY RODHAM CHAMELEON

IN 1983 Woody Allen released the mock documentary "Zelig," the story of Leonard Zelig, a walking medical phenomenon with the uncanny ability to transform his physical and psychological characteristics to those of the people around him. What at first seems like a gimmick in the film, which stars Allen as this chameleon man of mirrors, takes on a real and nearly tragic organicity as Zelig assumes identity after identity, so suddenly, so often and so totally, over time, that one suspects he's lost his grasp on the core identity that makes him ... Leonard Zelig.

Politics is transformational business; the candidate fights to change or influence voters' perception of him or her; if the candidate does this right, the voters change the candidate's perception of himself. Or herself.

We've seen this a lot in this crowded campaign year. A mob of candidates has thinned out to less than a handful, practically speaking, and the process of fine tuning themselves to the public taste has also gotten more distilled. We can see clearly now how it's done. And to this point in the campaign, none has done it more often than Sen. Hillary Clinton.

Her campaign, gamely fighting for oxygen against Sen. Barack Obama in the runup to the March 4 primaries in Ohio, Texas, Vermont and Rhode Island, has offered the public a number of candidate sub-identities. With 11 straight election defeats in the primary season, Clinton is thought to be near a tipping point for the very life of the campaign. Husband Bill Clinton even said so.

◊ ◊ ◊

So the latest rebranding of Hillary has started in Ohio. David Postman, Seattle Times political reporter, was on the road there on Feb. 23:

"Voters in Ohio started to see a new TV ad from Hillary Rodham Clinton on Saturday, one her supporters say shows the *real* Clinton.

Michael E. Ross

"That'd be the emotional, religious and humble Clinton from the final moments of her debate last week with Barack Obama, not the Clinton full of facts, figures and policies she recites with a dose of braggadocio.

"The 60 seconds of political vérité — an edited clip from the debate — presents voters with the third *real* candidate Clinton since the New Year."

Has it been only three? We'd swear there've been more. There's Emo Hillary, who stopped just short of a mini-meltdown in Portsmouth, N.H. Then Wonk Hillary (a favorite) went on the offensive with a command of minutiae.

Strunk & White Hillary weighed in with pronouncements on plagiarism. Kum Ba Yah Hillary made nice with Obama in last week's one-on-one debate. Angry Hillary shouted on Saturday, waving Obama campaign literature and crying "Shame, shame!" Then Shakespeare Hillary arrived Monday with sarcasm (the last resource of the desperate), describing Obama as political Pollyanna, her body language sweeping and theatrical, arms open in mock supplication, playing to the cheap seats in the Globe Theater.

Leonard Zelig never changed so fast.

◊ ◊ ◊

It would be laughable if it weren't true, or seen as true by Clinton's supporters and those who might be. They ask themselves when she'll find the right strategy, when the tumblers in the lock will turn. They wonder which Hillary they'll see today.

They wonder because more and more, it appears, there's no baseline to Hillary Clinton's emotional rhythms, no defining persona for voters to get consistently comfortable with. For many voters, the tweaks and morphs that the campaign no doubt first thought were a display of versatility have come to reflect insincerity and calculation.

Hillary Clinton's talent for triangulation — for seeking the spongy, comfortable, navigable middle amid less-politically palatable extremes — may have finally found its most logical expression, in Hillary Clinton herself. Maybe when you do that long enough and often enough, sooner or later you can't express who You are anymore.

By now, after 11 straight contests, voters have sent the message that they want more than just someone to agree with, they want someone to believe in — the direct reflection of the inspirational desert the country's wandered in for almost eight years.

This is Clinton's dilemma, making the most of an opportunity not to tap into another guise, but to offer a necessary candor about Clinton the woman, the candidate, the American.

The politician, we already know her. This time, it's not about expressing a reason for being. It's about expressing a reason for being Hillary.

2/26/2008

'THE DESIGNATED HEBREW': BILLY CRYSTAL DIGS IN

HE almost looked mahvelous. But for taking a too-aggressive cut at a fastball moving at 88 miles an hour for a distance of 60 feet and six inches — a ball that needed just three-tenths of a second to trick his 60-year-old eyes — Billy Crystal, debuting as a New York Yankee, might have been a giant.

Crystal, believed to have been a Yankee fan in utero, realized a personal-best dream today when he made his debut — his first and last at-bat — with the team during spring training, playing the Pittsburgh Pirates at Legends Field in Tampa, Fla., after signing a one-game contract days earlier. "I think I'm the designated Hebrew," he said at a press conference.

Crystal's status as a Yankee fan has not been a casual thing. He frequently punctuated the commentary in Ken Burns' 1994 documentary "Baseball," and he directed the 2001 HBO movie "61*", - about the joys and agonies of Roger Maris' pursuit of the single-season league home-run record in 1961.

Still, the Yankees didn't cut him any slack. Invited by shortstop for the ages Derek Jeter, Crystal showed up and was (like all rookies, we'd guess) subject to team pranks, finding a drink spiked and the laces in his shoes disappeared.

Then, getting a standing O before he even got to the plate, one day before his 60th birthday, William Jacob Crystal dug in, the leadoff man in pinstripes.

Let the venerable Associated Press give you the play-by-play. Or maybe just the play:

Players on both teams perched on the top step of the dugout when Crystal came up. They almost saw something special as he took Jeter's advice: "Swing early in the count."

Batting leadoff as the Yankees' designated hitter in the first inning, he took a late-but-solid cut at a fastball from Pirates lefty Paul Maholm. Crystal hit a chopper that got past first baseman Adam LaRoche, but came down 3 feet foul.

Crystal showed a patient, good eye and got ahead in the count 3-1. Maholm came back with a pair of cutters, and the right-handed Crystal swung over both 88 mph pitches.

"I was mad at myself for swinging at 'em," he said.

Especially the last one.

"It was ball four," said plate umpire Mark Carlson, who shook hands with Crystal before the at-bat.

Said Maholm: "I tried to lay it in there for him. I definitely didn't try to blow it by him."

"It was definitely a little nerve-racking," he said. "I'm glad I didn't have to watch it every day, him getting a hit off me."

◊ ◊ ◊

"I can always say I led off for the New York Yankees," Crystal said. "That's an amazing feeling. I don't even know how to describe it. It was so intensely good."

The New York Yankees Web site played it up right: "Yanks lose despite Mussina, Crystal," read the headline in the story published after the game.

But some bloggers on the sports Web sites were weirdly uncharitable, calling it a stunt that cheapened the Yankee pinstripes. Hello folks — before it was a tradition, it was a game, a kid's game. Crystal never forgot that.

Whether the humorless chuckleheads who put him down know it or not, he took a hack at a dream, which is more than most of us can say. A goof? A stunt? Get real. Billy Crystal doesn't need any more publicity, and God knows the Yankees don't.

What happened today was a nod to the persistence of childhood, a short laugh at the advances of maturity and the relentless march of time. Billy Crystal took a shot for all of us. He was up three and one and went down swinging. That's a scenario we all relate to, sooner or later.

"There's more Met than Yankee in all of us," the great sportswriter Roger Angell once observed. And if that's true, and it is, there's more Billy Crystal in all of us than maybe we'd ever admit.

3/13/2008

.

INDIANA JONES
AND THE EVIL EMPIRE

O N MAY 22, the fourth installment of the Indiana Jones movie franchise/industry, "Indiana Jones and the Kingdom of the Crystal Skull," directed by Steven Spielberg, "opens wide" in about 4,000 theaters in the United States. Harrison Ford returns as maverick archeologist Henry (Indiana) Jones in a film likely to gain old Indy fans and newcomers who'd until now thought Indiana Jones was a second-string forward for the Pacers.

This fourth nod to the jungle movie serials of the 1930s would seem to be hamstrung by its own history. Rooted as it has been, in the years leading to World War II, the Indy saga could have been trapped in a nightmare limbo for its screenwriters: a movie without the designated villain of the Nazis. But with the choice of Russians as the bad guys, the "Crystal Skull" filmmakers have made use of history and, shudder, current events.

The latest story is set in 1957, and this time Dr. Jones confronts the Soviets in what Americans thought then was their march to world domination. They might have called it "Indy's Last Stand."

Consider: According to the Indiana Jones wiki, our favorite archeologist was born on July 1, 1899, in Princeton, N.J. The Indy template, "Indiana Jones and Raiders of the Lost Ark," (set in 1936) was released in 1981. The last one to date, "Indiana Jones and the Last Crusade," set in 1938, was released in 1989. That whole time, Indy was dispatching Nazis, Thuggees, assassins and various other evildoers in Europe, Asia and South America at a brisk clip.

But with so many years between the last Indiana Jones film and the new one coming in May — to say nothing of the time between the *first* Indy film and the one coming in May — sending him up against bad guys in the 1930's or 1940's wouldn't work logistically.

The Vietnam War wouldn't start cooking until the 1960's, and any number of other baddies — from Noriega's regime in

Panama to the rise of Saddam Hussein to the Islamist terrorists we fear today — didn't arrive on the scene until after that.

That leaves the Russians of 1957 as the only credible villains left for Indy to fight without doing it as a senior citizen.

◊ ◊ ◊

It would have been more of a problem for Spielberg and screenwriter George Lucas not many years ago, when the Soviet Union dissolved and the people of the Russian Republic were discovering the first heady whiff of capitalist freedom — not that long after President Reagan's now-timeless depiction of the Soviet Union as "the evil empire."

More recently, the more severe policies of Russian President (now prime minister) Vladimir Putin have made it easy to recast Russia as the Evil Empire Redux. By growing wages and playing to the nationalist desire for a strong leadership unafraid to stare down the West — and with the benefits of an unprecedented oil boom that's given the economy new clout on the world stage — Putin has returned Russia to a global swagger and military power that remind many analysts and world leaders of the old Soviet Union.

In February 2007, Putin essentially read the riot act to U.S. Defense Secretary Robert Gates and other Western officials, at a meeting in Munich. "Putin's 'Munich speech' drew instant comparisons to another diplomatic outburst: Soviet leader Nikita Khrushchev's notorious shoe-thumping at the United Nations 50 years ago, during an angry outburst against Western imperialism," NPR correspondent Gregory Feifer reported last year.

"The president has ended democratic reforms and reinstituted authoritarian rule, curtailed freedoms and returned parts of the economy to state control. And he has introduced an aggressive foreign policy that opposes Western countries on issues such as the war in Iraq and the expansion of NATO," Feifer reported.

With other actions such as a crackdown on dissidents, and the government's possible complicity in the deaths of some vocal critics of the Kremlin, it's clear that, for movie purposes at least, Ronald Reagan's "evil empire" has made something of a comeback.

CLOSE SHOT: INDIANA JONES, COLD WAR. DAY.

◊ ◊ ◊

Diehard fans are looking forward to the release of "Crystal Skull" with anticipation, but however well-received this film is, it's almost certain to be the last in a series.

You can see it in the latest poster art. Harrison Ford looks tired; there's not much of the spark of athletic defiance seen in poster art for the previous trio of films.

It's understandable. At age 65, Ford is seven years older in real life than the character he portrays. We like Harrison Ford — hell, we like *any* A-list actor with the stones to insist on doing his own stunts after the age of 60. To his eternal credit, Ford did just that in the "Crystal Skull" installment of the Indiana Jones saga.

But still, 65 years old is 65 years old. You have to think that with a personal net worth in excess of $300 million, five of his best efforts in the National Film Registry, four grown children and his health and good looks intact, Harrison Ford may be ready to commit his most celebrated character to another enduring life-movie: Indiana Jones and the Perils of Retirement.

3/15/2008

A DEFINING MOMENT

TODAY at the National Constitution Center in Philadelphia, Sen. Barack Obama delivered what must be considered the best speech of his political career. Eighteen days from the inevitable and necessary observation of the 40th anniversary of the assassination of the Rev. Dr. Martin Luther King, the contender for the presidency laid bare the great American stain in an address that brilliantly, eloquently posited an American racial future unchained from America's past.

Responding to a mounting series of attacks on him and his campaign in the wake of incendiary comments from his former pastor, Rev. Jeremiah Wright, and amid a growing queasiness about the role of race in a campaign that until recently has avoided the third-rail issue of our time, Obama addressed the issue head-on and set the tone — if not the bar — for any similarly frank discussions about race from his challengers for the presidency.

Obama's proven talent for uniting seemingly disparate elements of the American electorate — look at the diversity of the states he's won so far in the primary season — was validated again today. By conflating the experiences of all Americans of all races and ethnicities, Obama's deprived his challengers — though most notably Sen. Hillary Clinton, grappling with him for the Democratic nomination — of the *sub rosa* racial suspicions they might seek to arouse, specifically in Pennsylvania, the next delegate-rich state of the primary season.

◊ ◊ ◊

"I have already condemned, in unequivocal terms, the statements of Reverend Wright that have caused such controversy," Obama said of the pastor of Trinity United Church of Christ, an 8,000-member megachurch in Chicago. "For some, nagging questions remain. Did I know him to be an occasionally fierce critic of American domestic and foreign policy? Of course. Did I ever hear him make remarks that could be considered controversial while I sat in church? Yes. Did I strongly disagree with many of his political views? Absolutely — just as I'm sure many of you have heard remarks from your pastors, priests, or rabbis with which you strongly disagreed.

"But the remarks that have caused this recent firestorm weren't simply controversial. They weren't simply a religious leader's effort to speak out against perceived injustice. Instead, they expressed a profoundly distorted view of this country - a view that sees white racism as endemic, and that elevates what is wrong with America above all that we know is right with America; a view that sees the conflicts in the Middle East as rooted primarily in the actions of stalwart allies like Israel, instead of emanating from the perverse and hateful ideologies of radical Islam.

"As such, Reverend Wright's comments were not only wrong but divisive, divisive at a time when we need unity; racially charged at a time when we need to come together to solve a set of monumental problems — two wars, a terrorist threat, a falling economy, a chronic health care crisis and potentially devastating climate change; problems that are neither black or white or Latino or Asian, but rather problems that confront us all."

These excerpts, moving as they are, don't do the speech its proper justice but they reinforce the importance of Obama's basic principle — the nation as community — that has animated his campaign and provided the foundation for the coalition Obama has been building from the beginning.

◊ ◊ ◊

Columnists and the punditocracy comprehended the moment.

James Fellows, in Atlantic.com: "It was a moment that Obama made great through the seriousness, intelligence, eloquence, and courage of what he said. I don't recall another speech about race with as little pandering or posturing or shying from awkward points, and as much honest attempt to explain and connect, as this one."

Charles Kaiser in Radar: "He did it. No other presidential candidate in the last forty years has managed to speak so much truth so eloquently at such a crucial juncture in his campaign as Barack Obama did today. And he did it by speaking about race, the most persistent source of hatred among us since America began.

"It turns out that a candidate for president with a white mother and a black father has a capacity that no one else has ever had before: he can articulate an equal understanding of black racism and white racism --and that makes it possible for him to condemn both of them with equal passion."

Jon Robin Baitz, at The Huffington Post: "If there was any doubt about what we have missed in the anti-intellectual, ruthlessly incurious Bush years, and even the slippery Clinton ones, those doubts were laid to rest by Barack Obama's magisterial speech today. He reminded us that the dreams of black America do not come at the expense of white America. Someone running for the highest office in the land finally talked about it — the dark and secret swamp that we Americans dodge at every possible opportunity."

Trey Ellis, blogging at HuffPost: "Obama's speech just now was magnificent not because he relied on soaring rhetoric but because he eschewed it. ... His analysis was measured and brilliant in how he empathized with disgruntled and cynical black youths defeated by racism, but urged them to transcend; how he also empathized with struggling white workers unsympathetic to America's history of discrimination and yet urged them, too, to join in the fight to better this nation."

Andrew Sullivan, in Atlantic.com, said "this searing, nuanced, gut-wrenching, loyal, and deeply, deeply Christian speech is the most honest speech on race in America in my adult lifetime. It is a speech we have all been waiting for for a generation. Its ability to embrace both the legitimate fears and resentments of whites and the understandable anger and dashed hopes of many blacks was, in my view, unique in recent American history."

And MSNBC's "Hardball" host Chris Matthews was pitch-perfect in his placement of the speech in the wider American canon of that which explains America to itself:

"This should be, to me, an American tract, something you just check in with now and then, like reading 'The Great Gatsby' or 'Huckleberry Finn.'"

◊ ◊ ◊

The blogosphere weighed in big time. Citizen NickOhio, writing at HuffPost: "The speech was brilliant. It should show open up the debate and, for better or worse, allow us to see ourselves for what we are... a recovering racist nation. You may not agree with his comments nor his tone, but Senator Barack Obama has just raised the bar a few notches on the challenge to America. "

Monicall, also on HuffPost, smartly flips the script on the weight of Rev. Wright's words and Obama's own, asking the uncomfortable but necessary questions of an oratorical double standard in the national discourse:

"It's amazing to see those who are dismissing Obama's powerful heartfelt speech as 'just meaningless talk' or 'just political.' Yet those very same people are putting so much stock in what Rev. Wright says. So only negative rhetoric is believeable and energizing to you. If someone has something powerful and positive to say from their own mouths, you just can't buy that?! Why aren't you dismissing Rev. Wright's words so easily, as meaningless garble. Why are Wright's negative words viewed by you as so impactful, yet Obama's honesty from his own mouth dismissed as mere rhetoric?"

But Monique, at HuffPost, also makes a telling point – that Obama was under no pressure to stay in Wright's congregation in the face of language and attitude that offended him. There are, she implies, many ways to vote, first among them with your feet.

"If I heard a minister speak such anger and hatred, I would have the courage to pick myself up and walk right out -- whether the speaker was speaking against whites or blacks. As a leader, I would expect at least that much from Obama. But he not only failed to get up and walk out. He remained in that seat for 20 years.

Michael E. Ross

"Wright's words were not words of transcendence," Monique blogs. "They are the old, angry words of blame and hate. And not words that would keep me rooted in my seat for an hour, or twenty years."

◊ ◊ ◊

The media's tendency to offer immediate analysis is likely to be frustrated this time. The speech — its resonance, its appeal to Americans across the racial divide, its possible impact for voters in Pennsylvania — hasn't trickled down far enough yet, and probably won't for a few days.

But Rev. Jesse Jackson, writing on HuffPost, said that Obama "had turned crisis into opportunity." And that's likely to be the major takeaway from this speech: Rather than be put forever on the defensive about a pastor's comments — words Obama didn't make, had nothing to do with making, words he's rejected *and* denounced more than once — Obama has taken this inside fastball and parked it in the centerfield stands. Obama's speech was an absolute throwdown to the Clinton campaign, a dare to the forces of Hillary to raise their game in the remaining primary contests — to resist using the grim intimations of racial politics to advance a candidacy whose philosophical foundation seems to get shakier all the time.

In a speech already ranked as one of the finest in almost half a century, the biracial junior senator from Illinois hasn't so much reframed the debate on race — God knows, we've never really had one — as he has dared the American people to *have* a debate about race — dared the nation to stop retreating to the reflexive anger and resentment that litter the American past.

◊ ◊ ◊

The most reasoned, eloquent, passionate response to the speech from the blogosphere — maybe from anywhere — came from a place both alien and central to our lives. It came from Zipperupus, a Marine posting on HuffPost from Iraq, fighting one of two foreign wars, at a high burn rate of its lives, treasure and prestige, writing to a nation fighting its own ethnic war, at a high burn rate of its soul:

"The core reason that Obama is ahead of Hillary and will be the next President is because he speaks to our better selves. He doesn't simply cough up a bromide about God and country. He shows us the division, the left/right red/blue black/white divide and tells us that we can fix it by striving for the commonwealth. This is a huge deal.

"I'm tired of fighting. My sword wants to be beaten into a plowshare so bad... I want to go to work putting things back together, and i don't care if the person next to me voted for the other guy or gal. Now is the time to elect someone who stands for unity and healing, eloquence and sacrifice.

"Obama 08"

3/18/2008

FIVE YEARS AFTER

THE DEFENSE Department today announced the death of an American soldier.

"Spc. Lerando J. Brown, 27, of Gulfport, Miss., died March 15 in Balad, Iraq, from injuries suffered in an incident currently under investigation. He was assigned to the 288th Sapper Company, 223rd Engineer Battalion, Mississippi Army National Guard, Houston, Miss."

It is a succinct statement, but one profound in its communication of a national agony. Today we mark the anniversary of when those letters began.

Today five years ago — perhaps $600 billion, 3,991 American lives, at least 85,000 Iraqi lives, 29,400 combat injuries, and countless color-coded terror alerts ago — the United States embarked on what would become its longest war, a conflict that may yet prove to be its most inconclusive.

There's more than one measure of its cost. There's the human cost. For a truly comprehensive breakdown of the known casualty count, check out the excellent icasualties Web site. There in columns and rows of numbers are the figures that represent the human toll, the first most awful currency of the disaster of war. That tragedy, household by household, family by family, speaks eloquently for itself.

There's the financial cost. The National Priorities Project, an independent organization that analyzes and clarifies federal data to help Americans understand where their tax dollars are going, has a Web site with a counter that brings the issue home before your very eyes. The project estimates the cost of the war to date at almost $504 billion. By the time you read this, the figure will be higher than that.

It may be a lot higher. News outlets such as CBS and NBC today reported the actual cost at $600 billion.

With numbers that astronomical, you need some smaller metric to get your mind around it. How's this: CNN reported in November that "every minute troops are deployed in Iraq, the American public pays $200,000 to keep them there."

And that just tallies up what we've spent already. Some economists supported by the nonpartisan Congressional

Budget Office have estimated the eventual war's cost at about $1.7 trillion through 2017. But other economists, including Joseph Stiglitz, Nobel laureate and adviser to the Clinton administration, and Harvard economist Linda Bilmes have calculated that the real price tag may be closer to $3 trillion.

Stiglitz and Bilmes, who co-authored "The Three Trillion Dollar Conflict: The True Cost of the Iraq War," wrote that projections under $2 trillion don't include peripheral issues — collateral damage — such as the need to "reset" the U.S. military, basically the cost of repairing or replacing the material and man/woman power the current conflict is exhausting at an unsustainable rate.

◊ ◊ ◊

Then, to these mind-boggling expenses of life and treasure, add the intangible but real cost of the United States' sense of itself.

Since the war started (and certainly since the singular catastrophe of Sept 11, 2001), this nation has so deeply embraced a defensive psychological position concerning Islamist terrorism — the United States as victim — that it has thoroughly conceded control of the perception by which victory, or anything like it in the context of asymmetrical war, is to be determined.

Often we've been told that to leave Iraq with a publicly-known timetable would be an implicit admission of defeat, a strange and presumptuous concession that lets "the enemy" decide the terms of victory and defeat.

But who's conceding anything to the shadowy "enemy"? Who says they won — even if *they* say it?

Just as convincing, and even more logical in the classic calculus of war, is the idea that, when the United States exits Iraq it will have won the war, having achieved most of at least its initial stated objectives, and having realized that the objectives left unfinished can mainly, properly be achieved by the people of Iraq.

The conservative obsession with leaving Iraq "with honor" has parallels with the Vietnam experience that should be concerning, if not alarming, to the Republicans. It forces this nation into a victimology that is at odds with everything it stands for. It overlooks many of the usual benchmarks by which a war's winner and loser are decided.

When you leave the field of battle and the people in a conquered land are working *for* you instead of against you; when the might of your military has been absolutely validated; when you have vanquished or executed the old regime; when you have helped establish at least the foundations of a participatory democracy … you've won. No matter what "the enemy" says.

The defenders of America's ongoing role in Iraq have fashioned a rationale by which that war, and our personal and financial obligation to it, should stretch on indefinitely under the gauzy pretext of national security. It's this principle that animated John McCain's recent, celebrated vow that, if he were president, this country would fight in Iraq for "a hundred years" if necessary to achieve American objectives. War without end, amen.

◊ ◊ ◊

One of the bigger unresolved problems for the United States is coming to terms with a concrete definition of "victory" in the context of an asymmetrical war whose boundaries are less geographical than they are religious and philosophical.

Talking with NPR's Alex Chadwick, Gen. David Petraeus offered his own definition, saying that victory would mean "an Iraq that is at peace with itself, at peace with its neighbors, that has a government that is representative of — and responsive to — its citizenry and is a contributing member of the global community."

"There is a degree of hope in the Iraqi population that probably was not present back at that time," Petraeus said, adding that, success would hinge on "progress in the security arena, providing basic services to the Iraqi people, the Iraqi government getting their ministries functioning in a way that they are not right now, and getting the economy overall growing so that it can employ what is a fairly substantial unemployed and underemployed population."

◊ ◊ ◊

While the Petraeus explanation seeks to be a thoughtfully comprehensive one, there are flaws built in. An Iraq "at peace with itself" and "with its neighbors" is beyond the scope of the American military to oversee. With tribal strife between the Sunnis and Shiites that comprise the majority of the population going back not decades but centuries — centuries before the United States existed — an Iraq "at peace with itself and neighbors" can only be achieved on the terms of those who live there.

The United States can no more broker a truce in an 800-year-old tribal dispute than any other foreign power could come to the United States and militarily preside over a resolution of the racial divisions that stretch back in our history only 230 years. And for most of the same reasons.

An Iraq with "a government that is representative of — and responsive to — its citizenry" has already been achieved. The coalition and its diplomatic proxies helped usher in Interim and Transitional Governments until 2006, when they were replaced with the country's permanent government, after an election that international monitors deemed free and fair. CNN reported that about 10 million of 15 million registered voters participated in the election for the Council of Representatives — the first such referendum since Saddam Hussein was removed. Pictures of Iraqis holding high fingers stained with the purple ink signifying their status as voters are still powerful symbols both of Iraq's democratic reality and its possibilities.

With the basic structure of a government in place, then, the role of the military gives way to a need for diplomacy and economic intervention as a way to establish and solidify the government's aspirations to be "a contributing member of the global community."

The principles of democracy ultimately can't be enforced at American gunpoint. The surest sign of a viable democracy is what happens when you take away the guns you need to start one. If those democratic principles have any traction with the people who live there, those principles and ideals will take hold and flourish on their own. If they don't, that form of democracy was never meant to be there, and won't be imposed there by an occupying army. Whether that army stays for a year or five years or fifty.

Or even a hundred.

◊ ◊ ◊

Other items on the Petraeus laundry list may well be the work done by a true global coalition — the sort of WWII Allies-style congregation the Bush administration has conjured for years — or by the Iraqi people.

"Progress in the security arena" will happen on its own terms, again depending on the ability of Sunnis and Shiites to *themselves* set aside differences in deference to an Iraq resistant to terrorism and extremists. The process of "providing basic services to the Iraqi people" is more a job for the Army Corps of Engineers than for 158,000 combat troops. Later, that effort properly gives way to private companies like Bechtel and Fluor to transform an infrastructure that, at this writing, only affords Iraqis eight hours of electricity a day.

Other tasks — such as aiding the Iraqi government in overcoming ministerial and constitutional gridlock, and bolstering the economy — are more properly achieved by the elected government's work with coalition partners, any number of experts from the United Nations, officials of the European Union, and leaders in businesses and industries from around the world.

"On this grim milestone, it is worth remembering how we got into this situation, and thinking about how best we can get out," said Democrat congressman John Dingell on Tuesday. "The tasks that remain in Iraq — to bring an end to sectarian conflict, to devise a way to share political power and to create a functioning government that is capable of providing for the needs of the Iraqi people — are tasks that only the Iraqis can complete."

◊ ◊ ◊

Sometime in the near future — maybe a week, maybe a month, maybe as soon as tomorrow — the Defense Department will announce the name of the 4,000th American military casualty of the Iraq war. The commentators and pundits will bow their heads; the editorialists will weigh in with assessments (much like this one); the members of some family somewhere in the United States will witness a military vehicle pulling into their driveway, and scream to themselves, if not out loud.

And a nation consumed with its future and grappling with the present will be forced to confront again a lesson from its recent past:

There is no war more unwinnable than a war that should never have been waged.

3/19/2008

MRS. CLINTON MISREMEMBERS

GAMELY soldiering on on the presidential campaign trail, Hillary Clinton last week recalled a trip to Bosnia in March 1996:"I remember landing under sniper fire," she said at George Washington University on March 17.

"There was supposed to be some kind of greeting ceremony there at the airport," she said,"but instead we just ran with our heads down to get into the vehicles to get to our base."

Gee! Whoa! Good harrowing stuff, the kind of imagery that makes for powerful campaign moments shoring up Clinton's claim to foreign policy experience. We can see it: Hillary Clinton as a modern Sgt. Rock, gritting her teeth in a war zone, toughing it out, coolly advancing American objectives under fire in an unfriendly part of the world.

If only it were true. Maybe it was just Hillary engaging in a bit of St. Patrick's Day blarney. Maybe Hillary forgot what era in which she's running for the presidency. But life in the era of YouTube makes confirmation of such dramatic claims a slam dunk. As it is, there's ample evidence that, well, this trip to the ninth circle of hell came up about eight circles short:

On a video Hillary Clinton is seen on a C-17 with her battle-hardened squad: daughter Chelsea Clinton, comedian Sinbad and singer Sheryl Crow, and immediately encountered such belligerents as the eight-year-old Bosnian girl who greeted her warmly on the tarmac.

Sinbad recalled the trip for The Sleuth, the Washington Post blog: "I think the only 'red-phone' moment was: 'Do we eat here or at the next place?'"

On the New York Times' politics blog, The Caucus, Helene Cooper, Times diplomatic correspondent, reported Monday:

"I spoke with William Nash, who was the commander of U.S. troops in Bosnia and was at the Tuzla airport with Hillary Clinton. He said there was no threat of sniper fire at the airport during her visit. He said that Mrs. Clinton was gracious during her visit and took pictures with the soldiers, but "she never had her head down. There was no sniper threat that I know of."

Longtime Democratic adviser and talking head Robert Shrum told NBC's "Today" that "what stuns me about this is the explicitness of her recollection."

◊ ◊ ◊

Others have been less charitable. "Who the hell makes shit up about getting shot at by snipers?" asked Reality Man, blogging at the Atlantic Web site.

And Craig, also commenting on the Atlantic Web site, nailed it:

"Just wait until the footage comes in proving Clinton's claims that she:

1) Tore down the Berlin Wall
2) Traveled into space on Sputnik
3) Cornered bin Laden in the hills of Tora Bora
4) Won American Idol in 1986
5) Wrote the bestselling novel "War and Peace"
6) Personally executed Che Guevara
7) Finished second in Star Search"

No word yet on any Clinton claims to creating the Internet.

Team Clinton went into immediate damage-control mode. When she was asked about the discrepancy at a meeting Monday with the editorial board of the Philadelphia Daily News, Clinton sought to spin things differently. "I went to 80 countries, you know. I gave contemporaneous accounts, I wrote about a lot of this in my book. You know, I think that, a minor blip, you know, if I said something that, you know, I say a lot of things -- millions of words a day -- so if I misspoke, that was just a misstatement."

Setting aside the misstatement in that correction of a misstatement — she talks a lot on the campaign trail but doesn't utter "millions of words a day" — the latest Clinton gaffe suggests other errors of fact.

Michael E. Ross

The Nation asked: "... if Clinton is distorting what happened in Bosnia — a key section of her foreign policy resume — what else is she fibbing about?"

◊ ◊ ◊

Well, if Lord Trimble of Lisnagarvey is to be believed, Clinton stretched the truth about a 1998 trip to Northern Ireland, too.

Toby Harnden of The Telegraph (UK) reported that "Hillary Clinton had no direct role in bringing peace to Northern Ireland and is a 'wee bit silly' for exaggerating the part she played, according to Lord Trimble, the Nobel Peace Prize winner and former First Minister of the province."

"I don't know there was much she did apart from accompanying Bill [Clinton] going around," Lord Trimble told The Telegraph.

Quoting Lord Trimble, Harnden reported that "Her recent statements about being deeply involved were merely 'the sort of thing people put in their canvassing leaflets' during elections.'

"She visited when things were happening, saw what was going on, she can certainly say it was part of her experience. I don't want to rain on the thing for her, but being a cheerleader for something is slightly different from being a principal player," Lord Trimble said.

Such inconvenient claims as these thoroughly deflate Clinton's primary claim to fame: the experience she's been touting since Day One of her campaign. They point to a growing disconnect between Clinton's reality and everyone else's reality. And reaction to these assertions suggests that voters already understand something that Clinton would just as soon have them forget: There's a world of difference between breathing the morning air of the commander-in-chief and *being* the commander-in-chief.

◊ ◊ ◊

With her less-than-elegant embroideries of the truth, Clinton joins such experiential fabulists as Jayson Blair, the New York Times reporter whose fabrications of time and space cost him his job, and cost the Times considerable prestige as a newsgathering organization; and James Frey, the author of "A Million Little Pieces," an autobiographical work published in 2005, some of its central elements outed in January 2006 as towering fraud.

Such mental conjuring doesn't stop with high-profile cases. It's apparently an all–too-human failing. In a 2002 study involving undergraduates at Midwestern and California universities, Dr. Elizabeth Loftus and behavioral researchers at the University of California at Irvine actually got many subjects in a research study to claim they shook hands with Bugs Bunny at Disneyland.

"There is good evidence that memories lose specificity over time and become more generalized, author Gillian Cohen writes in the book "Memory in the Real World." "False memories can be deliberately implanted and recognition tasks show a relatively high rate of false positive responses for false memories and false details of true memories."

Our fallible memories can have significant consequences. Juries have convicted suspects based on eyewitness testimony that turned out to be less than credible and open to the erosion of time, and the suggestion of prosecutors.

Luckily, the stakes this time aren't quite so high — just the presidency of the United States hangs in the balance.

Sen. Barack Obama had the good sense after a trying week to take some time off, vacationing with his family in the U.S. Virgin Islands. Maybe it's time for Clinton to take a break.

If Hill does go on furlough, there may be a campaign ad in the making:

ANNOUNCER: Hey, Hillary Clinton! You've just had a busy week on the presidential campaign trail. What are you gonna do now?

CLINTON: I'm going to Disneyland!

3/25/2008

183

THE McCAIN SCRUTINY III

EVEN as Sens. Barack Obama and Hillary Clinton engage in their current battle to the death for the Democratic nomination, to the glee of the John McCain presidential bid, there's indication that Obama and Clinton have begun a conflation of issues that may prove fatal to Republican fortunes in November. For all the acrimony of the Democratic campaign going on, the Democrats' increasing oratorical unity of the domestic economy and the war in Iraq — perhaps the two biggest issues in American lives — may spell doom for the Republicans in the fall.

Pretty much up to now, the campaigns have examined the domestic economy and the Iraq war as discrete phenomena, each deserving of being separated as bullet points in campaign rallies, and certainly separated in the media's questioning during the recent high season for debates.

But recent speeches at Obama and Clinton rallies, more recent estimates of the war's cost exceeding $600 billion, and McCain's tepid performance this week at a "major speech" on economic policy suggest strongly that the GOP drive for the White House may be more vulnerable to its own inadequacies than to the Democratic opposition, whoever that opposition is.

◊ ◊ ◊

On more than one occasion, well before the current campaign, McCain has admitted to being a neophyte in the world of economics, despite his role as the ranking Republican member of the Senate Commerce Committee. At first blush maybe some populist reflex reaction kicked in for Arizonans, something they could relate to: Hell, like a lot of Americans, they couldn't figure out the world of economics, either.

But the stakes are higher for McCain as a presidential candidate; what might play as endearingly sympathizable ignorance in your home state becomes more problematic at the national scale, with another 49 state treasuries under your watch.

In the speech McCain made Tuesday in Orange County, Calif., the senator emphasized two principal points. "First, it is time to convene a meeting of the nation's accounting professionals to discuss the current mark to market accounting systems. We are witnessing an unprecedented situation as banks and investors try to determine the appropriate value of the assets they are holding and there is widespread concern that this approach is exacerbating the credit crunch.

"We should also convene a meeting of the nation's top mortgage lenders. Working together, they should pledge to provide maximum support and help to their cash-strapped, but credit worthy customers. They should pledge to do everything possible to keep families in their homes and businesses growing."

For observers, it was pretty weak tea. "The bulk of McCain's speech's recaps the broad outlines of what has transpired in the housing sector and Wall Street over the past year and reads as if cribbed from various state-of-the-economy reports previously delivered by Treasury Secretary Hank Paulson and chairman of the Federal Reserve Ben Bernanke," said Salon's Andrew Leonard.

McCain didn't help himself much with one particular excerpt that was, well, breathtaking:

"Already-tight household budgets are ... getting tighter," he told an audience in southern California, an audience whose grasp of this insight surely rivals his own.

◊ ◊ ◊

Credit MSNBC's Keith Olbermann for a rundown of three of McCain's more overt admissions of fiscal ignorance:

In January 2000 McCain told The New Republic that "I didn't pay ... attention to [economic] issues in the past."

In November 2005 McCain told The Wall Street Journal that "I know a lot less about economics than I do about military and foreign policy issues."

In December 2007 McCain told the Baltimore Sun that "...[e]conomics is something that I've never understood as well as I should."

One quakes with fear for the status of the McCain family budget.

There's already been some spin; much of McCain's speech was a practical call for a variety of ideas on some economic course correction, a plurality of opinions from Alan Greenspan, Paul Volcker and others. At one level this makes sense; if you can't do something or do something well, hire a professional who does. But for a candidate whose political ascendancy has had much to do with cultivating a reputation as a maverick, there's precious little that's original about outsourcing your economic strategy.

Quietly, the word's gone out: This is the best antidote for the economy the Republicans have. This economic naiveté, this lack of understanding is the best they're going to get. And this is something they can't retrofit. It can't be "fixed." It's built into the candidate. For McCain, the lack of fresh, thoughtful, nuanced, doable strategies for healing the national economy isn't an Achilles heel, it's an Achilles appendage. For millions of the Americans he will need as voters, this issue is The Issue, and by his own admission, the ranking Republican member of the Senate Commerce Committee hasn't got a clue.

And that's where the Democrats come in.

◊ ◊ ◊

"When you're spending over $50 to fill up your car because the price of oil is four times what it was before Iraq, you're paying a price for this war," Obama said Thursday in Charleston, W. Va. "When Iraq is costing each household about $100 a month, you're paying a price for this war."

"For what folks in this state have been spending on the Iraq war, we could be giving health care to nearly 450,000 of your neighbors, hiring nearly 30,000 new elementary school teachers, and making college more affordable for over 300,000 students," he said, according to The Associated Press.

On March 3, The Washington Post's Peter Slevin reported that Obama and Clinton "ask audiences to imagine what $120 billion — the approximate annual cost of the conflict — would buy. They contend that bringing the troops home would liberate cash for economic investment, infrastructure improvements and ... improved care for hundreds of thousands of war veterans and their families."

"It's weird," said Steve Stivers, an Ohio Republican state senator seeking a congressional seat, to The Post. "The economy is just overshadowing everything. When people are worried about jobs and their pocketbook, they don't want to think about things across the world."

Obama, in particular, has traction in the domestic arena, having proposed creating stimulus packages for ordinary Americans, and having some foresight into the current housing mess, in 2007. Sam Graham-Felsen, blogging Tuesday on the Obama community site, observed:

"Almost one year ago to the day, Barack Obama sent a letter to Federal Reserve Chairman Ben Bernanke and Treasury Secretary Henry Paulson urging them to convene a homeownership preservation summit. Today, Clinton is proposing essentially the same thing."

◊ ◊ ◊

MSNBC analyst Rachel Maddow recently articulated the Cornelian dilemma on McCain's reputed strength in military affairs, did so with a grasp of its imprisoning illogic that Joseph Heller might have appreciated: "I think that McCain will make the case that if things get better we have to stay, and if things get worse, we have to stay." Thus is the napalm torch of this war, and its cost, passed to a new generation.

Obama and Clinton are thinking otherwise. "In domestic terms," The Post reported, "the candidates point to the war's cost, suggesting that taxpayer money directed to Iraq could make a difference at home if it were invested in the nation's battered roads and bridges or spent on schools and social services."

The Post continued: "The argument makes sense to Sen. Sherrod Brown (D-Ohio), who has heard about the war's budgetary impact while listening to constituents at 85 roundtables since early 2007. He said he hears from business owners and government officials that federal support for such things as police and utility improvements is drying up.

" 'They are starting to understand this economically," said Brown, who defeated Republican incumbent Mike DeWine in 2006 with a message that touched on the war, the economy and corruption. 'They are seeing that, because of tax cuts and because of the immense cost of the war, they aren't getting what they need locally.'"

And that's why — whether he faces Barack Obama, Hillary Clinton or a ham sandwich in the fall — John McCain is in trouble.

With his quiet snarling embrace of national security and our war footing, and not much else, McCain may be the one-trick pony of the presidential campaign, a one-issue candidate outflanked by the opposition's attention to that issue *and* the issue of the domestic economy. His inability to view those two central American matters as a single motive force requiring attention, his paucity of corrective ideas may be the greatest single shortcoming he carries into the fall — a shortcoming of vision, something way more damaging than revisionist Bosnian history or gotcha screen grabs of a volatile former pastor.

Democratic attack dog James Carville hasn't said it yet this year — *as far as we know* — but his legendary Clintonian bromide is true again: It's The Economy, Stupid. This is what matters to America. And it may already be too late to matter to John McCain.

3/26/2008

THE MCCAIN SCRUTINY IV

DAVID BELLAVIA has borne the battle. A former Army staff sergeant who served in Iraq in the 1st Infantry Division, Bellavia was recommended for the Medal of Honor, nominated for the Distinguished Service Cross, and received the Silver Star, the Bronze Star with valor, and the Conspicuous Service Cross. His 2007 book "House to House" recounted his experience fighting for control of Fallujah. Bellavia is vice chairman of Vets for Freedom, a veterans' advocacy organization. By any reasonable measure, Bellavia has served his country honorably.

But Bellavia, a supporter of Sen. John McCain for president, has a blind spot about certain matters on race and ethnicity in America, a blind spot that reflects poorly on McCain's candidacy, and raises questions about the candidate's own ability to make meaningful distinctions in a country waging its own sectarian battles.

On Tuesday, Bellavia introduced McCain at a Vets for Freedom rally in Washington, D.C., offering the fulsome praise for a veteran one would expect from another veteran.

"Senator John McCain has spent a lifetime in service to our nation. His example of unwavering courage is a model for every American," Bellavia said, in an allusion to McCain's five-plus years as a prisoner of war in Vietnam. "Rest assured that men like Senator McCain will be the goal and the men that my two young boys will emulate and admire. You can have your Tiger Woods, we've got Senator McCain."

He didn't. Oh yes he did. Not a typo. In a campaign endorsement meant to be a pre-emptive shot at Sen. Barack Obama, the Illinois senator who may be McCain's challenger in the fall, Bellavia conflated Obama with Tiger Woods, the world's greatest golfer and a cultural phenomenon in his own right.

◊ ◊ ◊

The first most obvious question is why? What in the world would connect Tiger Woods to Barack Obama? The first most

189

obvious answer is unsettling. The one thing that connects them is a multiracial heritage. Obama, of course, is the son of a Kenyan father and a white mother from Kansas; Woods' ancestry is African American, Thai, American Indian and Chinese.

The fact that Bellavia said it was bad enough. The author Michael Eric Dyson, speaking on MSNBC's "Countdown With Keith Olbermann," said the comment "bespeaks a sense of racial insensitivity at best, and at worst a kind of deliberate attempt to distance himself from black people."

It also reflects an inability or unwillingness to make distinctions between people as people; the suggestion is that, to borrow the phrase we recognize, We All Look Alike.

What made it worse is that, when McCain stepped to the microphone, the candidate had nothing to say about this monumental gaffe— letting it pass unchallenged as if Bellavia's sentiments, Bellavia's blind spot, were his own.

◊ ◊ ◊

There's other evidence pointing to McCain's possible discomfort on race matters. On Tuesday, The Politico, quoting from interviews with black leaders in McCain's home state of Arizona, found a candidate apparently of two minds on relations with black residents.

"Interviews with black civic and business leaders in Arizona found no one who suggested that McCain holds racial animus," The Politico reported. "And McCain can point to some warm personal and political associations with blacks, some of whom cited his responsiveness to their concerns when they approached him on official business.

"But the widespread perception of activists in the state's traditional civil rights organizations and the African-American press is that McCain has consistently treated them with indifference."

"I don't recall him ever attending any function with the NAACP," said Oscar Tillman, head of the NAACP's Phoenix chapter. "Each year we send them an invitation [to an annual banquet], and each year they say no."

A bigger question is why McCain would make distinctions between one bloc of his state's black constituents and another — and what those distinctions might say about how McCain would govern this multiracial nation.

McCain has shown signs suggesting that he "gets it," even if supporters like Bellavia don't. He's reportedly set to make campaign stops in Alabama and the Watts district of Los Angeles later this month, the better to shore up his bona fides among black voters.

But as a senator who initially opposed efforts to make Martin Luther King's birthday a federal holiday; as a senator who opposed making King's birthday a state holiday four years later; as someone who missed many of the touchstone events of the civil rights movement, John McCain has work to do in this regard between now and November. The man who would be president has as many bridges to build as he has fences to mend.

4/10/2008

THAT WAS THE NEWS MODEL
THAT WAS

IT'S A RUMOR with the weight of a fact, whether it becomes one or not. The Wall Street Journal reported Thursday that Katie Couric, the $15 million-a-year anchor, managing editor and iconic face of CBS News, may be leaving the network as soon as next year — years ahead of her contract's current expiration in 2011. (The Journal story follows one that The Philadelphia Inquirer published in 2007, saying essentially the same thing.)

The network, of course, denies loudly, issuing not one but two statements downplaying rumors of Couric's possible departure. The Journal quoted a "CBS Evening News" spokeswoman saying "We are very proud of the 'CBS Evening News,' particularly our political coverage, and we have no plans for any changes regarding Katie or the broadcast."

If the talk of her departure is true, there could be a lot of reasons. From almost the start of Couric's tenure at the Tiffany Network in September 2006, reports surfaced of Couric clashing over content and style with Rick Kaplan, the legendary (and some have said legendarily difficult) veteran executive producer. Couric has been said to be coveting the longform possibilities of a gig with "60 Minutes." And then there's the other grating fact: Except for one brief period, the Journal reported, "Ms. Couric never bested the ratings of interim anchor [longtime CBS Washington correspondent] Bob Schieffer," brought on in the wake of the Dan Rathergate scandal. When the temp outshines the franchise player on the bottom line, that's trouble.

From the network's viewpoint, the reason for Couric to go would have to do with money. For CBS, a network under pressure to cut rising costs, paying an anchor $15 million a year is hardly feasible in today's economy.

But another real reason for Couric's possible exit may have to do with a historic, or at least historical, sense of timing: The half-hour dinnertime news format she has inherited — the legacy of Douglas Edwards, Dan Rather and, yes, even Walter Cronkite — isn't where most of America lives anymore.

◊ ◊ ◊

James Poniewozik, blogging at Time.com, understands. "Katie was brought in on the premise that she and her star power — plus a revamping of the newscast format—could bring in new viewers to the evening news ... She cannot. God cannot. It is a losing proposition. ... Couric's newscast has been an expensive final refutation of the desperate belief that it is possible to reverse the slow, inexorable decline of network news.

"Network newscasts are a holding effort. They are a rearguard action. They are prisoners of demography and cultural shifts that are as irreversible as the physical laws of the universe. Namely: fewer Americans have the time or inclination to watch a half-hour TV newscast at 6:30 in the evening ..."

This is partly, even mostly true. What's inarguably in decline is the *broadcast* version of network news.

Cable network news programs are very much in the ascendancy of both shaping and being shaped by people's evolving expectations of television. Jon Lafayette of TV Week reported last August that ad-supported cable television had twice the viewers of broadcast television in prime time — a doubling of viewer share for the second straight year.

Ironically, it's the historical failure of broadcast news execs to grasp the implication of that distinction that's contributed to their model's demise. If/when Katie Couric exits from CBS, she may well be the one to turn off the studio lights on a news format whose fifteen minutes of pertinence to American lives expired ten years ago.

That's true for two good reasons:

First, the very idea of what news is is evolving at breathtaking speed. The shopworn definition of news according to the broadcast network model — a 23-minute recap of everything you've heard in the white noise of the modern world all day long, plus commercials — is dead as a rabbit-ears antenna.

That approach has been shattered by the velocities of modern life; the impact of popular culture; the crazyquilt of irregular work schedules, home-based businesses and graveyard shifts; the advance of the Internet; and a democratization of information so prevalent, so much the air we breathe that we take it for granted. Your news isn't my news isn't her news, and there's no turning back from that.

Second, that cultural time shift, that democratization of news and its increasingly viral and populist component, makes a longer time frame necessary. People want their news when they want it, and they want it the way they live their lives: around the clock. That demand for 24/7 information immediacy is something broadcast networks (beholden to affiliates wedded to local programming and syndicated shows) can't possibly provide.

Was it a coincidence? Weeks before the rumors of Couric leaving CBS arose, there were reports of CBS and CNN refloating an idea to create a newsgathering joint venture of sorts. The idea first emerged around 1998, and was thoroughly detailed in a cover story for the dear, departed Brill's Content magazine. The most recent plan called for CBS news stories filed from its Baghdad bureau to be included on CNN cable feeds.

The rationale? The move would have saved CBS about $7 million a year, according to the network, and would have at least peripherally extended the CBS news brand and personalities into the lucrative realm of cable.

The negotiations fell through, but that kind of tie-up may be the only reed for broadcast news left to grasp in the future. NBC, of course, is well-positioned, with partners throughout the cablescape (MSNBC, CNBC and Bravo, to name a few) that make the NBC broadcast model an example to follow. CBS and partner in misery ABC don't have such inroads into cable; theirs are the network news models that Poniewozik (and anyone with anything worthwhile to do at 6:30 in the evening) knows are in the sunset of their days. If Couric leaves, CBS may be the first to hit that wall.

Or not. It doesn't have to be like that. It's been said before: Broadcast TV news' survival depends on thinking outside the box it's in. For all of NBC's vast broadcast and cable presence, for instance, the Peacock Network has made scant use of its Telemundo unit, acquired in 2002, or of mun2, launched in 2001 as the first national cable enterprise to offer bilingual programming in Spanish and English. Those acquisitions, the growing number of Latino households, and the rising impact of Latino culture in the United States present a screaming opportunity to rewrite the playbook of broadcast news: Why not consider the culturally daring but financially lucrative move of a bilingual, one-hour prime-time news broadcast?

Couric apparently knows or senses something in the wind; there's talk that she may be positioning herself to replace Larry King, the long-of-tooth talk-show host whose CNN contract expires in 2009.

That need for change is something CBS brass hasn't internalized — yet. For the half-hour evening news, this isn't handwriting on the wall, it's a block-long billboard that the network suits can't ignore. A fickle, restless viewership and the dictates of economies of scale mean the only hope for yesterday's broadcast news model is to find out what time it is. And fast.

4/11/2008

'BITTER' PILL AND ANTIDOTE

WHEN is a controversy not a controversy? With the Pennsylvania primary hanging in the balance, the media's talkingest wags and the presidential campaigns of Hillary Clinton and John McCain have leaped on what was thought to be a fatal gaffe committed last week by Sen. Barack Obama.

But the lack of negative traction Obama's comments have gained for Clinton and McCain, and Obama's forthright defense of those comments, suggest that the expiration date for that kind of rabble-rousing by Obama's challengers for the presidency may have finally arrived.

Obama, speaking to campaign donors at an April 6 fundraiser in San Francisco, said the nation's smaller municipalities, heir to dismal economic circumstances, were subject to bitterness manifested in religion, and in some of the tropes of national intolerance.

"You go into these small towns in Pennsylvania and, like a lot of small towns in the Midwest, the jobs have been gone now for 25 years and nothing's replaced them," he said. "And they fell through the Clinton administration, and the Bush administration, and each successive administration has said that somehow these communities are going to regenerate and they have not.

"It's not surprising then they get bitter, they cling to guns or religion or antipathy to people who aren't like them or anti-immigrant sentiment or antitrade sentiment as a way to explain their frustrations."

◊ ◊ ◊

Fans of events of the World Wrestling Federation must have reveled in the political tag-team attack that followed.

First Clinton jumped off the turnbuckle, calling his comments "elitist" and "out of touch" on Saturday, in a reflexive play to the rural vote that Clinton hopes to curry favor with in Pennsylvania on April 22.

"I think his comments were elitist and divisive," she said on Monday. "You don't have to think back too far to remember that good men running for president were viewed as being elitist and out of touch with the values and the lives of millions of Americans," she added, referring to Al Gore and John Kerry, the 2000 and 2004 Democratic nominees.

"I think it's very critical that the Democrats really focus in on this and make it clear that we are not (elitist). We are going to stand up and fight for all Americans," Clinton said.

Then McCain scuttled into the ring on Monday at the Associated Press Editors Annual Meeting in Washington: calling Obama's comments "elitist" and saying they were a "contradiction from what I believe America is all about."

"These are the people that produced a generation that made the world safe for democracy," he said. "These are the people that have fundamental cultural, spiritual, and other values that in my view have very little to do with their economic condition."

◊ ◊ ◊

It was not Obama's best choice of words; actually, coming from the most oratorically gifted American politician on the scene, it seems curiously offhand and tone-deaf to the sensibilities of the very people he needs to win between now and November. More important, the comments suggested an insensitivity to traditions and values that are, for better or worse, some of the nation's most deeply embraced.

"Are working people bitter? There's no doubt that many are extremely bitter over the economic hand they've been dealt," The New York Times Bob Herbert wrote today. " … But 'bitter' has a connotation that is generally not helpful in a political campaign. Bitter suggests powerlessness and a smallness of spirit. Most people would prefer to be characterized as 'angry' — a term that suggests empowerment — rather than 'bitter,' with its undertone of defeat."

Hoping to capitalize, Clinton went so far as to including on her campaign music playlist the John Mellencamp song

"Small Town" at at least one campaign rally. Once again, the naysayers envisioned Obama circling the drain.

But what happened next — what's happened since — has been one of the latest surprises in a campaign full of them.

Obama proved he could stand in the fire, even a fire of his own making, and turn a negative into a possible positive. Simply put, he didn't back down from what he said days before. And by standing his ground, he may have done himself more good than harm.

At a CNN "Compassion Forum" on Sunday last night, Obama expanded on the April 6 comment.

"What I was saying is that when economic hardship hits in these communities, what people have is they've got family, they've got their faith, they've got the traditions that have been passed onto them from generation to generation. Those aren't bad things. That's what they have left. And, unfortunately, what people have become bitter about -- and oftentimes have told me about, as I traveled through not just Pennsylvania, but I was referring to states all across the Midwest, including my home state -- is any confidence that the government is listening to them. They don't think that government is listening to them."

On Monday, at the AP meeting in Washington, Obama addressed again both his comments and the knee-jerk critiques to those comments.

"I may have made a mistake last week in the words that I chose," he said. "But the other party has made a much more damaging mistake in the failed policies they've chosen and the bankrupt philosophy they've embraced for the last three decades."

"If John McCain wants to turn this election into a contest about which party is out of touch with the struggles and hopes of working America, that's a debate I'm happy to have. I think it's a debate that we *have* to have ... I believe that the real insult to the millions of hard-working Americans out there would be a continuation of the economic agenda that's dominated Washington for far too long."

"If I had to carry the banner for eight years of George Bush's failures, I'd be looking for something else to talk about, too."

◊ ◊ ◊

Clinton's piling-on didn't go unnoticed. Arianna Huffington blogged at The Huffington Post: "By cynically twisting Obama's comments about small town voters in a way that confirms every right-wing demagogic caricature of her own Party, Hillary Clinton has adopted the frames, lies, stereotypes and destructive clichés long embraced by the likes of Lee Atwater and Karl Rove. She has clearly decided that the road to victory runs through scorched earth. The question is, if she succeeds, what kind of Party will she be left to lead?"

What should be more worrying to the Clinton campaign is that, as reported by The AP's Mark Scolforo on Monday, some Pennsylvanians found Obama's comments were no big damn deal.

The AP: "Truck salesman Bob Bildheiser, 49, said he is tentatively supporting Obama and that he agreed with the point that Obama was trying to make about the nation's economic problems.

"'The people are bitter about the economy, about jobs, about the gas prices. It's terrible,' he said. ...

"Dennis Yezulinas, [a] Clinton supporter in Shenandoah, said he is more offended by the rhetorical fight that followed Obama's comment than by the remark itself.

"'Not just for the good of the Democratic Party, but for the good of the country, they need to make it less contentious," said Yezulinas."

Mary Ellen Matunis, a Clinton backer from Shenandoah, said, "I was not offended. Poor choice of words, but I think it was just misspoken."

"People are bitter in small towns," said Thomas Frank, author of "What's The Matter With Kansas?," a book on the shifting political dynamic of middle America. "People are bitter everywhere," Frank told The Huffington Post's Sam Stein. "I don't know if you have seen the stock market — people are bitter about their situation. It doesn't strike me as a very controversial statement."

Michael E. Ross

In his HuffPost column on Saturday, Robert Creamer used a headline that made pretty plain the hypocrisies behind the latest spate of Obama bashing: "It Takes Real Chutzpah for a Guy Who Owns Eight Houses (McCain) to Call Barack Obama an 'Elitist.'"

And Hillary Clinton, whose gold-plated tax returns were released recently, is similarly vulnerable to being revisualized in a hurting blue-collar state, despite her best working-class guises. How can anyone who's half of a matrimonial/political corporation whose assets over seven years topped $109 million make any credible claims to being anything *but* an elitist?

◊ ◊ ◊

The Monday Gallup Daily Tracking Poll — an admittedly fluid thing based on daily snapshots of perception and which side of the bed you got up on — showed that, in the short term at least, the "bitter" pill didn't really need an antidote. Obama had maintained a 10-point lead over Clinton, a lead first established the week before.

The reasons why this hasn't exploded in Obama's face are anyone's guess. Maybe it's just campaign fatigue. Or Obama may have accidentally tapped into something that Pennsylvanians can relate to, deeply and personally: a willingness to stand one's ground. Rather than go into all-apologies mode after April 6, Obama stood up like a man who's *got* a pair, elaborating on what he'd said, sticking by it on principle. In doing so, he may have gained grudging respect, if nothing more, among the very people thought to be opposed to him on the basis of race alone.

(And maybe more respect than Hillary Clinton. Pennsylvania Gov. Ed Rendell's statement in February that "I think there are some whites who are probably not ready to vote for an African-American candidate" makes an inference that Clinton should be less than comfortable with: True enough, those Pennsylvanians unwilling to vote for Obama just because he's black may be predisposed to vote for Clinton just because she's white. On the basis of our historical and persisting patterns of bias, then, those same Pennsylvanians

200

would be just as likely to vote for McCain over Clinton because McCain's a white *man*.)

When is a controversy not a controversy? When something, anything happens in a presidential campaign so hard-wired to controversy itself that it's getting hard to make meaningful, enduring distinctions between one event and another.

When the ones who'd try to exploit it to their advantage get hoist higher on the same petard.

When the objects of that exploitation tell pollsters, reporters and neighbors at the corner bar: "The people are bitter. ... It's terrible."

4/15/2008

THE BURN RATE IN THREE PARTS

WITH the Democratic nomination for president all but a lock for Sen. Barack Obama, the obligatory early postmortems have started on what happened to the once-invincible campaign of Sen. Hillary Clinton.

It's a given that Clinton burned a lot of bridges to get here, "here" being either on the verge of the next phase in an increasingly quixotic pursuit of the Democratic nomination, or on the verge of ending that campaign altogether. She's been proving more recently that she's pretty good at spending money — the metric for the classic "burn rate" of the Internet economy.

But regardless of whatever salvation scenarios Team Clinton gins up between now and month's end, Hillary Clinton is where she is now (dependent on others to make or break her success, largely helpless to her own fate) for another reason. She's also proven to be adept at burning some of the very people she needed at more critical junctures of her failing campaign.

◊ ◊ ◊

Look at the bridges she's torched: Her recent adoptions of Republican rhetoric about the war and dealing with Iran, and her acceptance of the endorsement of conservative publisher Richard Mellon Scaife showed her taking her talent for triangulation to a new height. Clinton crossed into Republican territory with such ease and comfort that it's prompted several in the blogosphere to call for Hillary to own up to *being* a Republican, to make her conversion to the GOP official. (She did, after all, start her political life as a Goldwater Girl.)

This expedient abandonment of Democratic party principles and strategies reflected her desire to use a scorched-earth approach to campaigning, victory the ends achieved by any means necessary — even at the expense of the policy and practices native to the party she hoped to lead in the fall. Clinton is discovering the blowback of scorched-earth politics;

202

now, with party diehards rallying around Obama, the only earth left to scorch is the earth beneath her feet.

◊ ◊ ◊

The burn rate of campaign money — already a problem for a campaign that relied on top-of-the-pyramid, big-money donors in a national economy teetering on recession, a campaign that came late to aggressive use of the Internet as a platform for community and fundraising — only got worse in recent months. Clinton lent her campaign $5 million of her own money in March; it was revealed Wednesday that the candidate lent her presidential bid another $6.42 million for expenses in April and May.

Setting aside the obligatory press-release defense — such loans Only Underscore the Dedication of This Candidate to the Campaign — the Clinton hand-to-mouth ATM approach points to a failure of the basic strategy of counting on large donors to form the basis for a national coalition branded as a bottom-up effort.

Obama got this right away. Establishing a grassroots approach to fundraising, Obama tapped into a wider base of donors, everyday people who could kick in $25 here and $50 there, the "twos and fews" approach that's led to a highly liquid, easily replenished source of campaign funds.

Clinton's donors — faced with the impact of the same sputtering economy as everyone else — pulled back on big donations over time, forcing Clinton to tap her own kitty more than once.

McClatchy Newspapers asked the question in a headline: "If Clinton can't run a campaign, can she run the White House?"

Besides giving the country a relatively poor showing of her abilities as a financial manager, Clinton's problems reflected positively on how Obama would manage the national economy. His campaign balance sheet — flush with cash and small-money donors who've made regular donations a part of their *monthly budgets* — is a stark comparison and contrast with her own.

Michael E. Ross

◊ ◊ ◊

But these issues might have been safely navigated if Clinton hadn't committed the big one, the bonfire of the verities, the cardinal sin of American politics: She didn't dance with the ones who brung her to the party.

In October 2007, a CNN poll found that Clinton had a 57 percent to 33 percent lead over Obama among black registered Democrats overall — no doubt a base of support she largely inherited from her hubby, former president Bill Clinton, whose backing by African Americans continued to soar in the years after he left office. That poll result was up from 53 percent for Clinton and 36 percent for Obama in a poll carried out in April of that year.

"The 'sistah' vote is paying off handsomely for Hillary Clinton," Democratic political strategist Donna Brazile told CNN. "It's not only getting her the women's vote. It's also getting her the black vote."

◊ ◊ ◊

What a difference seven months make. Either with statements she uttered herself or through innuendo she mutely accepted on her behalf, Hillary turned her back on any serious nurturing of the storied Clinton relationship with African American voters. The result was quite the contrary.

With Bill Clinton's comments equating Obama's probable primary victory in South Carolina with Jesse Jackson's years before; with his derision of the Obama presidential bid as "a fairy tale"; with Hillary's derision of Obama's campaign ("let's get real about our future"); with her use of a passive-aggressive ethnicity dogwhistle (Obama was not a Muslim, "as far as I know"); and with the campaign's relentless pursuit of character assassinations borne of Obama's historical relationship with the Rev. Jeremiah Wright, black support of the Clinton campaign went south week by week, month by month, primary by primary.

By Tuesday, the results in the North Carolina primary found black voters in the state going for Obama by more than 90 percent. Clinton garnered just 6 percent of the state's black vote. Nationally, her core of black support isn't much better.

"Clinton failed to stand for African-American Democrats when the chance presented itself late last fall and into early January, even if doing so meant firing key staffers or dressing down her own husband," writes Thomas F. Schaller in Salon, in a piece published May 5 (before the Indiana and North Carolina votes).

"Doing that might have denied Barack Obama the near-universal claim to their support he now enjoys, and the black-white coalition he built from it. For Hillary Clinton, the price of that failure may turn out to be nothing less than the nomination itself."

Hillary Clinton's campaign is making history, all right: There hasn't been a faster dissipation of constituent good will in the history of American politics.

◊ ◊ ◊

It goes beyond race. Clinton disaffected many other activist supporters, such as the 3.2 million people affiliated with the liberal advocacy organization MoveOn.org.

Clinton spoke at a donors' fundraiser, which occurred sometime after Super Tuesday. On an audiotape from the event, excerpts of which were on The Huffington Post on April 18, Clinton blamed what she described as the "activist base" of the Democratic Party – with MoveOn.org singled out for special attention — for many of her Super Tuesday losses, claiming that those activists "flooded" state caucuses and "intimidated" her supporters.

At the fundraiser, Clinton said: "MoveOn.org endorsed [Obama] — which is like a gusher of money that never seems to slow down. We have been less successful in caucuses because it brings out the activist base of the Democratic Party. MoveOn didn't even want us to go into Afghanistan. I mean, that's what we're dealing with. And you know they turn out in great numbers. And they are very driven by their view of our positions, and it's primarily national security and foreign policy that drives them. I don't agree with them. They know I don't agree with them. So they flood into these caucuses and dominate them and really intimidate people who actually show up to support me."

Never mind that some parts of what she said weren't true (Eli Pariser, MoveOn's executive director, said the organization never opposed the war in Afghanistan). Clinton's remarks followed comments she made in April 2007, at the closing remarks during MoveOn.org Political Action's Virtual Town Hall meeting on Iraq, with highly favorable comments at odds with what she said after Super Tuesday.

This audiotape calls into question the fidelity Clinton has to the principles of the Democratic Party she wants to lead — and clearly indicates a willingness to diss the very people she needed to win.

◊ ◊ ◊

Those two keystones of the 21st-century Democratic Party — a longstanding foundation of black voters and a still-solidifying base of young, educated, upwardly mobile activists — would have made the difference between winning and losing this primary season. As a bad Super Tuesday in February gave way to a stunningly bad first Tuesday in May, Clinton was hemorrhaging the support of the people she consistently needed in the primaries, and would have needed in the fall.

In her bid for the presidency, Hillary Clinton has made fair use of a wide variety of political talents for the 2008 race. But besides the names of pollsters and analysts, advisers and specialists she'll no doubt keep on file in her BlackBerry, she'd be well advised to add others to the payroll for her campaign in 2012:

Having burned her people, her principles and her pocketbook this time, a good firefighter or two would come in handy.

5/8/2008

CAMPAIGN FOR AN UNDIGNIFIED CLIMBDOWN

"SHE'S had more incarnations than the Dalai Lama, and she's not as well-liked," said William Curry, former advisor to Bill Clinton, about Sen. Hillary Clinton, whose picture could be included in the next edition of the Webster's Dictionary in two places — next to the words "hubris" and "tenacity."

On Tuesday night, with the returns in from Indiana and North Carolina — Clinton's latest line-in-the-sand, game-changing, tide-turning, watershed Democratic primaries — many in the media ordered the horseshoe man-sized wreaths for her campaign, a presidential bid that is mathematically all but over.

Clinton's relentless competitive drive kicked in on Thursday, with the candidate vowing to press the fight to the end of May, seeking a resolution on the delegates from renegade states Florida and Michigan from the Democratic rules committee ... acting for all the world as if nothing had happened the night before ... oblivious to the world around her, a little like Norma Desmond at the end of "Sunset Boulevard," a nonentity descending a staircase, ready for her closeup, eyes focused on a camera, on a grandeur, only she can see.

◊ ◊ ◊

Clinton's pledge to continue the fight for the nomination over Sen. Barack Obama reflects the tenacity we've come to expect from the senator. But there's a point at which Clinton needs to weigh continuing to fight for a nomination that will never be the gift outright against what it would mean — what it would be worth — if she were to wrest the nomination from Obama, its likely heir.

Clinton's all-consuming hubris is such that now, victory is the only meaningful metric the Clinton campaign will entertain. Delegate count, states won, popular vote, donations raised, field advantage — all that stuff fades into insignificance.

Now the new Clinton measuring stick is electability, which is just as gauzy and imprecise as it sounds.

Clinton might well have looked at an NBC News poll conducted after Tuesday's vote. It found that 50 percent of the Republicans who voted in Tuesday's primaries said Obama would beat Sen. John McCain in the fall, compared to 37 percent who favored Clinton to beat McCain in November. So much for her electability advantage.

◊ ◊ ◊

Speaking Thursday in Shepherdstown, W. Va., Clinton pointed to her razor-thin win in Indiana as proof that she can deliver where Obama could not: garnering the older white voters that have eluded him, by comparison to Clinton, in his drive to the nomination. But even that proof may have been faulty.

Clinton won in Indiana, defeating Obama by about 18,400 votes. But some aspects of that victory have to be seen in grimmer, more ambiguous light, thanks to talk-radio Doberman and former pharmaceutical recreation enthusiast Rush Limbaugh.

Weeks ago, Limbaugh floated the idea that Republicans in primary states should register as Democrats (holding their noses if necessary) and vote for Clinton over Obama, the reasoning being that Clinton would be an easier candidate for the GOP to defeat in the fall. True to form, Limbaugh took credit for Clinton's win in Indiana, claiming his "Operation Chaos" with Republicans masquerading as Democrats gave her just enough to defeat Obama.

There's no way to know if it's true, of course. But because it's possible, it has to call into question the purity of the Clinton vote in Indiana. There's at least a chance that Clinton's marginal win in Indiana — and possibly other slim victories earlier in the campaign — were the result of mischief-making by Republicans who have no intention of voting for her in November.

Limbaugh's cheap strategem may do more to cement the reasoning for Clinton ending her campaign than Limbaugh's plan to keep it going.

◊ ◊ ◊

Clinton has now invested her hopes in winning West Virginia and Kentucky, two states that, on the basis of racial and ethnic demographics, would seem to be in her corner. Team Clinton is counting heavily on it.

But look at it another way. The good people of West Virginia and Kentucky, who can do math as well as anyone, may well decide that a vote based on little more than the candidate's sheer obstinacy — a vote that can't gain her the nomination even if she won every delegate at stake in both states — is the wrong symbolic signal to send.

With the economies of both states hit by the same economic headwinds as other states, and with the condition of the national economy looming as a central theme of the fall campaign, they may decide that a vote for the candidate reflecting the proven and evolving will of the Democratic party makes more sense than a vote for a candidate who can't deliver without winning, a candidate who can't win without tearing the party apart.

Maybe Clinton unintentionally betrayed the same feeling on Thursday, at the rally in Shepherdstown.

The New York Times reported that "[a]t one point in her 19-minute remarks, Mrs. Clinton promised that the United States would have universal health care 'if I'm president,' a deviation from her customary 'when I'm president.' "

Was it just accidental use of the wrong conditional conjunction? Maybe. But maybe not. And that's the issue for the people of West Virginia and Kentucky. No matter how dedicated voters might be to a candidate, it's hard to walk into a polling place and cast a vote for what you *know going in the door* will be the losing side, no matter what the vote totals are.

It's hard to be a true believer in a candidate when, deep down, the candidate talks like she's not a true believer herself.

When the candidate's opponent has 91.4 percent of the delegates needed to finish the game.

That's Hillary Clinton's dilemma: taking the risk of an undignified climbdown from a lofty unprecedented height while looking for a way out with honor intact, trying to put the brakes on a campaign bus that no longer needs brakes, a vehicle that's noisily skidding to a stop, the wheels having come off a long time ago.

5/9/2008

CASUALTY OF WAR

IF Hillary Clinton's pending defeat for the Democratic presidential nomination really does signal the end of the Clinton era of Democratic politics (or at least this iteration of it; 2012's not that far off), the twilight of that era may parallel the end of the Bush era of presidential politics. This phase of the Clinton saga dovetails with that of the Bushes most notably in the one thing they have in common: the war in Iraq.

For President Bush, the war's evangelist-in-chief, emotional sparkplug and public face, the direct damage is obvious. The war that has cost us more than four thousand lives, and which will exact social and economic damage we can't fathom yet will forever be laid at the feet of the 43rd president, and no one else. All the revisionist spin in the world won't change that.

For Clinton, pursuing among the last of her campaign's contests in Kentucky and Oregon, the wounds may be as serious in another way. As one who supported the war from its inception, and who has consistently avoided the issue of whether she'd vote the same way now, Clinton began her campaign with a liability built in from the beginning. Her support of a dangerous and ruinous war, and her stubborn resistance to discuss how six years of hindsight might have an effect on her judgment today, compromised her standing with a public that's already expressed its opposition to that elective conflict — in the voting booth in 2006.

◇ ◇ ◇

The fact that she misread or ignored that clear signal to Republicans, coupled with the hubris of her virtual self-coronation when she announced her candidacy, cemented in the minds of voters a disingenuousness, a tone-deafness to the national mood that ultimately couldn't be ignored.

Clinton's gradual backtracking from absolute support for the war, which we've seen on the campaign trail, was an early and frequent indicator of the half-truths and duplicities that followed.

Finally, with some recent rhetorical body blows to Barack Obama, the likely Democratic nominee, Clinton allied herself with John McCain — the Republican nominee — on matters of experience and national security, at Obama's expense.

The result? While it may have scored some cheap points in the primaries, Clinton's dance with the enemy underscores for voters nationally the long-held suspicion that her support for the Iraq war is only part of a wider Clinton triangulation agenda: presiding over a union of Democratic initiatives and Republican rhetoric. For voters with memories longer than the Rev. Jeremiah Wright, voters who oppose that rhetoric and its tragic consequences, the question has become a simple one: *If I oppose the war, and she supports the war —how can I support* her?

Lately, the primary exit polls haven't much focused on the wars in Iraq and Afghanistan as a front-and-center issue for how voters voted. Maybe the wars we're fighting are so much a subtext of the national white noise, we've stopped isolating them as a line item in the attention span. But for many primary voters, Hillary Clinton is a wanton casualty of war. Among all the things that have hobbled her historic but tragically flawed presidential campaign, her support for the war in Iraq cost her early and, for those untold unpolled voters, too often.

5/19/2008

WATERLOO, S.D.

THERE'S no reverse gear for a car heading off a cliff. The panoramically flawed, irreversibly doomed presidential campaign of Hillary Rodham Clinton learned this lesson — maybe its last — in the wildfire of reactions to her comments in South Dakota, a twisted speculative conflation of the chance of assassination and the rationale to continue a failed bid for the presidency.

Those comments, said Friday at a newspaper editorial meeting in Sioux Falls, S.D., and weakly explained later in the day at a supermarket in Brandon, S.D., said it all. Her Friday statements were really the fourth time Clinton either directly or obliquely referenced the June 1968 assassination of Robert F. Kennedy, en route to an expression of the potential for surprise as a reason for staying in a race she cannot win.

But this time was too over the top, too visible to ignore. In a streaming-live moment, Clinton invoked race and the specter of political violence in the service of a campaign whose appetite for self-destruction seems almost pathological. It's an Internet-time meltdown: Her comments distill in a moment what's been obvious in slow motion for months: we're witnessing not just a political campaign but a political career in free fall. We're watching a decline almost Nixonian in its arc.

"This does great damage to her persona and her biography," said Douglas Brinkley, presidential historian and professor at Rice University, on MSNBC's "Countdown." Brinkley clearly understood the cultural repercussions: "Leno and Letterman types can't even make a joke about the latest comment because it's just so dark ... it's almost become now a pathology we're dealing with. The humor of her not quitting is starting to not even be funny anymore."

In every political campaign, there's some distilling moment that puts everything in that campaign to that point in a clear and unmistakable perspective.

This was her watershed. Her Waterloo.

◊ ◊ ◊

Now Team Clinton faces the prospect of having to make their electoral-map case with little leverage at all; most of her positions are now politically untenable. Whatever leverage she may have had for gaining the vice-presidential spot on the Obama ticket has evaporated *tout court*. And whatever sway she may have possessed with the already dwindling number of superdelegates is gone too. In fact, according to a Friday story by independent journalist Al Giordano, on his Web site, The Field, a group of superdelegates — including some pledged Clinton delegates — is about to announce support for Obama.

There are few options left for Team Clinton. The opportunity for a dignified climbdown is pretty much off the table. She's seen to that. Damage control is more the order of the day than it had been already.

5/24/2008

THE IMAGINARY ADVANTAGE

IF the torrent of commentary in the blogosphere since recent comments by Hillary Clinton on Friday is any indication, Clinton is losing her grip on women voters — the one American cohort at the heart of her claim on the Democratic nomination. Her purported advantage with this crucial bloc of voters may have been illusory all along.

Women voters commenting in vast numbers on any number of news Web sites and campaign-fan Weblogs, are expressing feelings of being embarrassed by Clinton's abortive campaign, some to the point of outright anger that the first serious female contender for the presidency would persist in such a poor campaign, and persist in chasing a claim of electability that would overthrow the principles of the party she hopes to lead. These women voters are definitely in favor of a woman in the White House, just not Hillary Clinton. Not this time.

◊ ◊ ◊

Reactions to her Friday comments are deeply passionate: "I can't believe she said it. Forget that Ted Kennedy was just diagnosed with a brain tumor, but what about all of us over 50 something women, her base?, who lived through the shooting of Robert Kennedy. Doesn't she realize that there already is a twinge when we watch any large rally of supporters remembering back to what happened. I think the Clintons are desperate. We all know they have their own reality that doesn't necessarily go with the truth, but this was beyond insensitive and I think totally deliberate." [Joan Young, posting on the NYTimes Web site.]

"Hillary has finally done exactly what she had so desperately hoped Obama would do. She has made a definitive gaffe that can't be overcome. It can't be explained away or marginalized by self-proclaimed presidential attributes. Her words are now memorialized like the giant 'Mission Accomplished' banner, the final blow she personally delivered to her own campaign." [L Jeanne at NYTimes]

215

And other women responded to Clinton's campaign more generally. One writer blogging at The Huffington Post on Friday as (go figure) ObamaEdwards expressed feelings that have to send chills down the brain trust at the Clinton campaign. She is surely not alone:

"Once and for all: I am a feminist. A REAL feminist. That means: I don't applaud all women simply because they have female parts. I look at the individual's track record and character. I looked at Clinton a long time ago, and concluded that she is not a good leader, or a very good person. I waited. I hoped. And along came Obama, who has the character and good will and good nature and leadership ability I sought in a candidate. I will back him, and only him, all the way to the White House.

"To HELL with party solidarity. And to HELL with the sisterhood. We will make progress in all social areas when we have a good candidate, like Obama, to help us get there.

"Can we now stop making excuses for a woman who is a terrible role model? Please?"

◊ ◊ ◊

Rather than be swayed by Clinton's *sub rosa* argument that the Obama campaign is no friend to modern women voters, those voters and others may well be looking at how women are, in fact, greatly shaping the tone and focus of Team Obama's strategy as campaign directors and advisers.

First, there's the role of Michelle Obama. "As a lawyer and hospital executive, she provides evidence that Obama respects strong women even as he's campaigning against one," reported Nedra Pickler of The Associated Press.

Pickler's story also lists several women at or near the helm of the Obama campaign, including Valerie Jarrett, a senior adviser who has known the Obamas since before they married; finance chairwoman Penny Pritzker; finance director Julianna Smoot; policy director Heather Higginbottom; scheduling director Alyssa Mastromonaco, and foreign policy aide Susan

Rice, a former United States Assistant Secretary of State for African Affairs.

We can't know if Clinton's purported gender advantage is real or only assumed in the context of a general election. But recent polling suggests that Obama's not far behind among women voters. In a Gallup daily tracking poll published May 20, Obama trailed Clinton among women voters 18 to 49 years old by four percentage points, and trailed Clinton among women 50 and older by only three. These and other important constituencies are moving toward Obama, Gallup reported — days before Clinton's statements over Memorial Day weekend dropped.

Clinton's playing of the gender card may result in some short-term gains on her behalf. But what's clear is that women voters are no more monolithic in their preferences than black or Hispanic voters, and for many of the same reasons.

Rather than thinking and voting in the lockstep context of the herd, as Clinton seems to assume they will, women voters are using their own campaign math this primary season. They're thinking for themselves — a basic component of both civic responsibility and modern feminism. That may not be good news for Hillary Clinton.

5/27/2008

YES HE DID

THAT TREMOR you felt this evening at 6:01 p.m. PDT (9:01 p.m. EDT) was the sound of history arriving, the sound of our comfortable national realities, our long-held national expectations being irrevocably transformed.

Buoyed by millions of African American voters, and a broad cross-section of Americans across the racial and socioeconomic spectrum, Barack Obama, the biracial son of Africa and Europe, is now the presumptive Democratic nominee for the presidency of the United States of America. The iPod wins.

" ... [B]ecause of what you said; because you decided that change must come to Washington; because you believed that this year must be different than all the rest; because you chose to listen not to your doubts or your fears but to your greatest hopes and highest aspirations, tonight we mark the end of one historic journey with the beginning of another — a journey that will bring a new and better day to America," Obama said in Minneapolis-St. Paul, Minn., before a crowd of 17,000 (with another 15,000 reportedly waiting outside).

"Tonight, I can stand before you and say that I will be the Democratic nominee for President of the United States."

◊ ◊ ◊

It wasn't all movie moment. Hillary Clinton saw to that. In a campaign rally at Baruch College in Manhattan, Clinton performed a not-quite-dignified climbdown, in a curious valedictory that wasn't a concession speech despite the numerical evidence, that Obama was well over the 2,118 delegates he needed to win. Clinton congratulated Obama and his campaign "on the extraordinary race they have run." But she congratulated him in the context of the race going on rather than ending, offering a recap of the reasons (popular vote totals) why she should *still* be the nominee.

"In the coming days, I'll be consulting with supporters and party leaders to determine how to move forward with the best interests of our party and our country guiding my way," she said.

Republican strategist Alex Castellanos, on CNN, got the drift: "She did everything but offer Barack Obama the vice presidency."

It was obstinacy personified. The attitude even extended to the music on the Team Clinton campaign jukebox; her rally ended with Tina Turner's "Simply the Best" and, in an act of curious straight-up defiance, Tom Petty's "I Won't Back Down."

◊ ◊ ◊

Later, Obama extended an olive branch. "Senator Hillary Clinton has made history in this campaign not just because she's a woman who has done what no woman has done before, but because she's a leader who inspires millions of Americans with her strength, her courage, and her commitment to the causes that brought us here tonight."

Then Obama renewed his shift in attention to the general election. With both words and actions, he threw a jab at Republican challenger John McCain, the newly-minted nominee taking dead aim at McCain's relationship with the Bush administration — and the war that administration will be defined by.

"Change is a foreign policy that doesn't begin and end with a war that should've never been authorized and never been waged," Obama said at the Xcel Center in Minneapolis-St. Paul — the same Xcel Center where McCain will make his acceptance speech in September. "I won't stand here and pretend that there are many good options left in Iraq, but what's not an option is leaving our troops in that country for the next hundred years ..."

◊ ◊ ◊

"America, this is our moment. This is our time," Obama said tonight, reaching again for the Kennedyesque high ground, restating a theme (if not a phrase) he's used before, but better

Michael E. Ross

this time. Bigger. "Let us begin to work together. Let us unite in common effort to chart a new course for America."

Chris Matthews, co-directing the coverage for MSNBC, got outside his domestic political comfort zone and grasped the wider dimension of what was happening — that nothing less took place tonight than a change in the baseline of American possibility, a change with global resonance.

"Everywhere in the world in a few hours, in Europe and Africa, in Cape Town and Nairobi ... in Bangladesh and Asia, this is a huge story," Matthews said at the moment MSNBC called the South Dakota delegate count for Obama. "[I]n a world dominated by European powers — *forever*, it seems — this is the first time a major political power anywhere in that world has nominated ... a person of color. This is a unique, perhaps trend-setting change in our planet."

And if the population of the world could vote here, maybe they'd have echoed Thewrldneedsobama, posting at The Huffington Post:

"I'm so happy for America right now, you guys did it!!!! Thank you for give us Obama. I'm in tears ... And I'm in Mexico."

◊ ◊ ◊

Wednesday starts another kind of day one. Obama can be expected to fully make the change into general-election mode. First, there's unfinished business within the party. "At 11:06 p.m. EST, shortly after he left the rostrum in Minneapolis, Obama left Clinton a message congratulating her on winning South Dakota and asking her to call him back. At 12:16 a.m. she did, and offered to "sit down when it makes sense for you,'" Time.com reported.

Then there's Obama's plans to address what many in the punditburo see as his most glaring political weakness: connecting with the rural, blue-collar white voters who were largely absent for him in the primary season. Seth Colter Walls, reporting in The Huffington Post, reports that Obama plans to head Thursday to Virginia, "right smack in the heart of Appalachia, where he is often thought to be toast because of

220

his outsized losses to Senator Clinton in some of the region's primaries." James Webb is the state's Democratic senator.

For Barack Obama, an outsized improbable American dream has taken a huge step toward reality. "Politically, this is like landing on the moon," said MSNBC's Keith Olbermann when Obama passed the magic number. What's left may be the political equivalent of a mission to Mars, the landing exactly five months from Wednesday.

Ignition. Team Obama has cleared the tower.

6/5/2008

221

THE MCCAIN SCRUTINY VIII

WITH THE Democratic bloodbath suddenly, mercifully over, it's been expected that the presidential campaign of Sen. John McCain would have solidified its position, with McCain (the presumptive Republican nominee for almost four months) able to capitalize on the Democrats' endless barroom brawl by clearly defining himself, fortifying his strengths and shoring his campaign up in the broken places.

The luxury of time is wasted on some people, and John McCain has been one of them. In the weeks and months since his presumptive status, Team McCain has been plagued by internal missteps that are basic to the candidate and his organization. From problematic connections with the lobbyists larding his campaign to inconsistencies on positions about earmarks and the role of Hamas in the Middle East, from questions about character and temperament to continuing problems with characterizing facts about the Iraq war, the Iraqi people and national security (presumably his strong suit), the Arizona senator has shown an inconsistency and imprecision of message that's been breathtaking.

A statement made by McCain on Wednesday — that a timetable for returning American troops home from Iraq was "not too important" — has aroused doubts about his campaign's foundational claim that he represents a militarily strong America ... indeed, aroused doubts about whether McCain has the military capacity to be commander-in-chief.

Interviewed on the NBC "Today" show by Matt Lauer, and questioned about whether the purported success of the troop escalation known as the "surge" accelerated the value of a timetable for troop rotation from Iraq, McCain said, "that's not too important. What's important is the casualties in Iraq. Americans are in South Korea, Americans are in Japan, American troops are in Germany. That's all fine."

Besides the obvious insensitivity of the "not too important" statement, which Brandon Friedman of VoteVets.org, a veterans' service and advocacy organization, called "a morale crusher" for the troops in Iraq, it contradicted what McCain had said on May 15, at a speech in Columbus, Ohio:

"By January 2013, America has welcomed home most of the servicemen and women who has sacrificed terribly so that America might be secure in their freedom ... the Iraq war has been won."

"The job of the commander in chief is to understand the fundamentals of the conflict in which you have the troops engaged. And it is becoming crystal clear that John McCain doesn't understand it," said Sen. John Kerry, to The Huffington Post's Sam Stein. "This is an enormous flaw on his candidacy, which is supposedly hung on his ability to serve as commander in chief... There are series of contradictions in his statements that reflect a fundamental misunderstand[ing] of the conflict."

◊ ◊ ◊

The "Today" show debacle was only the latest disconnect between McCain's historical narrative and support for legislation that resonates with that personal narrative. McCain has consistently opposed passage of a new GI Bill that would increase educational and other benefits to Iraq war veterans — despite his long standing as a veteran and a presumed champion of the military.

The flip-flops are being noticed by others in the military — people prepared to call the senator on his shortcomings (maybe "call the emperor on his clothes" is a better analogy).

"I know he's trying to get traction by seeking to play to what he thinks is his strong suit of national security," Gen. Wesley Clark, former NATO commander, said of McCain in a June 11 interview with Seth Colter Walls of The Huffington Post. "The truth is that, in national security terms, he's largely untested and untried. He's never been responsible for policy formulation. He's never had leadership in a crisis, or in anything larger than his own element on an aircraft carrier or [in managing] his own congressional staff. It's not clear that this is going to be the strong suit that he thinks it is."

"McCain's weakness is that he's always been for the use of force, force and more force. In my experience, the only time to use force is as a last resort. ...

"When he talks about throwing Russia out of the G8 and makes ditties about bombing Iran, he betrays a disrespect for the office of the presidency."

Clark, whose name has infrequently surfaced as a possible contender for the vice presidential spot on an Obama ticket, said McCain "has pretty much bought the central thrust of the Bush administration's foreign policies: relying on threat and bluster [and] isolating people we don't agree with instead of engaging them."

That McCain association with the Bush White House is especially problematic now, in the wake of the latest bipartisan report on prewar Iraq intelligence released June 5 by Sen. Jay Rockefeller, chairman of the Senate Select Committee on Intelligence.

"Before taking the country to war, this Administration owed it to the American people to give them a 100 percent accurate picture of the threat we faced. Unfortunately, our Committee has concluded that the Administration made significant claims that were not supported by the intelligence," Rockefeller said in the report.

"In making the case for war, the Administration repeatedly presented intelligence as fact when in reality it was unsubstantiated, contradicted, or even non-existent," he said. "As a result, the American people were led to believe that the threat from Iraq was much greater than actually existed."

That McCain association with the Bush White House is especially troublesome, too, in the wake of a BBC News investigation that estimated that $23 billion in U.S. military equipment and materiel in Iraq is unaccounted for. "It may well turn out to be the largest war profiteering in history," said Rep. Henry Waxman, chairman of the House Committee on Oversight and Government Reform.

◊ ◊ ◊

The McCain campaign is facing a challenger that may be insurmountable: the McCain campaign.

Its problem is less political than it is existential, not so much what it says as what it is: a political campaign at odds with itself.

A Republican strategist thought he had the right prescription. The strategist told The Huffington Post's Thomas B. Edsall recently that "McCain has not claimed the maverick ground that should be his. He has not seized the mantle of 'change' and reform that he could own by going to Washington and saying, 'you know me. You know I've been a reformer all my life. Now, here's how I am going to change Washington if you elect me president.'"

But a strategy like that would be a hopeless enterprise even if Barack Obama hadn't previously and legitimately grabbed the brass-ring identity of change agent. A captive of his own political history, willingly tied to the mast of the ruinous Iraq war, and employing a campaign staff thick with K Street lobbyist insiders, McCain can't hope to lay claim to the mantle of Reformer. He's been inside the system for too long to be taken seriously as an outsider.

Launched with purpose and ambition and flags flying, the campaign of John McCain is in a dead calm, going nowhere, a ship with a compass whose philosophical magnetic north apparently doesn't exist, a ship that can't get any distance from the new wreck of the Hesperus that is the Bush administration.

There are no rescue boats on the horizon right now.

6/12/2008

TIM RUSSERT:
THE RIGHT KIND OF GOTCHA

SUNDAY mornings will never be the same again. Tim Russert, tireless fan of the Buffalo Bills, lawyer, journalist, author, moderator and prime mover of NBC's "Meet the Press," and the longest-serving host of the longest-running program in television history, died today — Friday the 13th — of a heart attack in Washington. He was a heartbreakingly young 58 years old.

About an hour before he was stricken, he was conducting a question-&-answer session with editors at MSNBC.com. TMZ reports that paramedics were summoned to the NBC Washington Bureau offices at 1:41 p.m. EDT. Russert was taken to at Sibley Memorial Hospital and pronounced dead at 4:15 p.m.

Russert's doctor, Michael Newman, told NBC News that cholesterol plaque ruptured in an artery, causing sudden coronary thrombosis.

Russert had been diagnosed with asymptomatic coronary artery disease, but it was being controlled with medication and exercise, and he had performed well on a stress test in late April, Newman told NBC. An autopsy showed that Russert also had an enlarged heart, Newman said.

◊ ◊ ◊

Without resorting to the bombastic insinuations of Bill O'Reilly or the prosecutorial pit-bull style of Chris Matthews, Timothy John Russert Jr. got closer to the heart of what makes American politics work, or fail to work, than any television political journalist of his generation, and quite possibly beyond his generation, and his medium.

In December 1991 he took over "Meet the Press," at that time a dry, vacuous, moribund Sunday-morning placeholder, and invested it with a drama and vigor that were a direct reflection of his passion for American politics and government.

His gift for political analysis was more than hobby or inclination; he learned his chops the hard way. Russert was special counsel to New York Sen. Daniel Patrick Moynihan for five years, and later an adviser to New York Gov. Mario Cuomo from 1983 to 1984. He later moved into the world of journalism, joining NBC in 1984.

"He was a real-life, old-school television journalist, but at the same time he was someone who really worked in the multichannel environment we have," said Robert J. Thompson, Trustee Professor of Television and Popular Culture at the S.I. Newhouse School of Public Communications at Syracuse University.

"He was America's host for election night," said Thompson in an interview from Syracuse, N.Y. "He was a major force for the civic life of this country."

The dry-erase board that Russert used repeatedly to explain the mathematical chaos after the 2000 presidential election was an icon of clarity — so much so that its first use by Russert on the air was named by TV Guide as one of the 100 most memorable moments in television history.

◊ ◊ ◊

In today's snapshot valedictories were reactions from the people who were his journalistic adversaries — the people in power or those who wanted to be in power. The one throughline? He was tough and fair.

"He was the standard-bearer for serious journalism," Sen. Barack Obama said. "There wasn't a better interviewer in television, not a more thoughtful analyst of our politics, and he was also one of the finest men I knew."

Sen. John McCain, Obama's rival for the presidency, called Russert "a great journalist and a great American. Tim Russert was at the top of his profession. He was a man of honesty and integrity. He was hard but he was always fair."

One aspect of Russert's fairness doctrine was, for those on the receiving end, probably a little terrifying. In his sixteen years on "Meet the Press," Russert evolved a deceptively effective interviewing style, a way of rebutting rebuttals that let a politician hoist himself or herself from the petard of their own words.

"The part that was really hard was that he would actually make you debate with yourself," said Madeline Albright, former U.S. secretary of state, to MSNBC's Keith Olbermann. "He would find some quote that you said many, many years before ... and you think, 'I couldn't possibly have said this' ... and he really made you walk through it and allow you the time to give an explanation ... It was a rare privilege to be on the show."

◊ ◊ ◊

The author and columnist Calvin Trillin once called the Sunday political programs collectively the "Sabbath gasbag" shows. But there was a difference. Under Russert, "Meet the Press" raised the bar on Sunday-morning political talk, effectively acting as a model, in tone and style of inquiry, for other Sunday talk shows that followed on cable TV.

Russert and "Meet the Press" made Sundays special. The civilized tone and breadth of discussion were the perfect way to begin the day. Whether what followed were hours of working in the yard or watching the day's customary sports programs, all too often "Meet the Press" was what got the heart started on Sundays.

GrouchoMarxist, in a comment at The Huffington Post:

Sunday morning:
1. Hangover
2. Coffee
3. Newspaper
4. Meet the Press
Won't be the same without you Tim.

◊ ◊ ◊

In an era embracing the rise of the "gotcha" aspect of journalism — those sudden and sometimes salacious disclosures that seem to be meant as much to embarrass as to enlighten — Russert tried to stand apart.

His was the right kind of gotcha: an attempt to show the ways politicians' positions were not always consistent, and to show it not with mud-slinging or sly opinionating, but simply by contrasting what a politician said back in the day (whenever "the day" was) and what a politician is saying now. He gladly left ridicule to others who were less talented, and frankly less principled. Russert took the high road.

Marysandra, in The Huffington Post:

As an Irish Catholic daughter of Buffalo, I think I always sort of "got" Tim Russert, we were brought up in a time and place that valued hard work, the Church, family loyalty, and respect and civility. You were never supposed to get "too big for your britches." South Buffalo was a place of fierce Democratic politics, humor, and the ability to tell a good story. Humility and Charity were your duty, after that loyalty to the Buffalo Bills was almost as important as loyalty to family ... He never really changed much from those roots, to my eyes, despite his remarkable career ...

◊ ◊ ◊

He was just hitting his stride. Russert was to be honored with a lifetime achievement award for service to journalism at the Newhouse School of Public Communication at Syracuse University on June 23.

On election night, any election night, Russert's eyes revealed a merry anticipation for what was to come. He displayed an animation, an intellect and a spirit that the indifferent lens of television couldn't help but love.

"The really sad thing about his passing now is that he was gearing up for what might have been his magnum opus," Thompson said in reference to what Russert undoubtedly planned for NBC's coverage of the presidential election night to come this November.

For sure, we're poorer already without Tim Russert's ability to distill the minutiae of presidential politics into something that everyday people can get their minds around.

Michael E. Ross

For sure, election night in November will have its usual hoopla and foolishness. But the election-night antics will ring hollow this year. As of today, there's a hugely empty chair at 4001 Nebraska Avenue NW, the address of the Washington bureau of NBC News.

As of today, there's a vacancy in the lives of a father, a wife, three sisters and a son.

As of today, there's a hole in the life of American journalism.

As of today, there's a cavernous absence of civility in the public discourse of America.

And there's no way to fill any of them.

6/13/2008

UNIFIED FIELD THEORY

UNION, N.J., wasn't quite right. Nor, apparently, were Harmony, R.I. or Accord, N.Y. But for the long-awaited Kum Ba Yah convention of Barack Obama and Hillary Clinton, Unity, New Hampshire (pop. 1,715, according to 2006 Census figures) was the proper setting — the right name on the right place for the former combatants for the Democratic presidential nomination to jointly appear Friday for the first time since Obama clinched that nomination.

There have been no news reports of any handholding and swaying among the 6,000 people attending the "Unite for Change" rally in that sunlit open field in Unity. In fact, some Clinton supporters have announced their intention to resist the building tide of good feeling, despite Clinton's outreach.

The immediate sense was that such sour grapes are best distilled and sweetened into table wine at the Democrats' new welcome table. But there may be something under that table. Something with teeth.

◊ ◊ ◊

It all sure sounded warm and fuzzy.

"To anyone who voted for me and is now considering not voting or voting for Senator (John) McCain, I strongly urge you to reconsider," said Clinton, calling on her supporters to hook up with Team Obama "to create an unstoppable force for change we can all believe in."

"We need them. We need them badly," Obama said of the two-for-one deal of Hillary and Bill Clinton. "Not just my campaign, but the American people need their service and their vision and their wisdom in the months and years to come because that's how we're going to bring about unity in the Democratic Party. And that's how we're going to bring about unity in America."

"We are one party; we are one America, and we are not going to rest until we take back our country and put it once again on the path to peace, prosperity and progress in the 21st century," Clinton said.

"For 16 months, Sen. Clinton and I have shared the stage as rivals for the nomination, but today I could not be happier and more honored and more moved that we're sharing this stage as allies to bring about the fundamental changes that this country so desperately needs," Obama said.

And in other, more substantial ways, the unity *was* real. They've apparently beaten their swords into donations: Both Clintons, Hillary and Bill, each made the maximum $2,300 donation to Obama's campaign Friday in an online transaction, aides said. The Obamas reciprocated with the same.

◊ ◊ ◊

All of which screams the question, the obvious one, about what one blogger called "Hillary's delegate condition": If all this goodwill, this unity is the real thing, why hasn't Hillary Clinton released her remaining delegates?

One blog, Clinton Democrats, reported that "In a conference call with delegates June 9, Hillary reiterated she has 'suspended' her campaign, which means she is holding on to her delegates. In addition, she said she is seeking 300 more delegates to take to the convention."

"Someone asked specifically if this meant Hillary would hold on to her delegates until the convention. [Clinton campaign manager Harold] Ickes said yes, so she can fight to make sure the platform includes issues central to her campaign, particularly universal health care. Ickes added that of course pledged delegates were free to work for Obama if they did not want to stay with Hillary until the convention in Denver."

But Hillary's gambit calls on Clinton delegates to willingly embark on an existential dilemma — pledged to one candidate while working actively for another. You have to assume that if they've decided to work for Obama, they realize the value of his policies, compared to John McCain. Since those same delegates can vote their consciences at the convention in August, and having already committed thousands of hours of effort for Team Obama, there's as much of a chance for Hillary Clinton to be embarrassed at the convention as Obama, and maybe more.

◊ ◊ ◊

What's left is to get the disgruntled Clinton supporters on the peace train bound for Denver. Some won't get on board no matter what.

"I will not vote for BO — it was a STOLEN election," posts Rita on Marc Ambinder's blog at TheAtlantic.com.

"Many of us Hillary Clinton supporters are now John McCain supporters. Hillary and Obama campaigning together will not sway us to vote for Obama," – says S.A., posting on the Los Angeles Times blog.

Others would disagree.

"There is a stark difference between the Democratic and Republican platforms. I advise S.A. to read both before making a choice. If she supported Senator Clinton because of her policies than the choice is obvious. If she supported Senator Clinton because she is a white woman, well that's another choice." – says P.C. Chapman, on the LATimes blog.

"I know many Hillary supporters who are behind Obama. Hey, I know it hurts, but the pain of losing the Supreme Court to the Conservative Right, the loss of a woman's right to choose, continuing to have our democracy morph into the fascist state that the Republicans have been creating, the pain of knowing that Mobil, Chevron and other oil companies have been awarded NO-BID contracts for Iraq's Oil, and that's why so many people had to die in Iraq... how can you possibly vote for McCain? ..." writes Barbara Brockelman, at LATimes.

◊ ◊ ◊

The idea — the theory, if you will — of Obama and Clinton achieving unity in New Hampshire is a fine one, like theories often are on paper. But the torrent of angry pro-Hillary posts and fledgling Web sites launched after Obama secured the nomination suggest that bringing that idea to reality is still an uphill thing. Clinton's backers still harbor grim suspicions.

In politics as in physics, a unified field theory attempts to bring fundamental forces together under a single framework. But the political version may be harder to achieve:

Gluons and photons don't write blog posts.

6/28/2008

MALEFACTION JACKSON

THERE'S no denying that Jesse Louis Jackson has been a soldier on the ramparts of the civil rights movement. His role in black American life since the assassination of Rev. Martin Luther King Jr. in 1968, his in-your-face method of speaking truth to power, helped to fill a vacuum of inspiration and leadership at a critical time. But in more recent years, Jackson's been a self-fulfilling parody, a loose cannon of half-baked strategies, slurs and personal missteps that have badly compromised his standing as a national leader.

That decline on the national stage got worse this week. By now you probably know the dirt: Jackson was preparing for an interview on "Fox & Friends" on Sunday, and sitting before a microphone he didn't know was live. Responding to a fellow guest's inquiry about speeches on personal responsibility that Obama has given recently at black churches, Jackson whispered what may be his real feelings about Sen. Barack Obama, the presumptive Democratic nominee — the man who realized what Jackson had failed to achieve in his two abortive runs for the presidency.

◊ ◊ ◊

The whispering Jackson appeared to barely suppress anger at Obama, in the wake of the senator's Father's Day speech in which Obama called for black fathers to more fully assume the responsibilities of fatherhood and reject the pernicious legacy of out-of-wedlock births, part of the panorama of nihilistic behavior that vexes black America today.

"We need fathers to realize that responsibility does not end at conception. We need them to realize that what makes you a man is not the ability to have a child - it's the courage to raise one." Obama said as a part of a wide-ranging speech that addressed many issues of black social pathology — a speech that really didn't say anything that hasn't been said before by others in the black community, from Bill Cosby to Louis Farrakhan — to Jackson himself (remember his condemnation of "babies making babies"?).

235

Jackson, apparently, lost sight of that historical perspective that he's a part of when he made his comments Sunday on the Fox News set. When he said … what he said.

"I wanna cut his nuts off."

There hasn't been more attention paid to the word "nuts" since 101st Airborne Division commander Gen. Anthony McAuliffe, besieged by the Nazis during the Battle of the Bulge and offered the chance to surrender, sent that one-word reply to the Germans, in a much-celebrated show of American determination.

Jackson's use of the word was hardly so heroic. There may be no more psychically corrosive symbol of the subjugation of black Americans than the prospect of castration — a fate suffered by countless black men through American history. Castration was part of the ritual degradation of lynching stretching back to Reconstruction, after the Civil War. Jackson's *sotto voce* call for symbolic emasculation of the most successful black presidential candidate in American history spoke volumes about a lingering history we can't put behind us fast enough.

◊ ◊ ◊

Apologizing later, after his comments were broadcast Wednesday on Fox's "O'Reilly Report," and after the gravity of what he'd said began to resonate, Jackson called Obama's campaign "a redemptive moment for America."

"For any harm or hurt that this hot-mike private conversation may have caused, I apologize," Jackson said in a written apology released Wednesday. "My support for Sen. Obama's campaign is wide, deep and unequivocal."

It was part of an All Apologies Tour for Jackson, who furthered the written mea culpa with a series of televised appearances essentially repeating the same thing.

It's a long comedown for Jackson, perhaps the last beneficiary of the perception of unified black thinking in America, in the wake of King's assassination. It was he who, according to an Associated Press-AOL Black Voices poll in February 2006, was voted "the most important black leader" trailed by none other than Secretary of State Condoleezza Rice.

The whisper incident was maybe the best evidence of something black America has known for years: Long ago, the mantle of black national leadership moved, not to one individual in the mold of King or Malcolm X or Louis Farrakhan or any other singular personality, but to no one in particular. With King's passing 40 years ago, the notion of one person speaking for a monolithic black America largely vanished — right along with the idea of there ever having been a monolithic black America in the first place.

"We have formally entered the post-Jackson reality," said Rev. Eugene Rivers of the Azusa Christian Community Church, on MSNBC's "Hardball" on Thursday. The question going forward, he said, "is how do we frame a post-civil rights agenda that ... dovetails with the pragmatic politics that Senator Obama brilliantly personifies?"

◊ ◊ ◊

But other questions remain: Were Jackson's sentiments merely the proof of a once-powerful spiritual and political leader realizing the degree of his own eclipse? Or were they evidence of a generational divide within black America — the same kind of split apparent in the controversy over comments by Rev. Jeremiah Wright, earlier this year?

Despite the fulsome apologies, how valuable can Jackson possibly be now in solidifying black support for Obama in his quest for the presidency?

And finally ... after two generations in the public eye, how could Jesse Jackson be so tone-deaf to the history of his own people? How could he just get it so wrong, after so long?

King, Jackson's spiritual mentor, referred to himself more than once in his too-brief lifetime as a "drum major for justice." With this latest accidental revelation, Jesse Jackson's shown that he's a drum major marching in his own parade.

7/11/2008

ICH BIN EIN BÜRGER DER WELT

L OCATED about a mile west of the Brandenburg Gate, and maligned as a tribute to Prussia's brute military defeat of three of its neighbors, the Siegesschul, the Victory Column gracing Berlin's Tiergarten Park, was today the site of a kind of world sociopolitical Woodstock. This time there was only one player; it was Sen. Barack Obama in the role of Jimi Hendrix, and like Hendrix, Obama unfurled his own Star-Spangled Banner, but this time with global overtures.

In what may have been the most anticipated campaign address in American political history, and certainly the one geographically farthest from the American political arena, Obama took the stage before an estimated 200,000 people and began to redraw the world's perception of the United States of America.

And more: In a speech that touched on a range of global issues — race relations, environmental concerns, the proliferation of nuclear weapons, immigration and the need to refortify the trans-Atlantic alliance — Obama grafted the themes of commonality he frequently used in the primary campaign onto a message for global consumption: now is the time to look for what connects us, rather than what conflicts us.

"I come to Berlin as so many of my countrymen have come before," he said. "Tonight, I speak to you not as a candidate for President, but as a citizen – a proud citizen of the United States, and a fellow citizen of the world."

◊ ◊ ◊

In Obama's rhetorical hands, the dismantling of the Berlin Wall in November 1989 was symbolic of the need to tear down walls of race and ethnicity, governmental suspicion and class warfare, in Germany, the United States and the world beyond.

"The walls between old allies on either side of the Atlantic cannot stand," he said. "The walls between the countries with the most and those with the least cannot stand. The walls between races and tribes; natives and immigrants; Christian and Muslim and Jew cannot stand. These now are the walls we must tear down."

"In Europe, the view that America is part of what has gone wrong in our world, rather than a force to help make it right, has become all too common. In America, there are voices that deride and deny the importance of Europe's role in our security and our future. Both views miss the truth – that Europeans today are bearing new burdens and taking more responsibility in critical parts of the world; and that just as American bases built in the last century still help to defend the security of this continent, so does our country still sacrifice greatly for freedom around the globe.

"Yes, there have been differences between America and Europe. No doubt, there will be differences in the future. But the burdens of global citizenship continue to bind us together. A change of leadership in Washington will not lift this burden. In this new century, Americans and Europeans alike will be required to do more – not less. Partnership and cooperation among nations is not a choice; it is the one way, the only way, to protect our common security and advance our common humanity. ...

"People of Berlin – and people of the world – the scale of our challenge is great. The road ahead will be long. But I come before you to say that we are heirs to a struggle for freedom. We are a people of improbable hope. With an eye toward the future, with resolve in our hearts, let us remember this history, and answer our destiny, and remake the world once again."

◊ ◊ ◊

The point of the event, the centerpiece of Obama's tour of Europe and the Middle East, was for Obama to deliver what the campaign called "a major speech on the historic U.S.-German partnership, and the need to strengthen Transatlantic relations to meet 21st century challenges." But implicit in his presence, just his being there, Obama announced something more revelatory to Europe, the world, and the folks back home.

Obama reached for global commonalities, and more. He never uttered these words, but he might as well have, in a tweak of President Kennedy's statement at the nearby Brandenburg Gate: *Ich bin ein Amerikaner. I am an American, and I represent a new iteration of the country you thought you knew.* For Germany — struggling with its own problems with unemployment, an economy under challenge and the fractious process of integrating foreigners into its society — Obama may seem like exactly the distillation of intelligence, toughness and pragmatism its citizens have come to expect from the United States.

And for the crowd in Berlin, Obama ratified both the possibilities of a black man, and of a recalibration of American potential. For the first time since the ascension of Rev. Martin Luther King Jr. — and in a political context the first time ever — a black man assumed the default position of what defines an American to the world. It can't have been lost on the Berlin crowd, or the millions who watched around the world, that this son of America embodies the ethnic mosaic America has long purported to be.

"Germans differentiate between America and the Bush administration. They are not anti-American per se; on the contrary," said Andreas Etges, a Berlin professor and museum curator, to Stephanie Kirchner of Time. "Obama, not only because of his skin color, for many represents the other, better America."

◊ ◊ ◊

Some have proposed that Europe's obsession with all things Obama may be a way for Europeans to exorcise the demons of their own countries' troubled history with racial assimilation by embracing the stranger from far away.

"It's a vicarious thrill," said Reginald Dale, a senior fellow at the Center for Strategic and International Studies' Europe Program. "After they've switched off their TV screens they're not going to go out and find a black candidate to put forward to lead their own country," he told The Associated Press on Tuesday.

But what European Obamamania is all about may, ironically, have less to do with Obama than with what Obama represents: a United States returning to the ideals and aspirations that made America the place all countries aspired to be. The ideals and aspirations that make America the nation that *America* aspires to be.

That's what Barack Obama symbolized today: another idea of the United States, a fresh version of a familiar favorite — a nation not exactly New! but quite likely, almost probably, soon to be Improved.

7/24/2008

OBAMA'S HIPHOP TANGO: CONSEQUENCES OF A COURTSHIP

"YOU always hurt the one you love." The song's been in the American songbook for generations. The Mills Brothers covered it during World War II; the pop evergreen has been covered by everyone from Spike Jones to Peggy Lee. But probably as many people embrace the title's wise irony as know the song itself. Sen. Barack Obama is one of them.

For almost two years now, the Illinois senator has been the beneficiary of the support of Christopher (Ludacris) Bridges, the Grammy-winning hip-hop artist, producer and emerging actor whose forthright street style and topical broadsides have garnered sales in the multimillions. In 2006, in the run-up to his presidential campaign, and as a bid for some needed street cred, Obama met with Ludacris to talk over strategies for empowering younger voters.

Their relationship, already expedient, just got more complicated. On Wednesday, Ludacris released a video of his latest song, "Politics," on YouTube. By all accounts, it's straight-up Luda firing on all cylinders, with shots at Sen. Hillary Clinton, President Bush and Sen. John McCain, Obama's presidential challenger. In a corrosive two minutes and change, Ludacris calls Clinton an "irrelevant [bitch]," posits McCain in a wheelchair, calls Bush "mentally handicapped … You're the worst of 43 presidents," and summons America to "paint the White House black" with the election of Obama in November.

The Obama campaign, adept at fast damage control, launched countermeasures quickly. Obama campaign spokesman Bill Burton told The Politico, "As Barack Obama has said many, many times in the past, rap lyrics today too often perpetuate misogyny, materialism and degrading images that he doesn't want his daughters or any children exposed to. This song is not only outrageously offensive to Senator Clinton, Senator McCain and President Bush, it is offensive to all of us who are trying to raise our children with the values we hold dear. While Ludacris is a talented individual, he should be ashamed of these lyrics."

◊ ◊ ◊

Less easily resolved is the issue of generational reach; Obama needs the support of the millions of voters, black and white alike, for whom Ludacris is a simpatico social and political voice. The 45 million registered voters between 25 and 44 — a cohort that's almost certainly right in Luda's demographic sweet spot for sales — are vital to Obama's chances to attain the presidency. This latest diss of Luda's world view can't help Obama's relationship with younger voters for whom hip-hop matters, deeply.

The Obama-Ludacris situation reveals one of the ironies of the Obama presidential campaign and its bid for broad appeal: that his speaking truth to power would go up against that of one of his most ardent — and necessary — supporters. Luda will of course say that he and Obama are in lockstep on one truth basic to politics and business: You never forget your loyal constituents. You never turn your back on your base.

But there's the challenge for Obama: figuring how to appeal to a younger, culturally adventurous and frighteningly intelligent segment of the American electorate without scaring off the wider range of voters — many of whom are still terrified of and confused by hip-hop culture and its drive-by velocity into the mainstream of American life. The conservatives have been only too ready to exploit that fear.

◊ ◊ ◊

That wider range of voters forms the base of Obama's support; and it seems that a détente is possible between Obama and the Luda demographic. Hiphop impresario Russell Simmons endorsed Obama in March. And in the June 12 edition of The Stranger, a Seattle alternative weekly, writer Charles Mudede interviewed a group of Seattle rap artists, and found a consensus that could be true of hiphop artists in general: Even though some were late getting on the Obama train, they're very much on board now.

Thig, half of the Seattle hiphop duo The Physics, told Mudede: "As a person of color, I think it's just plain crazy that someone can transcend race in this country. But that's what just happened and it surprised the hell out of me that [white] people could look beyond color ...

"When I went to my caucus, there was like two black people there. And the white people were hella pumped — Obama hats, Obama buttons, Obama this, Obama that. It's like we are on the brink of going beyond race ... I know America will not change overnight, but it's still damn impressive."

And Jace, of Seattle's Silent Lambs Project, observed that Obama's campaign means "change is now on a higher level ... It's not just: I can change the way I dress, I can change my ideology. It's: Look at this brother who's about to be president of the United States, with a beautiful wife and children, and he hasn't changed. And he's the most celebrated individual in this country. So what he's showing brothers is: There is another way to do this. You can still be cool, still have your street cred, still have a beautiful woman, still make money — all that shit that you envy, you can do it now in a way that is right."

◊ ◊ ◊

How the controversy over Luda's "Politics" changes things, or even if it does, remains to be seen. Some are already saying it's no big damn deal. "Hiphoppers and black folks understand the game," Jeff Johnson, an activist and host of an upcoming BET news and public affairs show, told The Associated Press. "They're thinking, 'An Obama who knows how to play the game is still better for me than a McCain.'"

"There are a ton of people who clearly are looking for [Obama] to denounce this in order to continue to view him as credible," Johnson said. "He, for political purposes, has to separate himself from anything controversially black."

But John McWhorter, a senior fellow at the Manhattan Institute — a *conservative* think tank — told The AP that "I'm not aware of hip-hop music affecting any election so far, and I don't think that this is going to be one, either," McWhorter is a supporter of Obama.

◊ ◊ ◊

Ironically enough, there's thinking that hiphop, so famously ahead of the curve — if not defining what the curve is — was caught off guard by the ascendancy of Obama. The Stranger's Mudede observed that "hiphop, at a mainstream level, did not see Obama coming, and this might be a sign of its age or its loss of relevance. From 50 Cent to RZA, support famously went to Hillary Clinton's run at the office. Hiphop missed the future."

Hip-hop and Team Obama appear to be narrowing their differences fast, the better to thwart the possibility of yet another intraracial divide: Obama's allegiance to Hiphop Nation is every bit as much a generational issue as Obama's relationship with the Rev. Jeremiah Wright. For Obama, both raise questions over how best to wade in the mainstream — how best not to be portrayed as "controversially black."

No small thing when (as hip-hop has made clear for a generation, and American race relations has made clear forever) to be black in the United States is to be born controversial.

8/1/2008

GANGS OF AMERICA

THE presidential campaign of 2008 has gifted the American lexicon with its own clutch of signature words and phrases. We've still got some 80-odd days before the election, but "metric," "downticket," "scorched-earth" and "dogwhistle" have been part of the political vocabulary for months.

But Sen. Barack Obama's transcendent presidential campaign has led someone more inspired by Obama's meaning than his message to come up with a gem of a phrase, a real flight of fantasy: "postracial politics" has entered not just the language but the national psyche in ways that are at least concerning, and maybe even disturbing.

The phrase suggests the ultimate Kum Ba Yah dream: that with Obama's claim to the Democratic nomination, and maybe the presidency beyond, America will have officially retired the issue and impact of race in American life. The phrase's gauzy promise also hints that black politics as we've come to know it for generations — a model of politics based on populist protest against the biases embedded in the national life — will cease to have a reason for being if Obama raises his hand to take the oath of office next Jan. 20.

"Postracial politics" is a fine idea, but one that fails to look at how black politics is as much a generational issue as a racial one. The flap over Obama's disagreements with the Rev. Jeremiah Wright over interpretations of American racial history, and more recently the rather ugly disagreements Jesse Jackson had with Obama over the familial responsibilities of young black men, are proof that, whether Obama wins or loses in November, you can't have postracial politics without first reconciling differences *within* the race.

It's as much a matter of cultural assimilation as anything else. Black Americans of Wright's and Jackson's generation came to maturity in a United States in which race was the absolute dividing line of the national experience. Back then black people regularly encountered the great national No at every level of their daily lives. From eating at lunch counters to drinking from a water fountain, from getting a quality education to the act of casting a vote, blacks were faced with the persistence of No. Those who dared to try and violate that great No often paid with their lives.

Now, many of the old ways have passed away. Race may well have become less a third rail than a line in the sand: present but ever-shifting, subject to smudging and sometimes capable of being erased altogether. Aspects of black American culture and language are today more often revealed to be what they've always been: part of the national bedrock.

And for blacks of the Jim Crow generation, the change that Barack Obama represents is unsettling. For the first time in their history, they're forced to think outside their comfort zone on matters of race and identity, to confront a social equation that doesn't always equate blackness with protest and pathology. They're required now to address the idea that race, while still a distinctive and inescapable fact of American life, doesn't matter the way it used to.

◊ ◊ ◊

Matt Bai, writing in Sunday's New York Times Magazine, grasps the shift going on in black politics, a shift that points to a new perception of what black politics can be, and is in the process of being:

"The generational transition that is reordering black politics didn't start this year," Bai writes. "It has been happening, gradually and quietly, for at least a decade, as younger African-Americans, Barack Obama among them, have challenged their elders in traditionally black districts. What this year's Democratic nomination fight did was to accelerate that transition and thrust it into the open as never before, exposing and intensifying friction that was already there.

"For a lot of younger African-Americans, the resistance of the civil rights generation to Obama's candidacy signified the failure of their parents to come to terms, at the dusk of their lives, with the success of their own struggle — to embrace the idea that black politics might now be disappearing into American politics in the same way that the Irish and Italian machines long ago joined the political mainstream."

Michael E. Ross

◊ ◊ ◊

This speaks to what's been for years one of the basic failings
of the Republican Party: its inability to look beyond the long-
persistent power structure of America, its inability (or its
unwillingness) to embrace the idea that the change Barack
Obama represents — not change as campaign meme but as a
foundational dynamic of America — is a perfectly natural thing,
and nothing less than proof of the evolution of America.

But that Republican failing is just as true for older black
Americans still trying to get their heads around the idea that the
comfortable black politics they've known for years is becoming
something they don't recognize.

As the rise of the Obama campaign shows, what's happening
in this country is no accident, no sudden chaotic transformation
sparked by a single event, or at the service of a revolution. This
is *supposed* to happen. The Framers, among other architects and
early champions of American democracy, *counted* on just such
an organic shift in political fortunes taking place.

They couldn't see the Obama campaign coming, and
consistent with the mores of their time may well have rejected
the idea of a biracial American president (Thomas Jefferson,
author of the Declaration of Independence, was a slave owner
himself). But the Obama campaign and its broad multiracial
appeal is the kind of ordered, principled, populist upheaval
that *makes* America America.

◊ ◊ ◊

You can't help but recall the schisms of generation and class
that Martin Scorsese brilliantly laid out in "Gangs of New
York," his 2002 film that explored, among other things, the
intra-ethnic clashes between native-born white Americans and
Irish immigrants arriving in America in the throes of the Civil
War. The newcomers were assaulted and condemned by the
nativists, who saw their immigrant brethren as opportunistic
interlopers and invaders.

248

As events unfolded in real life, though, the high tide of American possibility lifted all their boats; over the next two generations, Irish Americans would achieve power at every level of American social and political life, just like the Anglo-Saxon immigrant Americans who preceded them.

◊ ◊ ◊

As Bai suggests, much the same thing may now finally be playing out for black Americans. Despite old clashes over strategy and how best to become part of the American mosaic, black Americans collectively may be on the verge of a new experience of black politics as something that hasn't so much vanished as it's *evolved* to suit the needs and challenges of a new era. The internal disputes over strategy are giving way to recognition of the commonality of struggle and the social gains resulting from that struggle.

And to the extent that traditional black politics makes that pivot — as something integral to the national mainstream, rather than aggressively apart from it — other manifestations of identity politics are likely to go through the same change.

In such a scenario, the gangs of America we've come to know — the cohorts of population broken down along lines of race, ethnicity, gender, and religious and sexual preference — may themselves not disappear; over time their reasons for remaining separatist factions almost certainly will.

"Postracial politics" may not be any more possible than postgender politics or postreligious politics, at least not yet. But Obama's campaign — along with the successful mayoral campaigns of the late Tom Bradley in Los Angeles and the late Harold Washington in Chicago, and the successful gubernatorial campaigns of Douglas Wilder in Virginia and Deval Patrick in Massachusetts — reveal a nation that's slowly getting comfortable with reaching toward post-identity politics. Whether we actually get there is anyone's guess. But given the long and tragic national history on race matters, the reach for is as almost as valuable as the grasp of.

8/10/2008

OBAMA-BIDEN 2008

WELL ... OK. This is where everything seemed to be going for awhile now. With so many attacks on his national security cred and a short public-service resume, (relative to previous contenders for the presidency), it just makes sense that Barack Obama, the junior senator from Illinois, has tied up with clean, articulate Joseph Robinette Biden Jr., of Delaware, the warhorse with wit, the elder statesman of the Senate.

By picking Biden, a veteran of 35 years in the Senate, as his vice presidential running mate, Obama answers the critics who've long indicted him with the crime of relative inexperience. Biden is the lunch-bucket aspect to Obama's Ivy League mien, the gray hair to Obama's youthful drive, the inside game to Barack's three-pointer from downtown. Unlike his younger counterpart, Biden truly speaks Washington.

With this combination, Obama's message of change is married to the solidity of experience. When they appear together later today, at the Old State Capitol in Springfield, Ill. (where Obama's campaign began 560 days earlier), the stage just may be set for a photo-op of the future.

◊ ◊ ◊

It all came together in stealth mode, or something like it. Some time between 1 and 2 a.m. ET on Saturday morning, MSNBC, among how many others, announced via "Democratic officials" that Obama had selected Biden for the ticket. The Obama campaign had tried for weeks to keep the news a secret until supporters could be told first, by text message. The leak spoiled the texting party, but more surprising was the fact that, in the informational oxygen of the Internet age, the campaign kept this hushed-up as long as it did.

We were led to believe that the outcome might have gone in another direction. The media jabbered for weeks about a "short list" of potential running mates, a grab bag of names, including Indiana Sen. Evan Bayh.

Indeed, in what might have been a masterful head fake by Team Obama, KMBC-TV of Kansas City reported on Friday that "...the answer to who [Obama] would name as his running mate may have come down to a bumper sticker printed in Lenexa [Kan]. KMBC's Micheal Mahoney reported that the company, which specializes in political literature, has been printing Obama-Bayh material. That's Bayh as in U.S. Sen. Evan Bayh of Indiana. Word leaked out about the material as it was being printed up by Gill Studios of Lenexa."

Nice try.

◊ ◊ ◊

The choice of Biden shores up Obama in the broken places. In the Senate since 1972, Biden is the chairman of the Senate Foreign Relations Committee, and a strong presence on matters related to defense and national security. He's the former chairman of the Senate Judiciary Committee, and is no stranger to the rough & tumble of presidential politics, having run twice before.

Biden's working-class Catholic roots are thought likely to help Obama middle- and working-class voters in battleground states like Ohio, and in Pennsylvania, where Biden was born and raised. A son of Scranton, Pa., Biden shares a history in that city with Sen. Hillary Clinton, who made much of her roots there during the primaries.

Biden's life has been tempered by tragedy. His first wife and a daughter were killed in a traffic accident in 1972, before Biden even took office. Biden battled back from that personal disaster to become a mandarin of the Senate, widely respected by colleagues and by his constituents in Delaware. One of Biden's self-described high points as a senator was the 1994 passage of the Violence Against Women Act, something that's likely to help with women voters nursing the collapse of Hillary Clinton's campaign.

◊ ◊ ◊

That's on the plus side of the ledger. Unfortunately, Biden has a history of being long-winded, and has also committed more than one embarrassing gaffe on the campaign trail. This downside presents a challenge for the Obama campaign. "The big challenge for Biden is to going to be to stay focused, to keep his mouth shut, to not answer in 15 minutes when he can answer in two," said Newsweek's Howard Fineman on MSNBC this morning. Team Obama's immediate need, Fineman said, may be to "keep him on a pretty short leash, lest his enthusiasm run over the banks."

No sooner than the announcement been made than the opposition apparatus of Sen. John McCain, Obama's challenger, kicked into high gear, using some of Biden's own statements against Obama during the primaries. "There has been no harsher critic of Barack Obama's lack of experience than Joe Biden," said McCain spokesman Ben Porritt in a statement, conveniently forgetting the harsh criticism from McCain himself. "Biden has denounced Barack Obama's poor foreign policy judgment and has strongly argued in his own words what Americans are quickly realizing _ that Barack Obama is not ready to be president."

For her part, Clinton spoke glowingly of her primary-season antagonist, calling Biden "an exceptionally strong, experienced leader and devoted public servant."

"Sen. Biden will be a purposeful and dynamic vice president who will help Sen. Obama both win the presidency and govern this great country," said Clinton, whose persistent hopes for a vice-presidential nod officially evaporated this morning, but whose name will be placed in nomination in Denver, purely as a formality she and her supporters had insisted on for weeks.

◊ ◊ ◊

The Republicans will do their best to emphasize the previous differences between Obama and Biden, but McCain's options in this area are more limited. If McCain taps former Massachusetts governor Mitt Romney as his running mate, as has been more or less expected for months, McCain faces a new challenge based on the personal dynamic.

"If I were John McCain, I'd hear the footsteps already," said MSNBC's Chris Matthews, advancing the McCain-Romney tie-up scenario. "Romney and McCain don't like each other. That's more serious business than having had a tiff or a kerfuffle or two during the primary season. When you've got two guys who clearly don't have the right chemistry against a guy and another guy who might well have it ... I think the public's going to see a comparative advantage going to the D's on the question of who's got the right partner at the dance."

And if this turns into a battle of soundbites meant to embarrass a nominee for his choice of a running mate, McCain's gonna have splaining to do himself if he picks Romney:

That part of the general election equation has yet to play itself out; McCain's reportedly set to make his veep announcement on Aug. 29, his 72nd birthday, if it isn't leaked beforehand.

But for now, the Obama-Biden ticket has been received by Democrats as a tandem that makes sound political sense. Intelligently joining gravitas and youthful drive, and composed of two inspirational personal narratives, it's a ticket that could effectively unify working-class centrist voters and the millions of younger and minority voters who've already sided with the Obama machine.

An old Navy man, John McCain knows what "general quarters" means. It's a signal for a naval crew to prepare for battle. If the McCain campaign hasn't sounded that alarm before, it certainly will now.

8/23/2008

BARACK OBAMA 2.0

TONIGHT, forty-five years to the day after Rev. Martin Luther King Jr. dared America to embrace a dream, Barack Obama dared America to actualize it.

In a speech that encompassed the lives and sorrows of people from Iraq to New Orleans, in a straight-up callout to Sen. John McCain on the best way to lead the nation, Obama accepted "with profound gratitude and great humility" the Democratic nomination for the presidency of the United States. The address was smashmouth, it was wonkish, it was red meat, it was an asskicking of the first oratorical order. And it left no doubt — to the 84,000 at Invesco Field in Denver or millions more watching at home — that Barack Obama is more than ready for the combat of the next sixty-seven days.

For Team McCain, the call to "general quarters" just changed to "battle stations."

◊ ◊ ◊

"Tonight, I say to the American people, to Democrats and Republicans and Independents across this great land — enough! This moment, this election, is our chance to keep, in the 21st century, the American promise alive. Because next week, in Minnesota, the same party that brought you two terms of George Bush and Dick Cheney will ask this country for a third. And we are here because we love this country too much to let the next four years look like the last eight. On November 4th, we must stand up and say: "Eight is enough. ...

"John McCain has voted with George Bush ninety percent of the time. Senator McCain likes to talk about judgment, but really, what does it say about your judgment when you think George Bush has been right more than ninety percent of the time? I don't know about you, but I'm not ready to take a ten percent chance on change."

Obama drilled down into specifics, offering details on proposed policies ending tax breaks to corporations that outsource jobs, and creating tax cuts for the middle class and a

254

new energy infrastructure including wind and solar power and "the next generation" of biofuels.

And finally, forthrightly addressing those who said he didn't have the spine to take on McCain toe to toe, Obama threw down the glove, welcoming a national security debate with McCain.

"If John McCain wants to have a debate about who has the temperament and judgment to serve as the next Commander-in-Chief, that's a debate I'm ready to have," Obama said.

"You don't defeat a terrorist network that operates in eighty countries by occupying Iraq. You don't protect Israel and deter Iran just by talking tough in Washington. You can't truly stand up for Georgia when you've strained our oldest alliances. If John McCain wants to follow George Bush with more tough talk and bad strategy, that is his choice, but it is not the change we need.

"We are the party of Roosevelt. We are the party of Kennedy. So don't tell me that Democrats won't defend this country. Don't tell me that Democrats won't keep us safe. … I will never hesitate to defend this nation."

◊ ◊ ◊

"He took the gloves off but he never lost the smile on his face," said the Rev. Al Sharpton, one of MSNBC's commentator crew. "That's a dangerous opponent for John McCain."

Jacob Heilbrunn, blogging at The Huffington Post, said: "Obama's performance tonight should silence the doubters about his candidacy. He came out fighting tonight. He showed that he fully understands that the best defense is a good offense and after weeks of absorbing punishment from McCain. Obama went on the attack. His fluid, tough, and forcefully delivered speech indicates that he will be a formidable and potentially devastating opponent in the fall presidential debates. Anyone who can't see that just doesn't get it."

Also speaking on MSNBC, Rev. Jesse Jackson (chastened from his most recent personal misstep, but no less forthright about speaking truth to power) put the speech in its legitimate historical perspective: not as a sequel to anything, but its own identity as oratory for this place and time.

"He didn't make this a King Part II speech, he was smarter than that," Jackson said. "I think a lot of us were waiting for a King Part II speech. They didn't get King Part II, they got Barack Part I, and that's a good thing."

A slight quibble, though, with the ordinal number Jackson used: We've been getting Barack Part I for at least the last 566 days, in a variety of wise, streetwise, principled, passionate permutations.

What happened tonight was a restart, a reboot not of a campaign but of a sense of the vast national Possible, the moment when the software of a virally populist presidential campaign connected with the hard drive of millions of American people.

Tonight, amid fireworks both oratorical and literal, Barack Obama 2.0 went online. Do not expect this system to crash.

8/28/2008

MCCAIN-PALIN 2008:
THE ODD COUPLE

O N FRIDAY, his 72nd birthday, Arizona Sen. John McCain finally made his move for a running mate, again frustrating those within the Republican party, and blindsiding many, when he picked Sarah Palin, the one-term governor of Alaska, a rock-solid evangelical Christian conservative, to join him on the Republican presidential ticket.

It's an exceeding strange choice, from a campaign that's had something of a lock on strange for months. Despite its intent to energize a listless conservative base, and maybe play to disaffected women voters, it's a wrong choice that has more to do with who she's not than who she is.

There's a lot to recommend about Palin as a populist from the left field of the right wing: the former mayor of Wasilla (pop. 9,000) and a self-styled supporter of gun ownership and drilling in the ANWAR region, she's a self-described "hockey mom" of five children, one of whom was diagnosed with Down's syndrome. A former beauty queen and part-time sportscaster, Palin is a former union member and a true believer in every touchstone of the social conservative cause.

But McCain's choice of Palin dismantles the one claim McCain has had over Sen. Barack Obama, his Democratic rival.

The New York Times' Peter Baker synthesized it well this morning: "Senator John McCain spent the summer arguing that a 40-something candidate with four years in statewide office and no significant foreign policy experience was not ready to be president.

"And then on Friday he picked as his running mate a 40-something candidate with two years in statewide office and no significant foreign policy experience."

◊ ◊ ◊

By choosing Palin to be the first woman on a GOP ticket, McCain seems to have played into a first-blush sense of being a copycat, of trying to co-opt the meme of change that Obama has made a cornerstone of his campaign. It's a hasty bid to call into question Obama's credentials as a supporter of advances for women.

And there are questions about whether she's the right woman. All campaign long, McCain has doubled down on the idea of making a vice-presidential choice that would reflect wisdom, a shared world view, and political experience that— if he failed to complete a first term — would be pretty much equal to his own.

Palin as a statement of wisdom? Experience?

Here's one way to get your head around how bad this looks for the McCain campaign: When McCain announced her as his running mate, Sarah Palin had been in office as governor of Alaska for 635 days.

Barack Obama, already a sitting member of the U.S. Senate, accepted the Democratic presidential nomination on Thursday, 566 days after announcing his candidacy in February 2007.

Sixty-nine days separate their high-profile, bullet-point timelines. This is McCain's threshold for fitness to assume the presidency.

Newsweek's Howard Fineman, on "Countdown," nails it: "Sarah Palin makes Barack Obama look like John Adams."

◊ ◊ ◊

McCain gets no real distinguishing benefit from Palin's reformist life story. Palin has been around her version of the American block, has created her own unique and compelling personal narrative — just like Obama.

The problem for McCain is making Obama's narrative more unacceptable and out-of-the-mainstream than Palin's own. Note to Team McCain: When your running mate's favorite meat is moose, she's not exactly in the beef-eating American mainstream.

Bigger problems lurk. Besides having compatible philosophical talking points, Palin and McCain share what seems to be a basic component of the McCain campaign: flip-flops on the issues.

In 2006 Palin initially expressed support for GOP Sen. Ted Stevens' much-maligned $398 million pork-barrel project, a bridge from Ketchikan to Gravina Island, the so-called "bridge to nowhere."

In October 2006, Palin told the Anchorage Daily News that "I would like to see Alaska's infrastructure projects built sooner rather than later. The window is now, while our congressional delegation is in a strong position to assist."

Palin's support for this pork boondoggle ended only after it was clear federal funding for the project wasn't coming. Put another way: Palin was for the bridge to nowhere ... until she was against it.

Stevens was indicted in July on seven counts of failing to report $250,000 in gifts received from a corporation and its CEO on his Senate financial disclosure forms. Stevens pled not guilty and requested a trial date before the 2008 election.

At Friday's announcement, Palin took credit for telling Congress "thanks but no thanks on that bridge to nowhere. If our state wanted a bridge, I said, we'd build it ourselves."

A straight-up reversal of position in less than two years, and one you can count being an issue from now until November.

And already complicating her straight-talk pitch is an editorial posted Friday on the Daily News-Miner of Fairbanks, Alaska, stating that Palin is flat-out unqualified for the vice presidency.

You have to ask, who does this choice reach beyond the conservative, evangelical, right-wing base — those voters who will likely turn out for McCain, holding their noses if necessary, regardless of their differences with him?

The bigger challenge is wooing voters who aren't part of that conservative base. Baker in The Times: "His campaign now needs to convince the public that it can imagine in the Oval Office a candidate who has spent just two years as governor of a state with a quarter of the population of Brooklyn."

◊ ◊ ◊

If the choice of Palin was meant to reach into the demographic of older women voters previously conceded to Sen. Hillary Clinton's campaign, it fails. Palin's ardently anti-choice position on abortion rights is fundamentally at odds with those women voters. Clinton's full-throated convention call to those voters to back Obama seriously undercuts any attempt to pick them off now.

McCain's choice of Palin almost certainly would have had more traction, more of a galvanizing effect on that chunk of the electorate, if McCain hadn't *waited so long* to make it.

If he really wanted to be the maverick he's claimed to be, he would have made this pick in June. He could have further snagged the Democrats' process of selecting Obama, roiling the waters with white women voters by announcing Palin earlier in the summer. It would have given the country more time to get to know her.

If this was purely a McCain gender play, Sen. Kay Bailey Hutchison of Texas would have been just as good on that narrow basis, and better in terms of presence in the Senate and gravitas on national issues. Philosophically, Hutchison would have much in common with McCain. If McCain really meant to make the case as a maverick, the choice of Hutchison would have pointed to a willingness to break from the doctrinaire pack — to truly burnish his reformist brand with a running mate whose moderate position on social issues, including abortion, would broaden the party's reach and appeal.

And picking Hutchison — or just about anyone else — would have meant a lot less of the work the McCain campaign is obligated to do from now until November: Telling the American people who Sarah Palin is. When McCain should be focused on sharpening his distinctions with Obama and laying out his path to American governance, much of the campaign's energy and resources will have to be invested in laying out her biography and relevance for the voters.

We'll watch with great interest as the McCain campaign tries to do with Sarah Palin in 60-odd days what it's said the

Obama campaign hasn't done in a year and a half: make the nation comfortable with the candidate.

◊ ◊ ◊

With Palin aboard, McCain may have wounded himself on several fronts: He loses the battle for experience bona fides, or at best faces a stalemate. He undercuts the sharp differences he's tried to make between Obama's life narrative and the nation's by picking a running mate whose personal past bears its own exotica. And he's misinterpreted the politics of those 18 million people who voted for Hillary Clinton, assuming they're transferable by virtue of gender alone — a sad appeal to a herd instinct that modern women voters want no part of.

With the Republican convention set to start on Monday, hurricanes permitting, the McCain-Palin tandem finally distills the Republican ticket: experience and change, in interchangeably dubious quantities. Conservatives have long wondered whether McCain was experience they could believe in; now the nation's voters more generally will wonder if Palin represents change they can believe in. Once they figure out who she is in the first place.

Much about the newly-minted McCain-Palin ticket is a matter of preaching to the choir, shoring up the support of the conservative base. Team McCain has work to do with establishing its newest member in the public eye, work to do in getting what the McCain campaign needs to win in November: a bigger choir.

8/30/2008

THE LATE NO-SHOW

THE landscape of late-night television is a wild place to be. Sometimes unpredictable, sometimes unwatchable, late-night TV offers a cavalcade of content for millions of Americans, some of it serious, much of it utterly frivolous. But the carnival barkers that are the hosts of the late-night programs understand something about the after-hours personality of their medium: In many ways, theirs is an intimate relationship with America, they reliably have the captive conversation with the country that political candidates would kill for.

So it makes sense: When politicians have a chance to be part of that conversation, they damn well better show up.

Sen. John McCain violated that cardinal rule of modern American politics on Wednesday, stiffing David Letterman for a scheduled appearance on CBS's "Late Show With David Letterman," as bully a pulpit as a failing presidential contender could hope for. That was bad enough. But the details of McCain's no-show on Letterman made a bad situation even worse.

◊ ◊ ◊

McCain apparently called Letterman personally early on Wednesday to beg off from appearing on the show, claiming that his work in Washington on the bailout package would prevent him from taping the program. It all sounded principled enough: The Maverick® of the Senate couldn't take time out to sit and chat with Dave — he had Work to Do on behalf of the nation. Duty called.

It might have worked if not for someone at CBS who alerted Letterman to an internal news feed that revealed McCain had actually done an interview with CBS News anchor Katie Couric at about the time he was scheduled to tape the Letterman show. McCain wasn't going to Washington to Do the People's Business; he was actually nearby at the CBS Studios on West 57th Street, doing a sitdown with Couric, as the internal CBS news feed showed.

There's particular salt in the wound for Letterman. It was on the "Late Show" that McCain announced his candidacy for the presidency on Feb. 28, 2007.

◊ ◊ ◊

At least six million people watched Letterman on Wednesday as the veteran TV host, more emotional that usual, tore into the Arizona senator. More than once. More than twice.

"This is not the John McCain I know, by God," Letterman said. "It makes me believe something is going haywire with the campaign."

"I'm more than a little disappointed by this behavior," Letterman said. "This doesn't smell right. This is not the way a tested hero behaves. Somebody's putting something in his Metamucil."

Letterman made the internal feed of the Couric interview part of the show. "Doesn't seem to be racing to the airport, does he?" Letterman said as he watched. "This just gets uglier and uglier."

Later: "We're told now that the senator has concluded his interview with Katie Couric and he's now on Rachael Ray's show making veal piccata. ... What are you going to do?"

Letterman kept it up on Thursday night's program. "Good news: Paris Hilton is on the program tonight ... unless she needs to rush to Washington to fix the economy." We can expect this to be a running gag for Letterman — and a continuing populist complication for McCain — until the end of the campaign.

For all the experience John McCain would have the country believe he has, His Maverickness has overlooked a number of basic rules of politics and modern life in a 24/7 era — one in particular on Wednesday.

"Eighty percent of success is just showing up," Woody Allen once famously observed.

Someone should tell the senator.

9/26/2008

NORMAN WHITFIELD:
JUST HIS IMAGINATION

THEY BURIED Norman Whitfield on Saturday. He died in Los Angeles of complications from diabetes on Sept. 16. He was 68 years old. The name of the dear departed and the fact of his passing generated scant attention in today's breathless mediascape. But in a year already crowded with mourning, this was another huge loss to the world of music.

For anyone whose knowledge and embrace of modern music began in a more recent era, the name might well be no more than the answer to a trivia question or a citation in a musical encyclopedia. Norman Whitfield was responsible for music from an earlier time -- music that, like the oxygen we take for granted, is so much a part of the American songbook that it's hard to imagine modern music without his contributions.

With songs recorded by Marvin Gaye, Gladys Knight & the Pips, Edwin Starr and the Temptations, between 1966 and 1971 Whitfield and numerous songwriting partners (including Barrett Strong, his principal foil, and Eddie Holland) wrote some of the '60's most enduring radio staples, a string of hit tracks that came to define "the Motown Sound" in an era when black presence on radio was far more marginal than today.

And Whitfield solidified his idea of those songs as the producer for the Temptations' biggest hits between 1967 and 1974. As the man in the studio behind the mixing board, Whitfield concretized the music he heard in his head, turned those musical ideas into the sounds on the radio or stereo, anywhere in the world, right now.

◊ ◊ ◊

We may not remember when and where we first heard these songs, but we know them. The titles and melodies and lyrics have become part of the cultural ether, part of the air we breathe. "Ain't Too Proud to Beg." "I Heard It Through the Grapevine." "Just My Imagination (Runnin' Away With Me)." "Psychedelic Shack." We know the story lyrics of "Papa Was a

264

Rolling Stone," the topical stream of consciousness of "Ball of Confusion (That's What the World Is Today)," the cautionary tales of "Runaway Child, Running Wild," "Cloud Nine" and "Smiling Faces Sometimes."

These tracks were the foundation of urban radio in the 60's and 70's. And if it was someone else's lyrics we were singing, it was Whitfield's melodies and arrangements— classically romantic, sonically adventurous, almost cinematically evocative— that lingered and haunted, as only music can.

It'd be easy to throw Whitfield and his work under the bus of irrelevance, write him off as so much pop-culture history, if it weren't for the evolutionary aspects of his songwriting. He started his career in the early 60s, working with Strong and others writing the romantic ditties of the day to suit a radio format that couldn't accommodate songs much longer than three minutes. His early work with such groups as the Marvelettes and the Velveletts was very much locked in a static mold, the black equivalent of June-moon-croon.

But Whitfield's music paired with Strong's lyrics made the pivot from poetical romantic expressions to songs that reflected a growing concern with the civil rights movement; the culture's growing fascination with the psychedelic social experience; social problems that plagued America, from drug abuse to absentee fathers; and the agony of war. That he made such a change while working mostly with the Temptations, a vocal group in the classic Motown soul-music template, makes their work that much more compelling.

Maybe it's a bridge too far to credit Whitfield with the musical foundations that allowed the emergence of rap and hip-hop. But it's true that his approach to writing music – the pairing of meaningful lyrics and memorable music to address the social concerns of the day from a black perspective -- certainly helped make hip-hop possible.

◊ ◊ ◊

It may be hard to fathom the pertinence of Whitfield's work in the face of the more brittle sonic palette of 21st-century pop culture. But Whitfield's passing — so soon after the death of

Isaac Hayes, in early August — is another lost connection to the notion of soulfulness in black American music, the sound for which the phrase "back in the day" was invented.

We hear those songs from years ago and they're still fresh, and they're still pertinent, romantically, emotionally, socially. Thank Norman Whitfield for shaking off the stereotype of what a soul-music composer was supposed to write for singers in matching suits, doing matching moves on stage.

Thank Norman Whitfield for showing us how "back in the day" is very much today.

9/29/2008
As performed in The Root

OBAMA-MCCAIN DEBATE II: THAT ONE

AIN'T it always the way? Some revelations you only get after their precipitating events have already happened. That occurred on Tuesday night. Maybe the most telling moment of the second presidential debate took place when the second presidential debate was over.

It was pretty much impossible to see it on the cable networks, which reflexively cut back to the analysts and Learned Ones those networks are employing for the rest of the campaign. MSNBC, CNN, the broadcast nets sprinted back to the studios to tell us What It All Means.

Thank C-SPAN for *showing* us what it all means. The C-SPAN feed from the Mike Curb Center on the campus of Belmont University in Nashville lingered in the hall for many minutes after it was over, observing the interactions of Sen. John McCain and Barack Obama, the ways they played with the crowd. For a while, anyway.

It was, generously, ten minutes after the debate ended when it was clear something had happened with who was hogging the camera. I wasn't there and neither were you, but viewers could sense by the imbalance of who the camera focused on, that someone was conspicuous by his absence. The Maverick® had left the building. McCain and entourage had vanished, and done so quickly. It was a disappearing act that, in the context of the debate he'd just handsomely lost, was more than just bad campaign "optics." It further conveyed the sense of invisibility Team McCain has gravitated toward in these final days of the election campaign.

Obama was another matter entirely.

Slate's John Dickerson, who *was* there, caught the mood perfectly:

"[W]ith McCain out of the room, the affection from swing voters increased. [Obama] was mobbed, patted, beamed at, embraced. One woman wriggled up next to him. At one point, about 15 voters posed for a group picture like it was the last day of camp."

◊ ◊ ◊

We won't weigh this down with a full-on transcript of the debate last night. Suffice to say that for ninety minutes we — 63.2 million people in the United States and millions more around the world — saw exactly why this race is where it is. In the freewheeling town-hall format McCain has claimed is his strength, McCain met his match in Obama, a challenger who seemed to look more presidential as the event wore on.

Fielding questions on energy independence, national security, the nation's two foreign wars and the economy — the 80,000-pound gorilla in the room — the Democrat warmed to the format, breaking through what actors call "the fourth wall" between them and the audience. Obama made it personal again, with strong eye contact, a folksy demeanor and measured responses to his angry opponent.

Not that he didn't revert to type. When Citizen Katie Hamm lofts a softball to Obama about Pakistan, Barry got to wax sage and professorial, offering his long-standing (and increasingly accepted) rationale for that country and Afghanistan as the real nexus of the war on terrorism. And answering other questions, Obama elicited a self-possession and confidence that was reflected in the faces around the room.

Contrary to the barroom brawlers in the punditburo who have called for Obama to engage McCain directly in the same mud-wrestling pit McCain prefers, Obama showed the intelligent cool he's brandished all year. For many in the audience, there was an unspoken belief that Obama's bearing at the debate — part of the fundamental sang-froid he's exhibited on the campaign trail for many months — would be the same character trait he could be counted on to show as president. "A calm hand at the controls," some facial expressions seemed to say. "Isn't that what we want?"

◊ ◊ ◊

McCain again equated his own personal strength and character in the crucible of imprisonment in the Vietnam War with the strength and character required to run a wounded, battered nation, despite a growing body of evidence to the contrary.

He rightly wants to stand up for Georgia and Ukraine joining NATO, and for warning Moscow from further renewal of its historically brutal expansionism. At one moment there was real fellow feeling for a member of the audience, former Chief Petty Officer Terry Shirey, a fellow Navy man. And the crowd seemed to respond with a quiet warmth. So what if McCain didn't wear a flag-lapel pin for the second debate in a row? This was the cold warrior in twilight, recognizing another once-comrade in arms.

But this was the exception. For a man who supposedly loves the town-hall format, McCain was not on his A game. He launched into fulsome praise for "my hero, Teddy Roosevelt," instantly mangling one of TR's signature phrases ("Walk softly — talk softly, but carry a big stick"). (This is how you treat your *hero*?)

Then he trotted out that tired-ass line about looking into Putin's eyes and seeing the letters K, G and B. And again he floated the notion of forming a "League of Democracies" to oversee various regional instabilities — a body that, as generally described, wouldn't be any different from the United Nations Security Council we've had for 60 years.

◊ ◊ ◊

Consider the unspoken things, what happened between exchanges with the candidates. While McCain spoke, Obama often sat watching his opponent, unafraid of eye contact, visually staying in the game, his body open and accessible.

When Obama spoke, McCain appeared restless, either sitting and taking notes, sipping water, or standing, sometimes with the body language of an impatient man.

Throughout the evening the audience got the John McCain Rage Show, co-starring condescension, irritation and barely sublimated anger. It was there in a thoroughly condescending manner when McCain addressed a question from Oliver Clark about the mortgage crisis.

Michael E. Ross

"But you know, one of the real catalysts, really the match that lit this fire was Fannie Mae and Freddie Mac," McCain told Clark. "I'll bet you, you may never even have heard of them before this crisis."

And that anger was there when McCain committed the gaffe of the debate season thus far, committing to political folklore a phrase that will adhere to McCain — not like glory but more like manure — forever.

Attacking Obama on a vote on an energy bill on the floor of the Senate, McCain, suddenly physically animated, said the bill in question was "loaded down with goodies, billions for the oil companies, and it was sponsored by Bush and Cheney."

Then he said (with a cringe-inducing sarcasm more physical than rhetorical) "You know who voted for it? You might never know. *That* one. You know who voted against it? Me."

There was more rhetorical counterpunch, more thrust and parry: McCain's idea of a $5,000 refundable tax credit for health care that Obama dismantled as a plan to tax company health-care benefits, a zero-sum-game proposal in which one hand of government giveth and the other hand of government taketh away. Or McCain's GOP-ritual blame of minority homeowners for the gravity of the mortgage crisis. Or McCain's trial-balloon stunt of proposing that the Federal government take possession of $300 billion in bad mortgages — a bailout on top of the bailout!

But two words put the icing on a cake in the rain. With two words — *that one* — John McCain revealed the gravity of his dislocation, the degree of his disconnect not just from the candidate who opposes him, but also from the country he proposes to lead. Some in the audience in the hall were visibly tuning out, mentally heading for the exits, already plotting how to get into a post-debate photograph with *that one.*

◊ ◊ ◊

John McCain has over the years effectively crafted a political persona combining the instincts of a nonconformist with

270

the principles of a reform-minded politician. Some of those principles that he stood on and for have disappeared.

More recently, over the long and revelatory months of this campaign, McCain model 2008 has advanced his political star by equating a personal and military valor we've never doubted for a moment with the temperament, judgment, vision and character it takes to be president of the United States. The shortcomings in that comparison were obvious Tuesday night.

The people at the Mike Curb Center on the campus of Belmont University in Nashville didn't have any doubt, any more than the millions more around the country — many of whom have already voted. If the hordes that crowded Obama after the debate are a sign, they know who they want for president.

That one.

10/8/2008

OBAMA-MCCAIN III:
WALL OF AIRQUOTES

SENS. Barack Obama and John McCain showed up tonight for the third presidential debate at the Mack Sports & Exhibition Center at Hofstra University on Long Island. The winner was Joe Wurzelbacher.

The name of Wurzelbacher, apparently the GOP's new hypothetical American, the Toledo plumber whom Obama met on the campaign trail, was invoked twenty-five times tonight — twenty-one times by McCain. Never mind the audience of millions who watched the debate on television in the United States. Joe the Plumber was the judge and jury before whom McCain and Obama made their best final arguments on fitness to serve as president.

The verdict? Joe the Plumber reportedly went to bed shortly after the debate ended; he'll no doubt hold a press conference in the morning. But we saw no game-changer, only the product of another furious reboot of the McCain campaign, evidence of a McCain Software Service Pack 2.1.5. There are still bugs in the code and the drop-dead ship date is three weeks from today.

McCain was stronger tonight, more visibly forceful in ways that worked for him and against him. He was more reliably aggressive and on-message than he was in the first two debates, but only just barely. For the most part he was flustered, he was evasive, he was defensive. He made faces and squirmed, rolled his eyes and arched his eyebrows. He acted like the guy in the Preparation H commercial who can't sit still.

M'girl Arianna Huffington got it right:

"McCain's reliance on angry attacks on Obama has been an unequivocal failure. But instead of course-correcting, he doubled down -- coming across as angrier and meaner than ever before. This debate was won on the reaction shots. Every time Obama spoke, McCain grimaced, sneered, or rolled his eyes. By contrast, every time McCain was on the attack, Obama smiled. It was like watching a split-screen double feature -- Grumpy Old Men playing side by side with Cool Hand Luke."

And if word choice is indicative of a debater's emotional baseline, McCain was apparently "angry": he used the word at least five times — four times in the first ninety seconds of his opening comments at the debate.

McCain's biggest problem is one of consistency — both his own and Obama's. While a loudly floundering McCain has tried to pivot in response either to national crises or those of his own campaign, the Barack Obama we saw in the first debate was the same Barack Obama who showed up in Hempstead, L.I., tonight. Principled. Methodical. Passionate. Relaxed under fire. And that's a problem for John McCain.

◊ ◊ ◊

For weeks now, the McCain campaign has resorted to character assassination and broad innuendo against Obama, trying for forever to connect him body & soul with William Ayers, a Chicago professor and former leader of the Weather Underground, the radical group that conducted bombings of domestic locations in the early 1970's. Ayers served on a community board with Obama years after Ayers' insane antics in the heat of the Vietnam War.

Once he knew about Ayers' antiwar activities, Obama denounced them clearly, and did so more than once. But for a campaign increasingly empty of original ideas, Team McCain has used Obama's passing acquaintance with Ayers as the basis for a campaign of guilt by association — a poisonous strategy that's led to the ugliest kind of outbursts at McCain's rallies, and those of running mate Alaska Gov. Sarah Palin.

McCain promised to make Ayers Issue #1 for this third debate of presidential finalists. For a man who prides himself in not telegraphing his punches, McCain was generous in spelling out the strategy beforehand: make William Ayers the centerpiece of his campaign for the duration.

When the subject of Ayers finally came up tonight — because Obama forced the issue, boxing McCain into saying to his face what he'd been saying in front of supporters at rallies, waving like red meat — McCain seemed to dismiss the whole business with Ayers. "Mr. Ayers, I don't care about an old washed-up terrorist," he said, pressing for an explanation of a non-relationship that Obama had thoroughly explained, cutting off oxygen to the rationale for a controversy of his own making.

But without question, McCain's biggest gaffe of the evening wasn't a gaffe at all but the distilling evidence of a fundamental misreading of the American people, a powerfully telling moment that may well have cost him many of the women voters he needs for even a chance at the presidency — mostly the white women voters he thought he could sway by picking Sarah Palin to accompany him on an increasingly quixotic campaign.

Discussing abortion, the two had the following exchange:

Obama: "With respect to partial-birth abortion, I am completely supportive of a ban on late-term abortions, partial-birth or otherwise, as long as there's an exception for the mother's health and life, and this did not contain that exception ..."

McCain: "Just again, the example of the eloquence of Senator Obama. He's for the 'health' for the mother. You know, that's been stretched by the pro-abortion movement in America to mean almost anything.

"That's the extreme pro-abortion position, quote, 'health.'"

McCain's physical use of air quotes of insinuation around the word "health" — as though it were a code word for something else — was emphatically reinforced with body language and the use of the word 'quote' itself: For McCain, the issue of the health of the mother was being used by the pro-choice crowd to justify abortion as a convenience, rather than a medical necessity. McCain's tone and demeanor practically radiated the idea: the matter of abortion for the woman's health was just more political sleight of hand, and not to be taken seriously.

The very idea that a senior United States senator could spend a quarter century in that deliberative body and so blithely dismiss a central issue of the reproductive rights debate, could be so emotionally tone-deaf to the critical issue of women's health as to lard it with winks and innuendo, seems almost impossible to believe. Impossible but true: the health-in-airquotes moment may have finally sealed the electoral fate of John McCain like nothing else could.

If, as some have said, women voters are the pivotal American demographic in this year's vote, they may well have decided themselves tonight, on the impact of that toweringly insensitive remark, that John Sidney McCain II will not be the president of the United States in 2008. Years from now, historians may look back and point to this night, that dismissive utterance, as the moment that he lost not only the debate, but also the election.

◊ ◊ ◊

There are still twenty-one days left for McCain to make his case. A week is a year is seventeen seconds in politics — whatever the metric is this week. But however much time there's left, there's not enough for another reinvention. John McCain said he had Barack Obama right where he wanted him. Trouble is, John McCain had John McCain right where Barack Obama wanted *him*.

There's clearly a level of desperation in the McCain campaign that has gone past the merely political. There is a mortal aspect to this thing now, the barely suppressed rage of the candidate and the thunderously bad advice of too many of the wrong handlers. The McCain campaign has begun to show the signs, the desperate strategies of a candidate for whom the words "last chance" have begun to reverberate in his ears, in the 3 o'clock in the morning that for John McCain right now is not hypothetical but real.

10/15/2008

LEVI STUBBS:
NOT THE SAME OLD SONG

A BAD YEAR for the sound of music just got worse. First we said goodbye to Bo Diddley, then Isaac Hayes, then Norman Whitfield. Then on Friday we lost Levi Stubbs, leader of the Four Tops, the Voice of Motown, the baritone whose urgent vocal passion launched a thousand thousand love affairs.

Stubbs, ill for years with cancer and the effects of a stroke, stole home in his sleep on Friday, at his home in Detroit, at the age of 72.

You know those songs in *your* sleep. "Baby I Need Your Loving," "Walk Away Renee," "Bernadette." "I Can't Help Myself (Sugar Pie Honey Bunch)," "Same Old Song." "Reach Out I'll Be There." "Standing in the Shadows of Love." "There Ain't No Woman (Like the One I Got)." These and more besides, all powered by that unmistakable take-charge baritone, a voice Stubbs himself once described for the Los Angeles Times as "rather loud and raw," but a voice without which Motown wouldn't, couldn't be the motive cultural force it was for 20 years.

The Four Tops, which began in the 1950s in Detroit as the Four Aims, consisted of Stubbs, Abdul (Duke) Fakir, Lawrence Payton and Renaldo (Obie) Benson — and it stayed that way for decades. In an era when bands changed members at the slightest sign of friction or difficulty, the original lineup didn't change for more than 40 years, a record of longevity and tolerance. Recording at least 32 albums for seven different labels, selling 50 million copies, the Tops had staying power.

Gary Susman of Entertainment Weekly grasped the tree-ring sense of the group's endurance: "Unlike many of the label's own hand-groomed and manufactured bands, the quartet was around long before Motown started, and its original lineup continued decades after most Motown bands had become tribute acts filled with ringers."

As the group that helped establish the power of the Holland-Dozier-Holland songwriting team, the Four Tops were effectively American ambassadors to the world.

The Berry Gordy finishing-school approach to stagecraft was part of what gave the Tops their panache. Karen Grigsby Bates, writing on the NPR Web site, observed: "In an era when broken-down bell bottoms, scruffy hair and Army-Navy surplus coats were de rigueur, the Tops were always elegant onstage, whether they were in tuxedos or silk Nehru jackets and medallions."

But Stubbs' voice was the signature of their signature sound. With a voice that always seemed on the edge of despair, a curious blend of strength and weakness, Stubbs became the frontman for the group that, with only the Temptations and the Supremes as competition, defined soul music for millions around the planet.

Break out your cassettes, start up your iPod. Listen to "Baby I Need Your Loving." Revel in the chorus, and the way Stubbs made time stop for that fraction of a second that seemed to go on forever.

"Baby I need your loving ... *Got!* to have all your loving."

Play "Bernadette": Hear Stubbs again, in a performance that wedded menace and loneliness — the way his voice emerges from a silence to cry a woman's name like a man at the end of his rope.

Stubbs, who was known as "the Captain," had been in declining health for years after a cancer diagnosis and a series of strokes in 2000. By then Payton had died (1997); Benson would follow in 2005. With Stubbs' passing, only Duke Fakir remains of the original Four Tops lineup.

Remember the voice that personified emotional honesty, joy and heartbreak so naked and plain you almost can't stand it. Remember Levi Stubbs.

It's not the same old song anymore. It'll never be the same old song again.

10/18/2008
As first performed on The Root

THE ALL-AMERICAN FAMILY CRISIS

IF there was ever any doubt about Sen. Barack Obama's ability to connect with the American people, as his strategically brilliant campaign has shown he's capable of doing, that doubt should soon be put to rest, in the wake of a personal tragedy now facing the Democratic nominee—the same tragedy being faced by millions of Americans every day.

The campaign announced on Monday that Obama would be taking time away from the campaign this week to fly to Hawaii to attend to the health of his maternal grandmother, Madelyn Payne Dunham, said to be gravely ill as a result of a broken hip and other health problems, the nature of which are none of your business or mine. Obama is expected to return to the campaign on Saturday, somewhere in the western United States.

The importance of Dunham in Obama's life has been the stuff of many of his campaign rallies. It's common knowledge that after attending schools in Jakarta, Indonesia, until he was 10 years old, Obama moved back to Honolulu to live with his maternal grandparents, Stanley and Madelyn Dunham, starting in the fifth grade and lasting until he graduated from high school. Obama has often credited Madelyn Dunham with giving him much of the motivation and the drive he needed to succeed—to in effect become the man he has become. "She poured everything she had into me,"the candidate said at the Democratic National Convention in August.

So there was never any question about Barack going back to Hawaii. Family is family. Full damned stop. End of discussion.

At least you would think so. No sooner had the campaign made the announcement, the punditburo —the D.C./N.Y. axis of campaign commentators, analysts and talking heads— weighed in with their somewhat clinical assessments of how Obama's absence would affect that campaign with two weeks left until Election Day. Already there's been dire but silly talk about his momentum slowing, suggesting that this unexpected event could be the unintended October surprise, the deus ex machina desperately needed by Sen. John McCain.

Really? To the contrary, this unexpected turn may end up solidifying Obama's connection to voters because his personal tragedy is a universal one. It is certainly an American one, as the country's population ages and stressed out middle-aged citizens find themselves struggling to deal with both the demands of their own jobs and the families they are raising, but also the failing health of the loved ones who raised them.

There's practically no one in this country who has not or will not, sooner or later, be forced to confront the illness of a relative or loved one. It is a human rite of passage. What Obama faces today strongly reinforces a sense of kinship with the American people. Confronting his own personal agony, and entirely at the hand of fate, Obama has connected with Americans on the matter of health care for aging relatives, the prospect of caring for someone who was once a caregiver and the ways in which the unexpected often trumps the best-laid plans.

Obama's response to this blow mirrors that of all Americans confronting a relative's imminent mortality: When things go south, you drop what you're doing and take care of business. Period. That response underscores the humanistic aspect of his personal narrative, and how it dovetails with that of millions of Americans. No matter what your party is, no matter your affiliation, you can relate to this. Or you will someday.

Setting aside his trajectory into the political life of the nation, his soaring oratory, his rapport with the crowd, his almost preternatural calm on the frenzied campaign trail, what the country is witnessing now from Barack Obama may well be his most moving communion with the American people.

In ways the pundits don't fully grasp yet, and more than at any other time in this long campaign, Barack Obama is us. Not the African-American us. The American us.

10/23/2008
As first performed on The Root

AMERICA 2.0:
THE UNITED STATES OF A MIRACLE

8:01 P.M. PT. Bells are ringing tonight. Car alarms whooping and car hornswailing. In Seattle they're shooting off fireworks in the cold air. Somebody just screamed. Somewhere, servers are crashing from the sudden traffic, cell phone lines are briefly jammed.

And somewhere, everywhere, people are laughing. And people are crying. Tonight, against all odds and truly, undeniably resetting the baseline of American possibility, Barack Hussein Obama, son of Kenya and Kansas, has been elected the 44th President of the United States of America.

The President-elect of the United States spoke after his victory, in Chicago's Grant Park before at least 250,000 people. "If there is anyone out there who still doubts that America is a place where all things are possible; who still wonders if the dream of our founders is alive in our time; who still questions the power of our democracy, tonight is your answer.

"It's the answer told by lines that stretched around schools and churches in numbers this nation has never seen; by people who waited three hours and four hours, many for the very first time in their lives, because they believed that this time must be different; that their voice could be that difference.

"It's the answer spoken by young and old, rich and poor, Democrat and Republican, black, white, Latino, Asian, Native American, gay, straight, disabled and not disabled - Americans who sent a message to the world that we have never been a collection of Red States and Blue States: we are, and always will be, the United States of America."

◊ ◊ ◊

The election of Barack Obama resets that baseline to what we as a nation have told ourselves — in story and song and national lore, in our education and our popular culture, from the first moment we put our hands over our hearts — this nation stands for. The very concept of a "level playing field" has never meant more, has never been closer to being an absolute American reality, than it does and is today.

For the first time at this nation's highest elective level, the Idea of America has fully become Praxis and become so in a way that is, more centrally than by coincidence, the single greatest act of bridging the racial divide in the history of this nation.

And there's a more enduring sweetness of the moment: this was not achieved through some sudden exercise of the powers of succession, not through some blind accident or extraconstitutional emergency, but through a regular, orderly canvass of the American people's desires in a national election. He won the gift outright.

The people of this brilliant, fractious, sentimental, argumentative, utterly unpredictable country *chose* someone to lead them and represent them to the world, and they chose a black man.

◊ ◊ ◊

There are few words to really express the power of what happened tonight. Nov. 4, 2008 is a new national ground-zero date, a soft ground zero. 11/4 is the day when black and minority Americans moved through the ceiling of our presumptive aspirations.

Not all the way through it, to be sure, but with head and shoulders clear, getting a glimpse of what, for all purposes, is a new world. *From today*, generations of black and minority children will never know a world without a black American president. The old threshold of what's truly possible will not exist for them. This is terra incognita, and is an existential liberation the likes of which we've never known before as a people.

And this election invites the rest of us, the ones with a perspective of life B.O. (before Obama) and A.O. (after Obama), to a serious reevaluation of the balance of our own lives, and how — with a change at the very top — they might be put to the best and highest use. Something to Shoot For. Unlike before, something completely attainable. For a people hobbled historically and today by an unending series of social and economic woes, and the vacancy of spirit that follows in their wake, that's huge beyond measure.

◊ ◊ ◊

Obama's pursuit of the presidency was a 50-state journey, conducted at a breathless, relentless pace that raises the bar on what successful campaigns will require in the future. Expect a new Rule #1 for campaigning to emerge: No more conceding states to the enemy. If you presume to run all of the United States, you've got to run *in* all of the United States.

Obama's campaign has rebranded the American political dynamic, and done it with a lean and vivid African American face. Is there a more telling symbol of this nation than the young eager politician, chock-full of the drive and energy that typify us, the campaigner relishing the sheer physicality of American politics?

Historically the visual symbols of that kind of politics, and the beneficiaries of their templatizing effect on popular expectations, have been white men. FDR. Truman. Three of the Kennedys. Reagan. Clinton. The Bushes. These are what highly successful presidential candidates look like. It's always been this way.

Well, not no more. Obama crashed through that old iconography. The white male stranglehold on the perception of political dynamism, endangered when he began his quest, formally ended tonight.

That fact need not be an obituary so much as a birth announcement. The idea of a successful American politician has a different look tonight than it did yesterday. A look more like all of America. That's more of a cause for celebration than anything else.

◊ ◊ ◊

It's pleasantly ironic that the first president of the Internet age comes from an American demographic that has, until fairly recently, been behind the curve of Internet access and knowledge. Leave it to the African American way with the drum, and adaptability.

It was that adaptability that sprang from Obama's earliest public incarnation that makes his victory at the polls tonight such a transforming thing.

Sen. John McCain and Alaska Gov. Sarah Palin ran down Obama on the campaign trail, more than once belittling his experience as a community organizer in Chicago. In doing that, they and the Republican Party missed the move Obama made to the hole — overlooked the bigger, broader, deeper truth of his organizing experience and what could be done with it in the age of the Internet.

McCain and the Republicans generally articulated the notion of a community organizer in outdated, stereotypical, central-casting terms: the scruffy kid in a peacoat and jeans sticking photocopied leaflets under windshield wipers before retreating to the storefront headquarters for coffee and face time with the hot new help.

They failed to see (right along with most of the country) the genius of Obama's uncanny way with the new drum of the Internet, and his adaptation of the principles of community organizing — an embrace of the grassroots; developing an agenda among like-minded people; accessibility by the public; a populist approach to fundraising; an unwavering sense of the objective — in the service of a national presidential campaign.

They failed to see it all until the end: For Barack Obama, community organizer, the United States was another necessary and doable undertaking. A bigger community to be better, more perfectly organized.

◊ ◊ ◊

Bells will ring tomorrow. Car alarms'll go off. And somewhere, everywhere, people will laugh and cry like every other day in life. But make no mistake, this nation has changed tonight, has shifted in its moorings to a different place.

The old equations of race and society are being changed, if not discarded. One of the social obstacles that have defined us and divided us for generations has been called into question, and set aside at the highest level, for the first time in our history. And we are better tonight as a nation than we've ever been before.

Briefly in some ways, forever in others, we're witness to life in the United States of a miracle.

11/4/2008

THE MCCAIN SCRUTINY XIX

O N TUESDAY night, not long after Barack Obama defeated him for the presidency of the United States, Sen. John McCain made a concession speech from a stage outside the Arizona Biltmore Hotel in Phoenix, a speech that was startling in its humility, grace and wisdom.

"My friends, we have — we have come to the end of a long journey. The American people have spoken, and they have spoken clearly. A little while ago, I had the honor of calling Senator Barack Obama to congratulate him.

"In a contest as long and difficult as this campaign has been, his success alone commands my respect for his ability and perseverance. But that he managed to do so by inspiring the hopes of so many millions of Americans who had once wrongly believed that they had little at stake or little influence in the election of an American president is something I deeply admire and commend him for achieving," said McCain (or an amazing simulation of him).

"This is an historic election, and I recognize the special significance it has for African-Americans and for the special pride that must be theirs tonight. I've always believed that America offers opportunities to all who have the industry and will to seize it. Senator Obama believes that, too. ...

"I urge all Americans who supported me to join me in not just congratulating him, but offering our next president our good will and earnest effort to find ways to come together to find the necessary compromises to bridge our differences and help restore our prosperity, defend our security in a dangerous world, and leave our children and grandchildren a stronger, better country than we inherited."

◊ ◊ ◊

That crack about "an amazing simulation of him" a few paragraphs back isn't just taking a shot. Almost as soon as McCain had uttered what must be one of the more moving political valedictories of recent times, the blogosphere, the punditburo and people in general asked the logical question:

Who is this man? What have you done with John McCain? And if that's *really* John McCain up there … where has this sense of fair play and principle and rhetorical even-handedness been for the last six months?

Irony of ironies: Even in the concession speech, there's another layer to contend with, another John McCain that contradicts the ones we've come to know, or at least experience, for the last ten months.

It's gotta be said: At campaign's end John McCain was ill-served by a horde of advisers who miscalculated the national hunger for change, the power of the Internet and the intellectual command of a little known governor from Alaska whose fall from grace would parallel his own. He got bad advice from a campaign manager who said, apparently with a straight face, that this pivotal presidential election wasn't really about issues, it was about personalities.

The candidate became known by the company he kept, too. People don't like to be told they live in "a nation of whiners," especially when the man who said it was serving as a lobbyist for an international banking and subprime mortgage corporation that had a hand in the mortgage meltdown. Even as he advised the McCain campaign on economic matters.

◊ ◊ ◊

But make no mistake, much of this fall had to do with John McCain himself. He was bullheaded and impetuous when the nation screamed for compromising and deliberate. He was tics and edges and sharp elbows when the country yearned for curves and poise and cool. He chastised those who invoked race and ethnicity in an already-heated campaign, even while he was either the wink-and-a-nod beneficiary of everything they did, or a passive participant in their character assassination of Barack Obama.

He was tirelessly focused on the peripheral when the country screamed for attention to the issues that matter. He admitted to knowing next to nothing about the economy when the economy was for many voters the *only* thing that mattered. He was convinced the United States economy was fundamentally sound, when the people of the United States knew better. He couldn't remember how many homes he owned, something the people of America can't afford to forget.

There have been existential contradictions in the McCain persona for some time now. His hiring of a lobbyist to run his Senate office, even as he championed campaign finance reform that impugned lobbyists.

His role in creating the Reform Institute, a nonprofit group promoting tighter campaign finance rules, followed by his resignation from the group after news reports found the group was getting the very unlimited corporate contributions he opposed.

And how could a man with such a supposed command of global affairs and national security, a senator well traveled abroad be so *wrong*, so laughably out of touch about the world he's traveled in?

Voters through the primaries and into the general campaign discovered the McCain World Atlas, a curious gazetteer in which Czechoslovakia still exists, Iraq and Pakistan share a common border, Shiites and Sunnis are interchangeable blocs of the Iraqi people, Somalia and Sudan have traded places (as well as Spain and all of Latin America), and Vladimir Putin is the president of Germany.

You're forced to wonder if a President McCain sent planes to bomb bomb bomb bomb bomb Iran, if they'd actually wind up dropping ordnance down smokestacks in Greenland.

◊ ◊ ◊

But John McCain finally failed to achieve the presidency because he wanted the prize more than he valued what the prize is worth. We're a nation whose natural inclination is to look forward, before moving forward. We don't do reverse gear very well. We never have and never will. That's what the prize of the presidency reflects: our investment in the future, in the wide untapped Possible of this amazing, unpredictable nation. Not what advertises itself as the future in campaign literature.

We want the real thing. The iPod, not the phonograph.

In a splendid essay in The Huffington Post, written three weeks before the deal went down on Election Night, columnist Mike Barnicle nailed the outcome, even then:

"It is a sad story: a proud and independent man permits a handful of advisers to take his hard-earned reputation and alter it to such an extent that the original is now hard to recognize, nearly invisible behind a curtain of cynical ads and the preposterous pronouncements of a woman whose candidacy is an insult to intelligence. ...

"Soon, the 'Straight Talk Express' will bank west and head for the Arizona desert and election eve. And John McCain will sit up front, staring out the window, exhausted, as the plane crosses the land he loves and the people -- millions of them -- he failed to connect with because while he was once indeed a prisoner of war, he has spent the last ten weeks letting himself become a prisoner of the past."

Mercifully, campaigns end — the relentless examination of the candidate and his statements and jokes, practices and policies gives way to something else.

Vaya con Dios, John McCain, you old sidewinder you. For now, we've seen enough. There's nothing to scrutinize anymore.

11/10/2008

A RUSSIAN FORECAST FOR AMERICA

THE LONG relationship between the United States and the Russian Republic has been bubbling at a low ebb for years. The last eight years of the Bush administration and its bellicose, hubristic attitude toward the so-called axis of evil (and anyone else the Bushies decided they didn't or may not like) has led to a kind of hot cold war, with weapons of rhetoric rather than missiles being lobbed back and forth between Washington and Moscow.

In 2007 there was the Bush missile defense shield plan, under which an American-made deterrent to nuclear strikes on eastern Europe would be placed in Poland and the Czech Republic by 2012.

The plan aroused the ire of then-Prime Minister Vladimir Putin. The Bush plan surely helped to bolster Putin's blatant appeal to the militaristic spirit of the Russian people (the Leader was seen in news reports presiding over teen education camps meant to cultivate animosities among young people — Putin Youth? — towards the United States).

American pop culture's even weighed in: In the most recent Indiana Jones movie, set in the 1950's. Indy (too long in the tooth to go on bashing the Nazis that had by then decamped for South America) took on the Soviets of the Stalin era with his swashbuckling style.

But the war of words and images has escalated with the growing profile and audience of a little-known Russian military analyst and professor, a man who suggests, with unsettling preciseness, that the meter on the United States as a world power is about eighteen months from running out.

◊ ◊ ◊

In an interview in today's Wall Street Journal, Prof. Igor Panarin, revisiting a forecast he's been making for about ten years now, says that the United States will "disintegrate" in 2010, the victim of an economic and moral collapse that would trigger a civil war leaving the United States nothing so much as a pie whose slices would be devoured by other world powers.

289

"There's a 55-45% chance right now that disintegration will occur," he told WSJ's Andrew Osborn.

Perhaps understandably, given the rise of a virulent anti-Americanism loose in Mother Russia, this Nostradamus-on-the-Volga is the darling of Russian state media, and the Kremlin. Panarin, a former KGB analyst, is the dean of the Russian Foreign Ministry's academy for future diplomats, has a doctorate in political science, and has been a student of U.S. economics, Osborn reports.

"Mr. Panarin's views also fit neatly with the Kremlin's narrative that Russia is returning to its rightful place on the world stage after the weakness of the 1990s, when many feared that the country would go economically and politically bankrupt and break into separate territories," Osborn added.

What's so alarming is the level of detail Panarin brings to this American twilight. Like the dystopia of Aldous Huxley's "Brave New World," like George Orwell's "1984," Panarin's vision names names, establishes boundaries and sets a rationale for events that is, disturbingly, deeply rooted in reality.

Osborn: "Mr. Panarin posits, in brief, that mass immigration, economic decline, and moral degradation will trigger a civil war next fall and the collapse of the dollar. Around the end of June 2010, or early July, he says, the U.S. will break into six pieces -- with Alaska reverting to Russian control."

"He predicts that economic, financial and demographic trends will provoke a political and social crisis in the U.S. When the going gets tough, he says, wealthier states will withhold funds from the federal government and effectively secede from the union. Social unrest up to and including a civil war will follow. The U.S. will then split along ethnic lines, and foreign powers will move in."

◊ ◊ ◊

In the Panarin cosmology, California forms the heart of the Californian Republic, and will be a part of China or under Chinese influence, like Hong Kong.

Hawaii would suffer more or less the same fate, yielding either to China or to Japan.

Texas would form the stronghold of the Texas Republic, a region whose nine states would encompass what's now the Deep South, an area that would fall under Mexican control or influence.

Canada — *Canada!?* — would acquire control of a group of northern and central states dubbed the Central North American Republic.

Washington and New York would be part of Atlantic America, a group of states on the eastern seaboard that (Panarin says) could become part of the European Union. Oh, and Alaska will become a property of Russia.

"It would be reasonable for Russia to lay claim to Alaska," Panarin said. "It was part of the Russian Empire for a long time." Well, by all means, we do want to be *reasonable* about this, now, don't we?

For all the suggestions of dime-novel apocalypse Panarin summons for the United States in a year and a half, there's something even more disquieting than the forecast itself. It's not so much what he's saying as who he is saying it — he's speaking not as an academic or a scholar, but as a Russian, as a man who himself has witnessed in his own country the same disintegration he predicts for another. It's unspoken but implicit in his scenario: "we didn't think it would happen to *us*, either."

◊ ◊ ◊

For all of Panarin's chilling specificity, though, there's a lot he's overlooked. It's one thing to be a student of American economics; it's quite another to be a student of America.

Panarin's doomsday vision assumes that any attempt at foreign colonization by any foreign power would result in surrender. Panarin doesn't entertain the ways in which dogged American regional identities would coalesce in the cause of maintaining the central government necessary to remain a single nation.

The idea, for example, of Canada taking control of a portion of the United States as far south as Missouri, assumes Canada has a military strong enough, 18 months from now, to drive a thousand miles into the interior of this country without a serious fight. Canada has a standing armed forces of about 87,000 active and reserve personnel. There's more than that many people in Fargo, N.D., alone.

Texas taken by Mexico? We've been there before, and we know how that turned out. This time, expect Predators patrolling the skies over what's left of the old mission in San Antonio, and Abrams tanks outside. Alamo II. As chaotic as the U.S. posture might be in 18 months, it's hard to imagine the armed forces of Mexico prepared to exercise control over a region of nine states inhabited by people as fiercely proud of their independence as the Mexican people are proud of their own. People whose belief in the Second Amendment — the right to bear arms — is evidence of that independence.

California colonized by the Chinese? Not if Arnold Schwarzenegger is still in office.

Alaska re-taken by the Russians? Two words: Sarah Palin.

Seriously, what Panarin overlooks most of all are two facts of history it would seem impossible to ignore:

First, he ignores the shift in global economic dynamics that make the United States and Russia partners in a dance neither can get out of. The ways in which a global economy intermingles not just currencies but also circumstances aren't specific to the U.S. housing crisis, or the economic crisis that followed.

The Russian standard of living, steadily improving over the last decade, has done so largely using a benchmark of acquisitive, Western-style capitalism. An economic interdependence exists, one that suggests that if the United States dissolves, the potential is there for a shared fate. Panarin seems to sense this: "One could rejoice in that process," he said. "But if we're talking reasonably, it's not the best scenario —for Russia."

Second, and more important, Panarin apparently dismisses the same instincts for survival and self-definition that Napoleon and Hitler overlooked in their attempt to rule his country: the basic, innate, human resistance to domination by another.

Napoleon marched toward Russia with between 500,000 and 650,000 troops in June 1812; he wobbled back to France six months later with maybe 20,000 still alive. Hitler carpet-bombed Leningrad for almost 900 days, and look what good it did him; a year and five months later the Russian Army was raising the Russian flag over the Reichstag in Berlin.

For twenty years, the armies of North Vietnam fought a succession of armies, including that of the United States, in a drive to unify North and South Vietnam, ultimately defeating the greatest army in the world on the way to charting a destiny as one country, without foreign interference.

We'll have to revisit the predictions of the Moscow Strangelove a year from this June; we'll know for sure by then. Maybe before then, Panarin will introduce another variable to his scenario: the resistance factor: For all the internal strife that may characterize a country, for all the economic disasters that may come down, when survival and identity are at stake, never underestimate the ability of a nation's people to be the people of a Nation.

12/29/2008

MOVEMENT MUSIC: MOTOWN AT 50

IN JANUARY 1959, as Rev. Martin Luther King Jr. was refining the strategy and building the profile of the Southern Christian Leadership Conference, as Dick Clark's star-maker machinery recommended teen pop idols to airwaves on which African Americans were conspicuous by their absence, Detroit native Berry Gordy took an $800 family loan and started the process of transforming popular music.

Pop music, the civil rights movement and Motown—the company Gordy founded 50 years ago today—would dovetail over the next decade, as Motown came to both define the popular sound and create a spiritual soundtrack for the civil rights movement.

Motown wasn't the first black recording-industry vehicle. Other labels existed but failed to thrive: See-Bee Records, founded in 1922, disappeared in short order; Vee-Jay Records, launched in 1953, enjoyed some mainstream success (even a few early Beatles releases) but went bankrupt in 1966. For the most part, black artists were forced to record on white-owned labels that regarded their work as novelties, one-offs and curiosities. It was an ad hoc approach that both overlooked the wellspring of black American musical talent and underestimated the popular appeal for that music.

◊ ◊ ◊

When Gordy launched Motown Records (originally named Tamla), he capitalized on the growing popular fascination with black music, and the former Ford Motor Company worker would soon do it in assembly-line fashion, with a roster of talent big enough to definitively chronicle the vast diversity of "black music."

Early Motown songs didn't communicate the message of protest implicit in the civil rights movement, but the label's talents were hardly immune to the social agonies of the time. Between 1962 and 1965, the cream of the Motown roster, including the Miracles (with vocalist Smokey Robinson), the Temptations, Martha & the Vandellas, the Four Tops and the

Supremes, formed the Motortown Revue. They traveled by bus to perform at venues across America, including the Jim Crow South. There, they endured some of the same harrowing experiences as the early civil-rights activists moving through the region.

Early on, the message was never about sit-ins, riots and protests in the streets. But Motown—more as a spirit than a sound—was all of a piece with the civil rights movement in the way it carried and communicated itself to the wider world: witty, urbane, accessible, a conveyor of universal truths and desires and emotions that didn't care what color you were.

Gordy's fledgling company would capitalize on the changes in American society. With catchy songs and melodies, and thanks in part to Gordy's finishing-school technique of stagecraft, Motown acts held themselves up as behavioral models, the orchestrated, choreographed vision of poise and style.

That touch of class, the diversity of sounds under the Motown name, and the way those sounds captured the airwaves of urban America, were emblematic of what the civil-rights struggle really was: a resistance to being viewed as exceptions or pathological abstractions, a drive for black people to be perceived in the context of the American normal.

"Motown shaped the culture and did all the things that made the 1960s what they were," NAACP chairman Julian Bond told Vanity Fair last month. "So if you don't understand Motown and the influence it had on a generation of black and white young people, then you can't understand the United States, you can't understand America."

In time, the Motown sound made a shift to become the music of social conscience. The Supremes' "Love Child," a statement song tackling the stigma surrounding out-of-wedlock births, topped the charts in 1968; Edwin Starr's "War" (1970) launched a sonic assault on the Vietnam conflict; and Marvin Gaye's "What's Going On" and "Mercy Mercy Me (the Ecology)" (1971) helped elevate environmental awareness in the world of pop culture, as the first Earth Day had done in the political world the year before. In the 2002 book, Motown: Music, Money, Sex and Power, historian Gerald Posner quotes Gordy, who reveals a clear understanding of what Motown was capable of: "In all the camps there seemed to be one constant—Motown music," Gordy said. "They were all listening to it. Black and white. Militant and nonviolent. Anti-war demonstrators and the pro-war establishment."

This was Berry Gordy's assimilationist victory: producing music that emotionally resonated no matter where you were on the ideological spectrum.

◊ ◊ ◊

The Motown name, one of the most recognizable brands in the world, would come to represent numerous other stars. Fielding the work of stars from the Commodores to Rick James, from Boyz II Men to Brian McKnight, Motown adapted to the times as much as its artists helped define the music of the times.

For Edna Anderson-Owens, now co-CEO of the Gordy Company, the artists under the Motown banner were bigger than the sum of their parts. "I had come out of the civil-rights movement, had come from the South," Anderson-Owens, Gordy's administrative assistant in 1972, told Vanity Fair. "I never thought of [Motown] as just being a record company, even as an entertainment company. It was more than an entertainment company. In a sense, it replaced the civil-rights movement for me; it became another movement. It became more of a cause."

Thanks to Motown—and any number of other musicians remaking the popular idea of black music during one of the nation's most racially polarized eras—revolution wasn't just in the air. A revolution was on the air as well ... one you could dance to.

1/12/2009
As first performed on The Root

WE'LL BE SEEING YOU, NO. 6

THE ACTOR Patrick McGoohan died in Santa Monica, Calif., on Tuesday after a brief and undisclosed illness, at the age of 80. If you don't recognize the name, it might be understandable given the velocity and short attention span of the times. He hadn't worked in some time, no doubt a concession to advancing age and the relative absence of parts in Hollywood for actors with, uh, that much experience.

But in his prime, McGoohan brought consummate acting skills and a voice that could have made the phone book sound like Shakespeare to numerous roles in movies and on television, one in particular.

He first came to the attention of American TV viewers as "Secret Agent," in which he starred as John Drake, a British agent involved in various global intrigues. The series roughly dovetailed with the American fascination with espionage according to the 007 movies, followed by "The Avengers" and "The Man From U.N.C.L.E." series on the small screen. The show's theme song, "Secret Agent Man" by Johnny Rivers, became a pop music staple of the '60's.

◊ ◊ ◊

If McGoohan's career had gone no further than "Secret Agent," he might have been no more than a curious pop-culture footnote. But he went to produce, direct, write and star in a series that paved the way for television as a more daring and inventive medium than it had been before — in many ways, more daring than it's ever been since.

In 1967 McGoohan debuted in "The Prisoner," a series whose short life (it only ran for 17 episodes, from late 1967 to February 1968) belies its importance to the medium of television.

In the series, McGoohan plays a British agent who had been involved in various business in the service of Her Majesty. Fed up, the unnamed agent (Drake?) resigns from the service. On the day he quits, he rushes home to prepare to leave the country, ostensibly for a much-needed vacation. It's then the agent is drugged and spirited away to, well, a secret undisclosed location: a bucolic Village whose inhabitants are seemingly happy and inwardly resigned to their fate, despite their identities having been smudged, their names reduced to numbers.

They are prisoners, a fact never more obvious than when one tries to escape from this not-quite-idyllic situation, only to be pursued by large, white, balloon-like blobs that appeared from nowhere to chase the would-be escapee and induce a briefly suffocating paralysis.

As No. 6, McGoohan spent much of his time plotting his own escape, secretly huddling with others of the same fate and inclination — searching for a way out, a way to exit from a fate and a future that, however benign, was not of his choosing. Every week the show's opening sequence was punctuated with the following exchange, setting the storyline for newcomers:

No. 6: Where am I?
No. 2: In the Village.
No. 6: What do you want?
No. 2: Information.
No. 6: Whose side are you on?
No. 2: That would be telling. We want information ... information ... information.
No. 6: You won't get it.
No. 2: By hook or by crook ... we will.
No. 6: Who are you?
No. 2: The new No. 2.
No. 6: Who is No. 1?
No. 2: You are No. 6.

And then, No. 6's cri de coeur: "I am not a number ... I am a *free man!*"

◊ ◊ ◊

What might sound like a thin foundation for a television series was anything but. "The Prisoner" was and remains one of prime-time television's enduring existential statements, a show that raised issues of freedom, enslavement, conformity, identity and one's purpose in life that would find their way into entertainments from "The Truman Show" to the current hit TV series "Lost."

In a tribute published in May 2004, TV Guide noted that "[f]ans still puzzle over this weird, enigmatic drama, a Kafkaesque allegory about the individual's struggle in the modern age."

Part thriller, part science fiction, part Orwellian dystopia, "The Prisoner" changed the perception of prison, daring to propose the idea that incarceration need not be an exercise of iron bars and stone walls — that the deeper prisons are those of our own minds and imaginations.

"The Prisoner," which also starred a youngish Leo McKern as No. 2, was all of a piece with the obsession with Brit culture of the time; check the Village exteriors (shot in Wales) and No. 6's jacket, whose lapels (bordered in white piping) still scream "Briton on holiday!" today.

◊ ◊ ◊

McGoohan went on to other roles: starring in such films as "Ice Station Zebra," "Silver Streak," David Cronenberg's sci-fi cult classic "Scanners" (1981), and (in a clever turnabout) as the warden in "Escape From Alcatraz," with Clint Eastwood. He worked in television, from "Columbo" to "Mastepiece Theatre." More recently, and memorably, McGoohan starred opposite Mel Gibson in "Braveheart" (1995) portraying the 12th century Plantagenet King Edward I ("Longshanks"), conqueror of Wales and the nemesis of Scottish rebel William Wallace.

But for better or worse, McGoohan was "The Prisoner" to TV buffs and fans of cult television hits. The role was a kind of genial cement — a prison — for McGoohan, who never quite escaped the popular fascination for the series and his role in it. ("The Simpsons" even did a takeoff in 2000.)

But what a prison. Without his realizing it, "The Prisoner" set the bar high for television going forward, its sense of adventure and fun something that risk-averse, prime-time TV has rarely approached since.

That spirit of independence ran deep. In at least one episode, when confronted by a Village superior who demands his conformity to the new order around him, No. 6 utters his fully defining statement, and maybe McGoohan's own:

"I will not be pushed, filed, stamped, indexed, briefed, debriefed or numbered. My life is my own."

A fitting passion for his career; a worthy pursuit for our own lives.

1/14/2009

THE CHANGELING:
POP ICONOGRAPHY AND
BARACK OBAMA

ORGANICALLY — the way all real phenomena emerge, from a tsunami in the South Pacific to a nor'easter along the eastern seaboard — Barack Obama has become the first rock-star president of the United States. That fact is meaningless if you're not a fan of rock music, have no sense of its velocity into the wider culture, and don't believe that its erratic, flamboyant, unpredictable and potentially dangerous nature tells a story — maybe *the* story — of the postwar American dynamic.

But if you're at least open to rock culture's potential for social and cultural change, you can see how what's about to unfold in Washington five days from now will be the small-d democratic political expression of the same viral populism that's made rock, in the words of journalist Mikal Gilmore "such a great adventure and such a great disturbance in our culture, our arts, and our values."

◊ ◊ ◊

John F. Kennedy, for all his élan and youthful drive, could never have been the first rock-star president. His ascendancy, in fact the whole arc of his presidency, preceded many of the sensibilities of rock culture we embrace today, and overlooked most of the others. The cultural dimensions of Kennedy's presidency owed more to Palm Springs and Boston than to Muscle Shoals or the Mississippi Delta. Of all the myriad figures of culture high and low that attended the celebrated Kennedy inaugural gala, there wasn't a rocker in the house.

It's been widely thought that the title rightly belonged to Bill Clinton, the saxophone-wielding, Ray-Banned politician who Elvised his way into the White House almost a generation ago. But Clinton's relentless and improbable rise to the presidency, while it had its insurgent moments, didn't really have insurgent origins. For Clinton, and not least of all because of his race,

301

his presidential campaign borrowed from rock 'n' roll when it suited the campaign. The unpredictable (and therefore uncontrollable) aspects of rock culture were something he only dabbled in, capably but occasionally.

When he takes the office on Tuesday, Barack Obama becomes fully the beneficiary of the kind of pop-cultural iconography our culture has granted to only a few, to fewer still who were African American and, to this point, to no one who's been president. Like Elvis Presley, Bob Dylan and the Beatles, the next president has already attained a place in the iconosphere that, ironically, transcends the office itself.

Think of it in visual terms: Any U.S. president of modern times except Bill Clinton would have been a fitting subject for a portrait by Yousef Karsh. Clinton's portrait, of course, would be done by Annie Leibovitz. If he were still alive, Obama's portrait would be done by Andy Warhol — one of those legendary multi-panel works, with different interpretations of the same image awash in color and Warhol's jagged, freewheeling swatches and squiggles that vividly alluded to the energy and mystery of the subject on the canvas. (The work of Obama portraitist Shepard Fairey stands in nicely.)

◊ ◊ ◊

Obama's campaign exhibited a sense of rock style and immediacy that wasn't grafted on at the last minute; the rebel aspects of the rock esthetic were basic to the campaign. From the audacity of even running to the grassroots proliferation of a wildly successful Web-based fundraising apparatus to a primary-season soundtrack that spanned Motown and U2, Barack Obama brought rock 'n' roll to politics and politics to rock 'n' roll. Signed, sealed and delivered.

As with that of the music's best ambassadors, Obama's appeal finally spilled over the banks of the adoration of the early adopters, arriving more widely into our everyday world. The folks at Ben & Jerry's, whose brands of ice cream have been their own toothsome salute to movers & shakers (a scoop of Cherry Garcia, anyone?), have recently released Yes Pecan, the Vermont company's tribute to the 44th president.

And the artists and writers at Marvel Comics, discovering that Obama was a fan of Spider-Man comic books when he was a kid, have put him on the cover of at least half the run of the latest Spider-Man edition. The run's expected to sell out in … well, damn, guess what? They're already gone.

The challenge — the political danger — for Obama isn't so much in maintaining this level of adulation as much as maintaining this level of passion and energy on behalf of a wider social purpose. He said it many times during the campaign: that his bid for the American presidency was less about him than it was about all of us — U.S.

◊ ◊ ◊

There's a downside to pop iconography; it can be suddenly, weirdly perishable, subject to dissipation when least expected. A misstep real or perceived, one false move on the high wire and … in an instant, the Ben & Jerry's ice cream isn't selling anymore.

Even though Obama has more convincingly wed the right-now! aspects of pop culture to the more procedurally-driven ways of politics than anyone in American history, it doesn't mean the marriage won't have its frictions.

Some fissures between Obama and his earliest supporters farthest on the left have emerged, with them crying "abandonment!" saying he's walked away from the core principles that won their votes and got him elected — failing to see the distinctions between campaigning and governing, roughly the difference between playing in Washington Square Park and Carnegie Hall.

Americans are an impatient and fickle lot, and they will demand results — especially from a candidate who adopted one of the simplest words in the language as the central plank in his political platform. Change is now more than a campaign meme or part of a slogan; it's what the country will expect, and the sooner, the more tangible, the better.

We just hope this country's patient as Obama adjusts to his new role on a bigger stage. We hope they'll cut a brother a break while he tunes up, does a mic check and hits that first chord with a band he's never worked with before, in front of an audience the size of a nation.

The house lights go down on Tuesday. Rock 'n' roll.

1/15/2009

GOODBYE, FAREWELL & AMEN

UNLESS, of course, they've undertaken a coup d'etat overnight and subverted the United States Constitution again, George Bush and Dick Cheney are only hours from passing the torch of the national executive to Barack Obama and Joe Biden, formalizing what we've known for far too long: the Republican business model of presidential politics is a thing of the past.

In the morning — that great gettin' up morning — about nine hours from now, Barack Obama will take the oath of office as the 44th President of the United States and begin the process of dismantling the damage done by the Bush administration.

Much of that damage done by Crew Bush #43 was attitudinal, a different way of thinking about the United States' place in the modern world. And that damage to the nation's sense of itself, its well-being, its future, may be the worse damage of all.

For Bush & Cheney, there was finally no real strategy, no overarching theme beyond control and leverage for the sake of a gauzy, ill-defined and needlessly belligerent set of principles whose imposition drained the national treasury and alienated the greatest nation in the world *from* the world.

◊ ◊ ◊

We'll miss the phrase "axis of evil," that curious mix of words — the stuff of Churchill and World War II (and what would have been a great title for a Motley Crüe release). That twist of language set the emotional pretext for global aggression. It was the first sign of the Bush Doctrine, the principles formally lashed together in a National Security Council paper and published in September 2002 — a testament to unilateral and pre-emptive belligerence against any country even slightly considered a threat to the United States.

"Our security will require transforming the military you will lead — a military that must be ready to strike at a moment's notice in any dark corner of the world," President Bush told cadets at West Point in June 2002. "And our security

305

will require all Americans to be forward-looking and resolute, to be ready for pre-emptive action when necessary to defend our liberty and to defend our lives."

With that distillation of intent, the Bush administration lurched the nation into a war that continues, at a ruinous cost of our fortune, our standing, our precious human lives. What a legacy, guys.

◊ ◊ ◊

We'll miss that cute thing they did with the shredder and the Constitution, effectively suspending habeas corpus for inmates in a prison in Cuba, and doing it on the flimsiest of pretexts. We can't forget the way they manipulated the language, turning "prisoners" into "detainees." Or how they legitimized the phrase "War on Terror," a meaningless sobriquet whose objective is utterly unattainable.

We remember how they enabled one Attorney General who fired U.S. Attorneys on purely political grounds, and enabled another Attorney General who refused to call the torture of those "detainees" for what it was.

Their policy of wide-open economic deregulation contributed to a corporate gigantism that backfired badly on Wall Street, and a liberalization of credit access that lured impressionable Americans eager for the storied American Dream of homeownership into improvisational mortgages whose terms would ultimately break them, and shatter that dream for them, and millions of other people besides.

And after Hurricane Katrina, the single most devastating domestic meteorological event in modern times, the federal agency that should have made a difference in the aftermath, if not been prepared for the aftermath *before* the storm arrived, was a woeful evidence of Keystone Kops miscommunication presided over by a feckless administrator who couldn't find his ass in the Category 5 windstorm that cost too many people their lives.

All while the president did a flyover in Air Force One. And some of the poorest people in this nation were scattered by the water to the four winds, left to wonder if their government ever really gave a good goddamn. Like a lot of the rest of us.

And we were witness to a kind of swaggering cluelessness through the last eight years of the Bush-Cheney tandem; a cowboy rhetoric that put the deadly earnest business of modern warfare in the language of the dime-novel Western; a belligerence of style that saw the president manhandling the German Chancellor; a brandished backwardness with which the leader of the free world would bring his own wife to India and not even take her to see the Taj Mahal.

◊ ◊ ◊

Bush & Cheney. They left a lot of broken things in their wake, like the sloppy owners of the house who turn a mansion into a fixer-upper before handing over the keys. They nurtured a divisiveness and unease in the country that've managed to spill into every facet of our lives, from the economic to the cultural, the religious to the racial.

We're the heirs to their world view, and a trillion-dollar deficit, a housing market in free fall, a stock market in coma, a badly and needlessly tarnished international reputation, and an overall malaise they've done nothing to prevent or overcome. Not bad for eight years' work.

Let's raise a glass to Bush & Cheney — phrasally wed forever, like Laurel & Hardy. Or Mick & Keith. Or Archie & Jughead. It's them that brought us to where we are today, ladies and gentlemen. Remember them. And thank your personal Gods: In the morning, we won't have them to kick *us* around anymore.

1/19/2009

THE WHOLE WORLD IN HIS HANDS

W E'VE known this was coming for ten weeks now, and still, when it happened, the capacity for surprise and wonder and tears was very much intact. Today was one of those signal American moments, maybe The Signal American Moment: remarkable not because we recognized it, but precisely because we never have before. This is the terra incognita our nation was meant to be. This is, now, finally, the America that America has been waiting for.

When Barack Hussein Obama took the oath of office as the 44th president of the United States of America, the nation shifted in its foundation; its spiritual longitude, its emotional latitude were in a different place than the day before. Even as he took an oath that confirmed the vitality of some of our bedrock American certainties, his very presence as president called other sure things into question. The country thought it had the racial arithmetic, the calculus of individual achievement, all figured out. And now *this*.

And for African Americans, the descendants of the slaves who built the house he will now occupy for the next four years, today represents a psychic dividing line, a clear line of demarcation between one world view and another. The late Arthur C. Clarke might have envisioned something like this for a science-fiction novel: a day on which the future announces itself in breathtaking fashion; a world in which people long accustomed to being warmed and nourished by one sun woke up one morning to find, inexplicably, a second sun in the sky.

◊ ◊ ◊

The challenges facing Obama, and the country, are vast and serious: two foreign wars, one of them totally unnecessary; a disastrous economy; a domestic housing crisis that's sapped the energy and confidence of millions of homeowners; business closing at a rampant pace; and a physical and emotional infrastructure in need of serious repair.

But with all of that, despite all of that ... something in Obama, some happy collision of personal narrative, delivery of message and urgency of the hour, have made him the symbol of our aspirations in what may be the world's most desperate and dangerous era. His innate sense of confidence. An infectious sense of possibility. His almost-otherworldly calm. A smile that could launch the careers of a thousand dental hygienists.

It's these intangibles that, ironically enough, are a currency as valuable as any amount of money, any elaborate fiscal policy. That'll come — the hard numbers will be on the table, preferably sooner rather than later. But for now, the unity he's inspired in a broke, bone-weary, oratorically impoverished nation is enough.

The first stimulus package Barack Obama's delivered to the American people is Barack Obama himself.

◊ ◊ ◊

For black Americans, the inauguration of Barack Obama happily endangers the bifurcated identity they've known in this country for generations — the "two-ness" of black identity brilliantly lamented by W.E.B. DuBois in "The Souls of Black Folk." That two-ness for black America was a sense of isolation encountered in "a world which yields him no true self-consciousness, but only lets him see himself through the revelation of the other world. It is a peculiar sensation, this double-consciousness, this sense of always looking at one's self through the eyes of others, of measuring one's soul by the tape of a world that looks on with amused contempt and pity."

With a President Obama, those double strands of black American identity have merged, convincingly and totally. As president, Obama ratifies the realization of a dream whose depth in the black psyche ran deeper than Martin Luther King or even DuBois could know: the dream to be fully African American *and* American. Barack Obama didn't bring African Americans into the mainstream. His rise to the presidency widely announces what we've always known: they *are* the mainstream.

◊ ◊ ◊

This emotional stimulus doesn't stop at the water's edge. The cable networks showed feeds from other networks around the world: BBC, al-Jazeera and others recording how the world greeted the news: parties in Paris and London; quietly cautious optimism in Tehran; street dances in Kenya; cheering in Indonesia, the world's most populous Muslim nation.

All this global big fun has nothing to do with policies and practice, and everything to do with perception. But underestimate perception at your peril. Not for nothing did Time magazine recently portray Obama as a physical surrogate for Franklin Delano Roosevelt.

The president's ability to impart a sense of the possible is especially, necessarily directed at Americans, black Americans in particular. But that message is resonating around the world right now. The world is waiting, already more inspired and hopeful than they've had any reason to be for the last eight years.

Obama's gifts — rhetorical, intellectual, political, emotional — may serve him as well as FDR's did, in a time at least as dangerous as FDR's was. Chief among those gifts is one that's both the most ephemeral and the most important. It's the ability to communicate a crucial rule of recovery — for a patient, an economy, a nation, a world: The first step to getting better is believing you will.

1/20/2009

THE MOVERS ARE HERE:
OBAMA ASSUMES THE PRESIDENCY

I T'S the most unlikely, but most necessary visual evidence of the ritual of our orderly American transfer of power: For all the majesty of the transition of the awesome duties and leverages of the residents of the White House, sooner or later, somehow it all just comes down to a moving van.

For a moment at 1600 Pennsylvania Avenue, it looked like a scene from Anywhere U.S.A. The Ryder truck, the boxes, the obvious sense of something going on. It was as symbolic of a major change in America as any you could think of, and also a moment straight out of everyday life. *Honey, the movers are here.*

But on Tuesday, the real movers were 1.2 miles away, outside the United States Capitol amid a crowd of perhaps 2 million people. And at 12:05 ET on a dazzlingly bright January afternoon, the prime mover, Barack Hussein Obama, took the oath of office as the 44th President of the United States.

As the high point of an inaugural ceremony and days of festivities that looked and sounded like America, in a speech that borrowed from Roosevelt, Lincoln and Scripture, the son of Kenya and Kansas called on the nation to move its mindset, to re-imagine itself and its possibilities, and to renew a commitment to self-sacrifice in a time of challenge.

"Today I say to you that the challenges we face are real. They are serious and they are many. They will not be met easily or in a short span of time. But know this, America — they will be met. On this day, we gather because we have chosen hope over fear, unity of purpose over conflict and discord.

"On this day, we come to proclaim an end to the petty grievances and false promises, the recriminations and worn-out dogmas that for far too long have strangled our politics."

The former Illinois senator, who opposed the ruinous Iraq war from the beginning, similarly called on the world to re-imagine America, not as the belligerent cowboy bristling with weapons and cowboy rhetoric — the one we've been for the last eight years — but again as a force for principle and for good.

"Recall that earlier generations faced down fascism and communism not just with missiles and tanks, but with sturdy alliances and enduring convictions," the president said. "They understood that our power alone cannot protect us, nor does it entitle us to do as we please. Instead, they knew that our power grows through its prudent use; our security emanates from the justness of our cause, the force of our example, the tempering qualities of humility and restraint."

And President Obama — how damn fine it is to write that — put both the nation and the world on notice. Let the word go forth, the nation's fifth-youngest president seemed to say, we're back in the ideals business.

◊ ◊ ◊

That's not to dismiss the challenges that lie ahead. An online survey released Jan. 18 shows that U.S. foreign policy is favored by only two of 21 countries. India and Poland were the only nations with majorities giving favorable ratings of the United States. Clearly, one of the Obama administration's most pressing international challenges (besides Iraq and Afghanistan, and the just-ended hot war in the Middle East) is restoring America's moral and cultural world standing — its "soft power" of artful, congenial diplomacy; recognition of humanitarian and ecological concerns; and the intangible but very concrete benefits of a still-popular popular culture.

And the hard and fast realities of coming to grips with the greatest economic crisis since the Great Depression will visit the Obama administration soon enough. A housing and foreclosure crisis, a stock market in constant decline, and a host of hungry global trading partners will make economic concerns Job No. 1 at the Obama White House.

But in his first address to a nation President Obama addressed the diversities of people here at home, not in the context of a never-ending problem but as an indelible possibility.

"For we know that our patchwork heritage is a strength, not a weakness," he said Tuesday. "We are a nation of Christians and Muslims, Jews and Hindus — and non-believers. We are shaped by every language and culture, drawn from every end of this Earth; and because we have tasted the bitter swill of civil war and segregation, and emerged from that dark chapter stronger and more united, we cannot help but believe that the old hatreds shall someday pass; that the lines of tribe shall soon dissolve; that as the world grows smaller, our common humanity shall reveal itself; and that America must play its role in ushering in a new era of peace."

Within those powerful diversities, the new president said, is a better way forward. "We remain a young nation, but in the words of Scripture, the time has come to set aside childish things. The time has come to reaffirm our enduring spirit; to choose our better history; to carry forward that precious gift, that noble idea, passed on from generation to generation: the God-given promise that all are equal, all are free, and all deserve a chance to pursue their full measure of happiness."

Despite everything about to come at him with full force, there's no escaping the ways in which Obama's sense of style, irrepressible optimism and personal vigor have already transformed the presidency. With he and First Lady Michelle Obama (it's damn fine to write that, too) as the first occupants of the White House with young children since the Kennedys, 1600 Pennsylvania Avenue will be a scene of youthful energy and spirit of joy, if not downright playfulness, it hasn't seen in years.

He'll bring that optimism and style to the serious work to be done. "In reaffirming the greatness of our nation, we understand that greatness is never a given," the president said. "It must be earned. Our journey has never been one of short cuts or settling for less. It has not been the path for the faint-hearted — for those who prefer leisure to work, or seek only the pleasures of riches and fame. Rather, it has been the risk-takers, the doers, the makers of things — some celebrated, but more often men and women obscure in their labor, who have carried us up the long, rugged path towards prosperity and freedom."

That journey has begun again with an African American at the helm of the greatest nation in the world, at a time of the greatest challenges that nation has ever faced. But today the nation rejoices in its possibilities, in the brilliantly unpredictable people and events that drive the American dynamic.

With the inauguration of the 44th American president, we celebrate (maybe for the first time) the real meaning of democracy — that a skinny biracial kid with an unlikely resume and an Islamic middle name can become the leader of the United States … that that same leader can move us to tears, then cheers, then action on behalf of the nation and the world.

The movers are here, alright. Somebody say Amen.

1/21/2009
Published in TheLoop21

THE AGE OF UBIQUITY

YOU'VE seen it for years and you see it today in television advertising, in the movies, in news reports and still photographs: the black or minority man or woman literally on the edge of the frame, last in a visual series, on or near the very periphery of the visual space you're looking at. On the margins.

This is no accident. It's become such a basic aspect of our culture that its composition is rarely questioned, and infrequently tweaked. But it's a passive kind of poison: You can't see people who look like you constantly shunted to the visual sidelines without being affected by it.

The practice isn't as bad, as pervasive as it used to be; years of fitful advances by minorities in the studios and newsrooms and ad agencies of America have seen to that. But it's still one of the more corrosive features of our relentless teleculture.

It's going to be real hard to do that for the next four years. That formula changed permanently on Election Night 2008, and it changed again on Inauguration Day. Barack Obama has completed the long process of moving African Americans, and minorities generally, to a place among the larger pixels of American culture.

The word "pixels" isn't dropped casually. It speaks to the way the visual is our main avenue for communication. We prioritize what's important by what we see, how often we see it, and how much we pay attention to it, whether it's on the flat-screen in the living room or a billboard on the highway. It's how we order things of interest, influence, impact. Who's that on the box, what's he saying? Check it out. What the face says might be important. Especially if it's the president's face.

That face on television, online and in magazines and newspapers. That face we see every day as an index to what's crucial, maybe indispensable to the national life.

That face has never been a black face before. It is now, and will be for at least the next four years.

That fact changes the definition — the benchmark — of American normality. Forever.

The real moments of American self-discovery can't be withdrawn or undone or reversed on appeal. Obama's inauguration as president was one such moment. With the dignity of the office and a felicitous irony, it ratified what may be, vis-à-vis race, a central emotional principle of participatory democracy: You're not on the margins anymore when the President of the United States looks like you.

◊ ◊ ◊

African Americans have come close to this cultural ubiquity before. It's a fact for black people over a certain age, those who remember growing up in households where the triptych images of John F. Kennedy, Robert F. Kennedy and Rev. Martin Luther King Jr. hung on the walls or adorned the mantels. For many elders it was a kind of personal iconography; for a lot of folks in the 60's and 70's, these men were the accessible saints, the contemporary North Stars of our moral compass.

King had a divinely inspired capacity for summoning this nation to honor its basic principles, but all of King's transformative career occurred before the advent of modern television and the Internet. President Obama's ubiquity in American life will transcend King's own, because of the social advances that King made possible, the political advances Obama made possible, and the technological advances America made possible.

All due respect to Roland Burris, the new junior senator from Illinois, but he's not the self-described "magic man." President Obama is. The nation's new chief executive, everywhere at once, the elected arbiter of all things American, the baseline standard for our lives. The automatic normal.

And black people have never been in that situation before. This is new and exciting and maybe even faintly terrifying.

Oh, the presidential honeymoon will end. Bet that. Those ads for victory plates and presidential coins won't be on TV forever. The realities of the job will settle on that greyhound Obama frame; the challenges once theoretical and now real will hasten the appearance of the salt-and-pepper hair we know he's been hiding with Just For Men.

◊ ◊ ◊

And for too many millions of black and minority Americans, Obama's elevation to the presidency is no panacea. Nothing changes for those without work, in danger of foreclosure, recently laid off, under threat of being laid off. The panoply of social pathologies we are heir to and those we take on ourselves won't vanish. Theirs are lives already challenged everyday.

But even so, now for African Americans especially, there's something special that wasn't there before. There's a charge in the air that wasn't there before, a different fact of the undercurrent of our lives. It's what you tell yourself: A black man is running the country, a man who's made a pledge to make things better. Got to get up off this couch, out of these doldrums, away from this funk. *A black man is running the country*.

And as time passes, that's when it gets really, wonderfully interesting: when the newness of this ubiquitous moment wears off, and Barack Obama becomes to the American people as a leader what blacks and minorities have always sought to be to America as people: Not three-fifths of anything, but whole and sufficient. Not peripheral, but central. John Q. Citizen. Jane Q. Citizen. Everyday people. The automatic normal.

1/22/2009

COMIC RELIEF IN THE OBAMA AGE

CHANGE. While it's the word and spirit of the moment for the nation and the world, it has trickled more slowly into the world of comic books. Ethnic integration of characters in one of the legendary comic-book series hasn't been exactly faster than a speeding bullet. But this month, Superman, the granddaddy of them all, has finally, fully come around.

Some 37 years after the first African-American character was depicted in the celebrated comic-book series, created in 1933 by Jerry Siegel and Joe Shuster, DC Comics has released a Superman comic book with characters whose appearance fully announces Krypton as a racially integrated planet.

Can someone say Obama effect?

Issue No. 683, released around the first of the year, features a story line in which 100,000 Kryptonians with powers like Superman arriving on earth—some of them non-white Kryptonians.

◊ ◊ ◊

The Superman shift is a departure from the Man of Steel's past, back in the intergalactic day when blacks on Krypton resided on Vathlo Island, the "Home of a Highly Developed Black Race"— a curious parallel to the era of segregation in the United States, despite its location on another world.

The first Kryptonian of color made an appearance in 1971, long after the advent of the civil rights movement and advances in other genres of popular culture. "In issue 239, a two-page map showed that Kryptonians of color had an island all to themselves, which is pretty embarrassing," said Mark Waid, an expert in Superman arcana and periodic DC Comics writer, in Newsarama.com, a Web site devoted to science fiction and fantasy.

"It wasn't until the mid-70s, when more 'World of Krypton' back-up stories ran more regularly, that we really saw any ethnicity whatsoever on the planet," Waid said.

A true comic-book aficionado, Waid defends the omission as one might expect: It was an oversight borne of the '30s-era habits and experiences of creators Siegel and Shuster, and of those writers and artists who followed.

But it's inescapable that such an omission, well into the period of African Americans and minorities in the mainstream of American life, sent the message that comic books without blacks and minorities represented some idealized realm, an alternate world without the thorny, complicating issue of race.

Thankfully, earlier comic-book depictions were more in tune with reality. In Marvel Comics' Spider-Man series, launched in 1962, Joseph "Robbie" Robertson was the black editor in chief of the Daily Bugle, where Peter Parker (aka Spider-Man) worked as a photographer. Robertson, the rational right-hand man of the erratic publisher J. Jonah Jameson, was a trailblazer: one of the first meaningful black characters in mainstream comics.

◊ ◊ ◊

For years, the Nick Fury comic-book series, also published by Marvel, featured Sgt. Fury and the rough-and-ready Howling Commandos, one of whom was Gabriel Jones, the squad's sole African-American member, who played a horn before battles during World War II. Jones debuted in the series in 1963.

And the character of John Stewart, a former Marine, was the first African-American Green Lantern, debuting in DC Comics in late 1971.

Marvel has taken point most recently on the issue in a way that's certain to build its comic-book sales by capitalizing on the cresting wave of Obamamania.In issue 583 of Amazing Spider-Man, Marvel will present a bonus story about Barack Obama, a nod to the new president's childhood fascination with comic books. About half the publication run ($3.99 each copy) features Obama on the cover with the Webslinger.

"How great is that? The commander in chief to be is actually a nerd in chief," Joe Quesada, Marvel's editor-in-chief

Michael E. Ross

Quesada, told the AP. "It was really, really cool to see that we had a geek in the White House. We're all thrilled with that."

Spidey's hookup with the 44th president and Superman's encounter with Kryptonians who don't look like him are just more examples of the ways real life moves in on our popular culture, how pop culture takes its cues, if not its oxygen, from society—often years later than it should have.

◊ ◊ ◊

Blacks in comic-book roles have moved into that other outlet of the popular imagination: the movies. Halle Berry starred as Storm in two of the highly successful "X-Men" films, based on the celebrated Marvel-comic franchise.

And last February, MTV News reported that rapper Common (who's proven his acting chops in "American Gangster" and the upcoming "Terminator Salvation") had been cast for the role of Green Lantern in a film whose production has lurched forward by fits and starts.

They're all concessions to the fact that—this just in—black people have fantasy lives, too.

It's just wonderfully ironic that now, almost two generations after Superman first discovered black America, the nation as a whole has found and embraced a superhero who's transcended the pages of comic books. Spider-Man's sidekick in chief of the moment, that darker figure of flesh and blood who took the oath of office on Tuesday, must now take on demons and monsters the comic-book world never imagined.

1/23/2009
As first performed on The Root

MENDING GLOBAL FENCES

HE'S been president of the United States for all of 200 hours, give or take, and Barack Obama has been busy frustrating the critics and the professional polwatchers who keep thinking they know his every move.

The Guantánamo closure announcement, for example, was completely expected, the fulfillment of a longstanding Obama campaign pledge.

It's what came next that caught people off guard: an action thick with an inescapable symbolism, one with possibly unbelievable dividends. On Monday President Obama conducted his first formal one-on-one interview with a major news organization, but it wasn't granted to one of the Multiple Wise Men at the American broadcast or cable nets, or to Katie Couric at CBS.

President Obama sat in the White House with Hisham Melhem, Washington bureau chief for al-Arabiya, a Saudi-supported TV news channel based in Dubai, and a news organization with mainstream standing in the Muslim world.

The alphabet networks of the United States were left standing with their eyes against the keyhole of the Oval Office door, while inside that office, the leader of the United States put the concerns and fears of the Muslim world front and center.

This latest break with modern presidential tradition wasn't so much a diss of the U.S. media as it was a bid for reasserting a telegenic, conciliatory American presence on the world stage. The president took his case as a world leader directly to the world's Muslims, presenting the United States as a nation willing to act again as an honest broker (and in sharp distinction from the last eight years, an *involved* honest broker) in the interminable Israeli-Palestinian conflict; to begin the process of ending U.S. military presence in Iraq; and to continue the healing begun, however symbolically, when Obama ordered Gitmo closed.

It was an olive branch attached to a powerful message: the days of reflexive marginalization of Muslims, by a government bent on ostracizing and criminalizing them, are over.

321

Obama's was also a personal message for the other everyday people of the Middle East. "I have Muslim members of my family. I have lived in Muslim countries. ... My job to the Muslim world is to communicate that Americans are not your enemy," the president said in an act of outreach that would have been unthinkable under the Bush regime. "[T] he same respect and partnership that America had with the Muslim world as recently as 20, 30 years ago, there's no reason we can't restore that."

"My job is to communicate the fact that the United States has a stake in the well-being of the Muslim world, that the language we use has to be a language of respect," Obama said.

After his exclusive, Melhem told Time.com he was touched by the president. "You can feel the authenticity about him," he told the Web site of Time magazine. "The interview was his way of saying, 'There is a new wind coming from Washington.' Barack Obama definitely sees the world differently from a man named George W. Bush."

As they concluded the interview and shook hands, Melhem recalled, Obama told him, "There will be more."

◊ ◊ ◊

The bipartisan aspect that is shaping the Obama administration may also slowly be yielding political dividends; there's reason to believe that hands-across-the-water can mean hands-across-the-aisle, too.

Vin Weber, a former Minnesota Republican congressman who advised the Obama White House on Middle East relations, gave the new president high marks for his appearance.

"There are decades and decades of skepticism of the West ingrained in psyches in people of the Arab world, and that's not going to change on a dime simply because we have a new president," Weber told the National Journal Online.

"What we have is an opening, an opportunity to change the minds of people," Weber said. "And I think the president has taken the right first steps, and if they see that we're persistent and consistent, I think that we can slowly, over time, change minds."

◊ ◊ ◊

The specter of terrorism was addressed by the president in ways that made some in the U.S. media recall President Bush's tendency to demonize. Obama used the word "nervous" to describe the al-Qaida leadership (and Melhem agreed with Obama's assertion, using the word himself), and the president described al-Qaida's ideas as "bankrupt."

It put some wags in mind of Bush's swaggering "bring 'em on" and "dead or alive" comments during the height of the Iraq war. But there was more at work in Obama's comments.

Steve Clemons, the publisher of the foreign policy blog The Washington Note, got the wider implications. "What's important to understand — which George Bush never did understand — is that terrorists are actually political actors trying to achieve legitimacy in the eyes of certain publics. And Obama, rather than just trying to kill terrorists … is trying to steal their audience."

◊ ◊ ◊

All due props to Clemons, but President Obama is doing more than that. With this overture to the mainstream sensibilities of ordinary people in the Muslim world, the president has begun the process of depriving terrorists of the emotional oxygen required for terrorism to flourish.

His tone, his personality, his experience and his ethnicity all combine to undercut the rhetoric of separation without which terrorism cannot survive. This is an early indicator of the global reassertion of America's values and character — what Atlantic columnist Andrew Sullivan has called this nation's "soft power" of diplomacy and culture.

Beyond the impact of an unprecedented interview seen around the world, the world's sense of Obama as conciliator may already trickling into the global psyche:

Last week Agence France-Presse reported that a barber in Khartoum, Sudan, a man who had recently opened a barbershop in the city, named the shop for Barack Obama, adorning the façade of the shop with the likeness of the American president.

"I opened the shop just before the U.S. presidential election in November, but I waited for Obama's victory before naming it after the president-elect," said the shop owner, Muntasser Jacob. "If the Republican John McCain had won the election I would not have named my shop after him."

When fences are torn down, around the neighborhood or around the world, they're rebuilt one hammer and nail at a time.

1/28/2009

'KIND OF BLUE' AT 50

IT'S ONE of those records that's been around for so long, been so thoroughly a part of the furniture of our culture and our lives, it seems like it's *always* been there, like the air we breathe or the sunrise we take for granted, a sound that captures everything, the full range of our emotions, without a word being spoken.

"Kind of Blue," Miles Davis' lapidary classic of jazz, celebrates its 50th anniversary this year as something kind of immortal, one of those records that's managed the rare and difficult dance of being a part of its time and our time — whenever "our time" might be.

In its five tracks, some of the most accomplished talents of the jazz world set down music — spare but animated, lean but muscular — that's a celebration of serendipity, of kismet, of the straight-up good luck that happens when everything just falls together.

◊ ◊ ◊

That seemed to happen a lot for music in 1959. Motown was launched early that year; less than six months later the year welcomed the Grammy Awards, the recording industry's salute to the industry's best (according to the industry). Charles Mingus' signature record "Mingus Ah Um" was released, combining the mercurial bassist's post-bop sensibilities, lush Ellingtonian band arrangements and a feel for the urban drive that animated the nation in another landmark recording.

But Miles was *really* feeling it that year. When Davis gathered with his sidemen at Columbia Records' 30th Street Studio on March 2, 1959, he was riding high on the creative wave that had already led to "Miles Ahead," its own classic, the year before; the same wave that would lead to "Sketches of Spain" at the end of a crowded '59.

Miles could be irascible and confrontational, he did not suffer fools gladly, but he had long since developed a talent for detecting talent, for recognizing the best that was within the other musicians around him. That's nowhere more evident than on "Kind of Blue."

Miles was joined principally by bedrock bass player Paul Chambers, drummer Jimmy Cobb, the pianist Bill Evans, an old hand of sessions with Miles; and the battery of Julian "Cannonball" Adderley on alto sax and the immortal John Coltrane on tenor sax. (Wynton Kelly, a former sideman with Dizzy Gillespie, performed on one track.)

He'd worked with most of these musicians before, but what resulted on "Kind of Blue" was an ironic combination of a freshness borne of familiarity, the happiest of accidents.

◊ ◊ ◊

Listen to the opening track, "So What," the opening 10-note sequence as recognizable as anything in jazz. As the group coalesces around the melody, Davis pulls back on the throttle … and we're cleared for takeoff, soaring on a beat and melody that thrives on economy rather than flash, an understated virtuosity.

It's counter-intuitive to think of a full emotional palette being possible on as few as five songs, but "Kind of Blue" displays a range of emotions with a depth and richness of spirit that not many recordings have approached since. The humor of "Freddie Freeloader" (with Kelly on piano) gives way to the introspective "Blue in Green," with Miles in fine form as a soloist, questioning and plaintive.

"All Blues," an 11-minute classic within a classic, finds the group in a balanced, upbeat groove with Adderley and Coltrane playing some of their most inspired solos. And on "Flamenco Sketches," the power, the majesty of this group becomes truly evident in a quietly confident sound whose components fit together like the parts of a fine Swiss watch.

Here the solo performances — those places in a song that can arouse the temptation for musicians to show off, with displays of dexterity often as impenetrable as they are unnecessary — are moving in unanticipated ways. The solos follow logically, one following another; they're marvels of economy, a musical tribute to the idea that "less is more."

It all yields a musical document that — a rare thing — found favor with critics, other musicians and the public at large, a record that led Miles biographer Eric Nisenson to call "Kind of Blue" "one of the most important, as well as sublimely beautiful albums in the history of jazz."

◊ ◊ ◊

All fine art outlives its creators. We hear this music from 50 winters ago; once the work of ordinary men, now it's mostly the work of ghosts just above our heads. Jimmy Cobb, the drummer on every track of the album, is the leader of the So What Band, currently observing the record's golden anniversary. He's the last surviving member of the sextet that changed jazz, and music, forever.

Coltrane left us in 1967. Chambers died in 1969; Kelly in 1971, Adderley passed in 1975, Evans exited in 1980, and Miles himself died in California in the fall of 1991.

In the intervening years we've been witness to rock music's pre-eminence in the culture, the insurgency of rap and hip-hop, and any number of other musical styles that flash on the scene for a hot minute and then vanish.

But "Kind of Blue" endures, a modal, bluesy sequoia of jazz from a departed soul of music and his comrades in melody, an indelible gift to keep life thoughtful, rueful, soulful, joyful for those of us still on this side of the stars.

2/5/2009

NOTE TO THE PRESIDENT: TAKE THE SHOT

THE GREAT novelist and essayist John Edgar Wideman once observed that basketball, as best and most faithfully practiced, is an act of athletic levitation, a game performed in the air. When he wrote this, in an essay published in Esquire years ago, he was speaking of basketball, the literal, actual game. Perhaps he couldn't have seen the dance and bruise and flight of the game in a political context. And he couldn't have seen you coming, Barack Obama. No one did.

We've lived and breathed with you all through this brilliant career. You went from playing on the courts at the projects to slinging the rock with the pros at breathtaking speed. Primary after primary, you drained it from the top of the key or took it to the hole like nobody's business. And against all odds, you won the championship. And you did it, you played the game in the air, on your terms.

You've been making history from day one. And it's time to make some more.

◊ ◊ ◊

There is a quietly building chorus of Democratic leadership in Congress — less than a consensus but more than a few — calling for an investigation into the panorama of illegalities by the Bush administration, from warrantless wiretapping of American citizens to hiring and dismissal of Justice Department attorneys for brazenly political reasons, to a policy of torture of foreign nationals on the pretext of national security in the post-9/11 world.

Sen. Patrick Leahy of Vermont, the chairman of the Senate Judiciary Committee, has gone so far as to propose a commission with subpoena powers and the ability to grant immunity, levers by which to prosecute the suspected evildoers of the Bush White House and their enablers for what many are calling War Crimes.

328

None of this has escaped President Obama's attention. He said as much in his first presidential news conference of the administration on Monday. "Nobody is above the law," the president said, "and if there are clear instances of wrongdoing, people should be prosecuted just like any ordinary citizen. …"He'd have been fine if he stopped there. But then this little … qualifier messed up everything. "So I will take a look at Senator Leahy's proposal, but my general orientation is to say, 'let's get it right and moving forward.'"

◊ ◊ ◊

Not so subtly built into that full-steam-ahead call to action is an implied desire to Close the Door on this Sordid Chapter in American Life. *Moving forward*, eh? The president had already said basically the same thing on Jan. 11, on ABC's "This Week." Vice President Joe Biden said almost exactly the same thing in January, too.

And check out the president's words: "take a look at." Obama, as gifted an orator as we've had in generations, knows the power of words. There's a cursory, incidental aspect to *taking a look* at something, and the president knows it. He also knows, or strongly suspects, that to engage in a seemingly partisan inquiry into the misdeeds of his predecessor could derail the sense of national unity he's trying to enlist in pursuit of urgent business, and short-circuit his own domestic agenda.

That may not matter.

Those in the Democratic leadership — Rep. John Conyers, House Speaker Nancy Pelosi, Senators Barbara Boxer and Russ Feingold — have been taking up positions in support of independent inquiries into the Bush White House, in spite of how politically inconvenient it might be for the president.

Those in the rank and file, ordinary citizens, have let their feelings be known by the millions on the Change.gov Web site, millions of people who said in early January that addressing this matter was of top importance, even more important than some aspects of the evolving economic crisis.

This is where you expect to read something about the Chinese ideogram that doubles for "crisis" and "opportunity," and with good reason: For the Obama administration, in this crisis (not of their own making) there is real potential for change. It's a rare thing when an administration can, in the literal dawn of its powers, take actions of principle that reinforce, starkly and clearly, the principles this nation was founded on. Opportunities are rarely as distilled, as unambiguous, as this.

This is a door President Obama must step through. This — the power of a return to the rule of law — is what he campaigned on, what swayed this nation to elect him. Now, there's no turning back. If you're serious about walking it like you talk it, this is as good as it gets.

The warnings are already out there, tactful, nuanced and reasoned. Jonathan Turley, the eloquent constitutional law professor at Georgetown, and one of the watchdogs of the intelligentsia, said it plain Tuesday on MSNBC:

"We need to be honest. There's great love for President Obama and I have great respect for him. But you cannot say that no one is above the law and block the investigation of war crimes by your predecessor. It is a position without principle. It is because you believe it is politically inconvenient …"

"The Democrats," Turley said, "are going to have to decide whether they want to detach themselves from principle, start their control of this government with an act of the most unprincipled sort."

◊ ◊ ◊

It's on you, Mr. President. Sir. B. You've made phenomenal strides in nothing flat, but the very fact that the need for this kind of investigation is right now something you're only considering, only "taking a look at," is exactly the problem.

You're concerned about reanimating the red state/blue state division you campaigned to overcome. You've got unspoken fears of galvanizing the hard Republican right. Don't worry about them. Rest assured that nothing — *nothing* — will galvanize *your* base more than your insistence on following the rule of law that you confessed when you pursued the job you now hold. It's on you, sir. This will not wait. There's no backburner back enough to put this on. This should be one of those non-dilemma dilemmas for a president whose indelible sense of right and wrong resonated throughout the presidential campaign just ended. There's every reason to believe (to hope?) that the decision to follow where evidence leads into whether laws and treaties were violated by the Bush White House is one that you yourself have already made.

The world *will* long note and remember what you say and do here, or fail to say and do. Count on it. It will stay with you, for good or ill, better or worse, for the rest of your life.

It's on you, Barack. You got the ball. People in the stands are crazy on your side. No debates, no chin-pulling and no passing it off to someone else. You got the ball. You have to take the shot.

2/12/2009

'SLUMDOG MILLIONAIRE'
AND THE NEW AMERICAN MOVIE

NEXT time you go to a movie and quietly curse the seemingly endless parade of corporate logos you have to endure before the feature attraction, consider the state of the global economy, the new film "Slumdog Millionaire" and the way those logos tell a story before the movie even begins.

"Slumdog Millionaire", this year's little unknown movie that could, has garnered 10 Academy Award nominations, including Best Picture. It was the Best Film at the Los Angeles Critics Choice Awards and won Golden Globe awards for best drama, best director, best screenplay and best original score.

With 10 Oscar nods — the same as "Lawrence of Arabia"! — "Slumdog" is an odds-on favorite to score handsomely at the Oscar ceremonies on Feb. 22. It's also doing serious business at the bottom line. Made for about $15 million, it has grossed more than $77 million in North America so far, and $118 million worldwide, according to boxofficemojo.com.

This small-scale story of a orphan pilgrim's progress through modern Mumbai (formerly Bombay) and the rigors of competing in the Indian version of"Who Wants to Be a Millionaire" is the talk of Hollywood — and of Bollywood, the Mumbai district where an estimated 1,200 films are made annually, making that the real movie capital of the world. The idea that a movie with Third World stars and setting could outpoint the best from Hollywood in this year's Oscar derby may seem unlikely. But the rise of "Slumdog" from art-house obscurity tells the story of Hollywood's future.

The evolving relationship between Hollywood and Bollywood was dramatically underscored last September, when Steven Spielberg's DreamWorks SKG, one of Hollywood's signature properties, entered into a $1.2 billion partnership with the Reliance ADA Group, a Mumbai-based communications concern.

Bollywood films are rising partly because of the size of the added benefit of a potential audience in India — an estimated

1.14 billion people live there — and because of the relatively small cost of production. Filmmaking in Bollywood cost an average of under $2 million each, compared with the estimated $50 million negative cost of a Hollywood production.

As media companies face new headwinds in the current economic crisis (look at the $6.4 billion loss just announced by News Corporation, parent of Fox and Slumdog distributor Fox Searchlight Pictures) they'll seek more capital from foreign investors. That's to underwrite more of those costs with money from those investors — companies represented by those logos you have to sit through — accelerating a practice that's been going on for years.

Foreign investment in American films isn't new. Such companies as the French-based Studio Canal, a division of the Canal Plus cable TV operation, have long invested in U.S. films and television. The Hong Kong-based Media Asia Films helped finance The Departed, Martin Scorsese's 2006 hit that won him an Oscar for best director. The relationship between American movie knowhow and foreign capital is an old one.

But India is the new player in the game, and they've come strong to the table.

Mumbai-based UTV Software Communications, for example, has production development deals with Fox Searchlight and with Will Smith's Overbrook Entertainment imprint. Maybe it's no surprise that Walt Disney came calling in 2006, acquiring a sizable stake in the company for $14 million. U.S. conglomerate Viacom signed a pact with India's Network 18 conglomerate in 2007; that deal will eventually result in motion pictures, television and digital media.

What's happening between Hollywood and Bollywood isn't happening in a straight line. The success of Slumdog is a rare win; other Hollywood-Bollywod tie-ups haven't been as successful, partly due to a disconnect in the emphasis placed on scripts and the importance laced on marketing.

Everyone "so far is only worried about the output," Bollywood industry analyst Vikramjit Roy said to The Times of India. "You have grandiose marketing plans made and you have extensive exhibition plans chalked out but, at the script level, there is a lot left to be desired. In the West, studios rarely go wrong because they continuously research scripts, the script is doctored by various focus groups and bounced off experts.''

But somehow "Slumdog Millionaire" prevailed by not taking all of that advice. By combining a credible storyline and likable characters with the fanciful, balletic production style common to Bollywood (right down to the vibrant song-and-dance number at the end), the film realized a success that was something marketing or focus groups can't match: the lightning-in-a-bottle of being exactly the right movie at the right time.

From Billy Wilder and Sam Mendes to Wolfgang Peterson and Ridley Scott, the emigrant experience for directors coming to Hollywood has been largely a European one. The breakthrough of "Slumdog Millionaire" reflects both the public's willingness to embrace something new, and the inevitability of that something new arriving on these shores from the biggest movie market in the world.

The future of American movies will be filled with the names of stars Americans won't be able to pronounce. Until they do.

2/13/2009
Published in TheLoop21.com

SKIN IN THE GAME:
TWO SIDES OF PRESIDENT'S DAY

TODAY, the first President's Day of the Obama administration, the patriotism of the holiday reveals to black Americans both its blessings and its barbs. This dramatic leveling of the playing field of American possibility is still sinking in, for all of us. Even as new behavioral models are being road-tested, old habits die hard.

In The Root, William Jelani Cobb's poignant, beautifully written confession of his conflicted sense of observing President's Day laid bare just how corrosive history can be:

"There are cynical luxuries that come with being black in this country, like the ability to shrug off the dime-store rites of patriotism. We've seen America through a perpetually raised eyebrow, the yeah, whatever perspective that comes with the terrain on our side of American history. And here lies Presidents Day. Like July 4th, Thomas Jefferson and NASCAR— it comes awash in the crimson, white and navy trimming meant to remind us of our blessed status as Americans."

For Teresa Wiltz, also writing in The Root, the fascination with President Obama was evident in the faces and attitudes of people at the National Museum of American History in Washington, people posing besides the portrait of the 44th president: "This impromptu photo-op, say the black folks who work at the museum—the curators, the historians, the security guards—isn't something that you saw before. People just didn't pause to pose with say, Warren G. Harding or Grover Cleveland, or even old Abe, celebrating his 200th last week. This, they say, is something different. A first. A shift."

"You can feel the enthusiasm," Reuben Jackson, the museum's associate curator and archivist, told The Root. "It's not some old white guy with a powdered wig."

Wiltz's generally upbeat assessment mirrors that of many black Americans, who undoubtedly felt this President's Day that they really had something to celebrate, that they had more of a vested interest in the outcome of the improvisation collectively known as America. For blacks and minorities, there was finally a reason to salute the subjects of the holiday, beyond the obligatory public genuflections. For the first time in two-hundred-too-many years, black folks had skin in the game.

◊ ◊ ◊

Some of the loyal shoppers at the Peterson Air Force Base commissary in Colorado Springs, Colo., didn't get the message. It was there this week when the picture of the President of the United States was removed from a Presidents Day sign after customers complained. The base is the home of the North American Aerospace Defense Command (NORAD).

The Defense Commissary Agency, which runs the stores, says employees took down the image, which was accompanied by a sign listing store hours, after customers complained that the holiday is about Presidents Washington and Lincoln.

Two other matters, however, cast doubt on that tenuously legitimate objection on grounds of historicity:

A cashier at the commissary who requested anonymity told The Associated Press that pictures of recent past presidents, including Bush #43 and Bill Clinton, have accompanied the Presidents Day closure sign. The cashier told the AP that one customer, a military retiree, objected specifically because of Obama's race.

"He said they're not going to have no black man on the window where he shops," the cashier said.

They must be crazy for powdered wigs in that part of Colorado.

◊ ◊ ◊

Two sides of the same American coin, two halves of the same day experienced by the same people. And that duality makes perfect sense given human nature and the propensity for sudden change. It'd be silly to think that, all at once, President's Day would suddenly resonate for black Americans the way it has for white Americans for generations.

Cynicism, that narcotic of expectation based on past experience, takes time to wean yourself off of. And shoppers at an American military base prove there's always a drug dealer somewhere.

You don't get clear of that drug overnight. Recovery is a process. There'll be setbacks; you'll fall off the wagon sometimes. But there's no going backward, for you or this nation. Not now. Not this time.

Those 44 portraits on the presidential wall belong to you, too. They're part of the museum, the laboratory, the boxing ring, the chapel and synagogue and mosque of this nation, and they're yours, too. And the 44th picture, the one they couldn't deal at Peterson Air Force Base, is the one that confirms the promise symbolized by the other 43.

This is something different. A first. A shift.

2/16/2009

STIMULATION DAY

MAYBE Pennsylvania Sen. Arlen Specter was really bonding with the president on Super Bowl Day, when some of his constituents — the Pittsburgh Steelers — won the game.

Maybe Barack got Maine Sen. Olympia Snowe's martini just right. Who knows?

What's not up for debate, not anymore, is the status of the American Recovery and Reinvestment Act, a 1,071-page behemoth shorthanded as the stimulus bill, a piece of legislation that went from a proposal to a law today, as the first and only slightly mitigated triumph of the administration of President Barack Obama.

With the signing of the $787 billion stimulus package, President Obama fulfills a longtime campaign pledge and taken the first steps, baby though they might be, toward righting the badly listing ship of the American economy.

Signing the bill today at Denver's Museum of Nature and Science, the president (as usual) didn't sugarcoat the nation's dire situation, or try to paint the stim bill — the largest spending legislation in American history — as the magic bullet. "I don't want to pretend that today marks the end of our economic problems. Nor does it constitute all of what we're going to have to do to turn our economy around. But today does mark the beginning of the end."

If the New York Times' breakdown of where the money goes is accurate, the stimulus will attempt to spread relief wide across a number of areas, if not that deep: $282 billion in tax cuts (satisfying the Republicans), $100 billion in public works projects, $87.1 billion in state Medicaid assistance, $69.2 billion for education and job training, $50 billion for transportation projects, $35.8 billion in enhanced unemployment benefits, $25.1 billion in COBRA health care coverage for the unemployed, $21 billion in food assistance, and $17.2 billion for upgrades in health information technology.

◊ ◊ ◊

The Republican right held fast, almost uniformly resisting approval of the bill, with only relative moderates Specter, Snowe and Sen. Susan Collins of Maine voting to support the package, breaking ranks with the Republican leadership. The GOP party line was more or less consistent mantra: a bill of this size should more properly go for tax cuts for businesses.

If you wanted any sense of bipartisanship, you had to look beyond the Republican leaders and seek out some Republican governors; Charlie Crist of Florida and Arnold Schwarzenegger of California have signed on to the thrust of the stimulus bill.

The GOP brain trust would have none of it. On Friday, Senate Republican Leader Mitch McConnell said on the Senate floor that "the stimulus bill that was supposed to be timely, targeted and temporary is none of the above. And this means Congress is about to approve a stimulus that's unlikely to have much stimulative effect."

It all seems like, among other things, an ironically sad estimation of the worth of the American dollar in its own right. The idea that $787 billion injected into various sectors of the state and consumer economies wouldn't have a beneficial impact on them is a rhetorical devaluation of the currency: If three quarters of a trillion dollars can't defibrillate an ailing economy, what the hell can?

But just as important as the effect of the literal application of the stimulus law, whatever that effect might be, is the psychological effect — not just market psychology, but Main Street's mindset as well. For the first time in too long, people see something substantive happening about the economy, a corrective effort on the same scale as that which needs correcting.

People see someone making the effort to change things. How it all plays out is still to be seen, but President Obama and his advisers will reap the benefits of the immediate public perception as men and women of action, urgent, principled and absolutely determined to fix the disaster they inherited from the loyal opposition.

◊ ◊ ◊

The GOP, still very much in wilderness mode, has strategized itself into another dilemma of its identification with the public. Throughout the long process of the stim bill's passage through Congress, and solidly along party lines, the GOP leadership and wannabes have so solidly positioned itself against the bill's passage that their opposition has looked like opposition for its own sake — not objections based on economic principle so much as objections animated by plain old political obstinacy.

The Republicans may be boxed in now by a perception of being the worst kind of opportunistic obstructionist: opposing the stimulus bill (and the broad economic recovery that would at least have a chance of beginning, and without which things would certainly get worse) out of a nakedly partisan fear that it *will* succeed.

Far-fetched? Remember the fighting words of Republican voice box and former recreational pharmaceutical enthusiast Rush Limbaugh ("I hope he fails!"). With the bill's signing into law, the Republicans are faced not only with a defeat on the legislative merits, but also a loss in the court of public opinion.

◊ ◊ ◊

Maybe the most important thing about the stimulus package signed into is what hasn't been said yet about how much more will be necessary to do what the stimulus package intends. Remember what the man said?: "Nor does it constitute all of what we're going to have to do to turn our economy around." What took place in Denver today might well be considered Stimulus I, the first round of timed-release economic rescue. Hip & knee replacement? Open heart surgery? Chemotherapy? Insert your medical metaphor here.

Interviewed Monday by Keith Olbermann on MSNBC, Nobel Prize-winning economist and New York Times columnist Paul Krugman expressed what he thinks is needed: More of the same.

"Just about all of the spending looks like good stimulus," Krugman said. "The aid to state governments is really important, the infrastructure spending is really good, the aid to education, the aid to health care and unemployment benefits — those things are going to mitigate the pain of this thing. They're going to help people who are in trouble ..."

"Given the sausage-making in politics, it's not a bad bill at all. But the actual meat in the sausage is not enough to feed us in this famine."

◊ ◊ ◊

So ... to the number of big jobs Barack Obama has been and will be asked to do, you can add one more: Butcher. The president has made a good beginning, and given the economic farrago that greeted him on day one of his presidency, a *very* good beginning, achieved, no less on day 28. The phrase "hit the ground running" doesn't apply if you don't hit the ground at all.

We'll overlook the little Churchillian reference in his speech ("today does mark the beginning of the end"); we know he's a better orator than that. We're looking forward to the appearance of his other gifts — as an administrator, a wonk, a visionary, a listener and a leader — as he steers us to our finest hour.

At least one finer than now.

2/17/2009

A SEAT AT THE TABLE: MALCOLM X, 44 YEARS AFTER

WHEN MALCOLM X (El Hajj Malik El-Shabazz) was shot to death at 3:10 p.m., on Sunday, Feb. 21, 1965 at the Audubon Ballroom in New York City, it ended a part of the civil rights movement that the civil rights movement never fully embraced. This 44th anniversary of his assassination occurs with America in the midst of societal transition he would have no doubt relished — a transition resulting in great measure from his critical assessment of America and its various racial dishonesties, an assessment that helped lay the groundwork for vast social and political change.

In the years of his ascendancy as a harsh, incisive and necessary critic of the nation of his birth, Malcolm X spoke truth to power with a volcanic directness and urbane wit that fascinated and frightened white Americans. But it was his adoption of Islam in a Christian nation that more or less isolated him from the mainstream visibility and acceptance enjoyed by Rev. Dr. Martin Luther King Jr.

Malcolm has always been held at a figurative arm's length both by the media and by the national historical record; both tend even now to fixate on King and the more familiar (and palatable) narrative of the civil rights movement's origins in the Christian church. Today, more than two generations after his death, a philosophical dichotomy between King and Malcolm X has been erected and enforced, a schism that, in fact, may not ever have existed.

Malcolm X's place in the leadership of the civil rights movement as taught in schools and universities has certainly been more peripheral, if not downright marginal. You got the overview on King (however abbreviated it might be) in your American history class. You had to go to a black studies class to find out about Malcolm.

That simplistic, convenient division has been a persistent fiction in the national life; Malcolm X and Martin Luther King were taking different avenues to the same objective. Considering that both men had essentially the same goal in mind — social and economic empowerment of Americans of African descent — considering that both men found more common ground as the Jim Crow agonies of the 1960's continued — the time is past to weave Malcolm more fully into the fabric of the historical narrative on civil rights. Where he's always belonged. Where he's always been anyway.

◊ ◊ ◊

"The juxtaposition of the views of Malcolm and Martin defines the evolution of the struggle," Howard Dodson, director of the Schomburg Center for Research, told me in February 2005. "The tendency to create polar opposites, which is what media did at that time, doesn't reflect the struggle. ... they were part and parcel of the same program. Malcolm said in so many words, 'either you deal with Martin King or you deal with me.'"

The contrasts between the two men — one steeped in the body of the church, the other seared in the crucible of the street — embodied the duality of black Americans' lives. Both men were riveting public speakers, of course, but Malcolm's earliest addresses sharply, sometimes harshly made plain the stakes: nothing less than equal, whatever it takes. Period.

King was expressing much the same message from the loftier rhetorical precincts of the Baptist church, but his reverential homiletics had a resonance for a Christian nation that Malcolm, before his conversion to Islam and certainly after, could never hope to attain.

◊ ◊ ◊

What's been largely omitted from the histories of the civil rights movement is the commonalities that developed between the two men. Dodson told me, for example, that, well before the end, "Malcolm had shifted into a broader humanistic perspective, upgrading the position of black, Hispanic and native Americans." King had begun to widen the scope of his message to include a full-throated opposition to the Vietnam War.

And what's likely to be seen in the next episodes of the improvisation we call America — the history still to be written — is a matter of faith: the rising role of Islam in the United States, a nation still psychically scarred by the Sept. 11 terrorist attacks, a country never quite far away from the stealth xenophobia that informs its past and bird-dogs its future.

Dodson in 2005: "Americans will have to come to terms with Islam within the United States and outside, and formulate positions at individual and societal levels that bring the same respect to Islam that people bring to Christianity. ... It won't happen overnight."

◊ ◊ ◊

Malcolm X has been gone for 44 years. In that time, the varying expressions of the civil rights movement have transformed this nation at every level, ultimately making possible the new man of the moment, Barack Obama, the 44th president.

To the media, the academy, the namers of the pantheon, let the record show: The civil rights movement was as multidimensional as the people it was meant to empower. Malcolm X has always had a seat at that table. In his search for voice and identity is mirrored the search for our own. We stand on his shoulders as well. By acknowledging his obvious presence in the national narrative, by accepting his faith in the national panorama, we perform vital double duty:

We begin to listen to a voice from the past, one we often marginalized or ignored; we start to prepare for a future, one that's coming to meet us whether we like it or not.

2/21/09

THE DUKE, THE COIN, THE REALM

DEEP back in the day — when it was harder for black folks to get anywhere *near* money, much less on it — Edward Kennedy Ellington spoke to us all. From close to the dawn of jazz and well into an era crowded with uneven yet adventurous experimentations in the form, Duke Ellington set the standard for musicianship, invention and style. With between 3,000 and 5,000 compositions to his credit, much of it among the most indelible and necessary music this or any nation has ever produced, the Duke can claim the United States as his realm, first one crowded with inspiration, later one inhabited by legions of his still adoring fans.

"His grand aesthetic vision was to bring work songs, spirituals, blues, and ragtime together with jazz, that aesthetic idiom of great latitude," Stanley Crouch observed in a Slate essay in January 2005. "Ellington combined his sources with more blistering force, imagination, and understatement than anyone had before him, inventing variations and grooves along the way. He produced music that would not only extend the reaches of jazz but would become one of the largest and most original bodies of American music ever created."

Clearly, the Duke's realm was America. All that realm needed was a coin, and on Tuesday, courtesy of the United States Mint, we got one.

For the first time in American history, a coin placed in general circulation will feature the likeness of a single African American: Edward Kennedy Ellington sits at a piano on the reverse of the new quarters just issued by the Mint. They'll be available in bulk quantities (bags and rolls) for about another seven weeks or so.

The Ellington coin, part of the series documenting moments and figures in history from each of the 50 states, represents the District of Columbia, where he was born in April 1899 and where he lived, in the district's U Street Corridor, artistic if not literal home to Ella Fitzgerald, Cab Calloway, Billie Holiday and other titans of jazz. In some ways it's an obvious nod to the clout and presence of Black History Month and, to a lesser extent, the groundbreaker-in-chief now occupying the Oval Office.

But credit the Mint for a decision that recognizes the cultural symmetry regardless of the date on the calendar.

Rather than bearing the likeness of a statesman, writer or politician, or someone whose exploits resonated from the remove of an earlier national era, the first general-circulation coin portraying a solitary African American is of a man whose cultural influence is very much in general circulation — its style and rhythms and invention foundational to the American songbook, its presence part of the American fabric.

Duke won nine Grammy awards in his lifetime of 75 years, four more posthumously, along with any number of other plaudits and honoraries bestowed upon him. Live long enough and you'll get every accolade there is to get.

The ingenious triumph of this award from a grateful nation lies in its everyday grandeur, its ordinary ubiquity — the ubiquity of a quarter in your pocket and music in the air.

You can buy the new Duke Ellington quarters in counts of 100 for $32, and change.

The coins will tarnish long before the music does.

2/27/2009

THE ROCKY PAPER HORRORSHOW

THE ROCKY Mountain News closed its doors on Friday, eight weeks short of its 150th birthday. The death of one of the nation's leading daily papers, Colorado's oldest paper and the state's longest continually running business, is thought to be an early warning of what's likely to come for some of the country's other beleaguered dailies. Reports of the possible demise of the daily newspaper may not have been greatly exaggerated.

The Rocky's last edition bore a front page that was a stunningly, emotionally effective valedictory: It was a reproduction of the front page of the *first* edition of the Rocky — April 23, 1859 — surrounding the goodbye statement of 2009. With no words beyond the news of its closing on the front page, the Rocky made a statement of the coming and going of a newspaper, with a wistful typographical farewell to an era when newspapers weren't an option but a necessity.

The Rocky's owner, E.W. Scripps Company, weary of hemorrhaging cash and with no gains in circulation; absorbing the body blows of a classified ad market decimated by the Internet; and reeling (like everyone else) from the ravages of the current downturn, threw in the already bloody towel and shut operations of the newsroom on West Colfax Avenue for good.

As much as anything, the Rocky was a victim of the speed and relentlessness of the times we live in. News isn't something we have the time to savor or linger over; for more and more of us, the day's information diet is gained through the rapid infusers of television and the Internet.

"I don't know anyone my age who has time in the morning to read a newspaper," said Chris Olivier, 37, to The New York Times. Olivier, a retail manager, said he gets his daily news from the Internet and niche neighborhood publications. "It's sad to see such a huge part of our state's history lost, but the market is moving, and newspapers haven't moved with it. They don't get the Web."

One Rocky reader gets it, understands the importance of contrasting voices to a vibrant democracy. Terrance D.

347

Carroll, a Democrat and the speaker of the Colorado House of Representatives, told The Times he hated the absence of those contrasting civic voices with the Rocky shutting down.

"I'm afraid of the echo chambers that are emerging because more people are choosing to get their news only from sources that reinforce what they want to believe," he said.

◊ ◊ ◊

The journalists and photographers and designers of the Rocky Mountain News, a resourceful lot, have already parlayed their professional talents and their personal pain into a Web site, I Want My Rocky, a collection of local news, reviews and ruminations, much of it written from the wounded and justifiably bitter perspective that's only normal a few days after your job is shot out from under you.

In the months and days preceding the Rocky's fall, there were news reports of other newspapers and their owners considering how to stay financially afloat.

The Tribune Company, owner of the Los Angeles Times and Chicago Tribune, 23 television stations and the Chicago Cubs, filed for bankruptcy protection in mid-December.

The Hearst Corporation, owners of both the San Francisco Chronicle and the Seattle Post-Intelligencer, was said to be perhaps weeks away from a decision about closing both papers if no buyers can be found. Hearst execs said in January that the Post-Intelligencer would be either closed outright or converted to an online-only publication — with a staff a fraction of the size it is now — within 60 days if no buyer came forward.

The brain trust at Newsday, the icon of Long Island, may be poised to truly break out of the box with a reported decision to convert its news Web site to a paid-content model — actually trying to get people to pony up for news online.

"We plan to end the distribution of free Web content and make our newsgathering capabilities a service to our customers," said Tom Rutledge, chief operating officer of Cablevision Systems, Newsday's parent company.

And some are even considering going a step further, following on the oft-stated dictum that journalism is a public trust and subordinating the profit motive. They're exploring the potential for news organizations to reform as L3Cs, low-profit variations on the limited liability company (LLC) that would allow such organizations to combine pursuit of work of a proven social benefit with a secondary profit motive.

Emily Chan, staff editor of the UC Hastings Constitutional Law Quarterly, wrote last July on the Nonprofit Law Blog:

"The low-profit, limited liability company, or L3C, is a hybrid of a nonprofit and for-profit organization. More specifically, it is a new type of limited liability company (LLC) designed to attract private investments and philanthropic capital in ventures designed to provide a social benefit. ...

"On April 30, 2008, Vermont became the first State to recognize the L3C as an official legal structure. Similar legislation has since been pushed in other States such as Georgia, Michigan, Montana and North Carolina. Although Vermont currently remains the only State to authorize the L3C, it has national applicability because L3Cs formed in Vermont can be used in any State or Territory.

◊ ◊ ◊

All of which comes too late for the Rocky Mountain News. Some of the Rocky reporting staff has reportedly been snapped up by The Denver Post, for decades the Rocky's loyal opposition, the adversary in a sometimes bitter newspaper war — and as of now the only Denver daily newspaper, and the surviving member of a newspaper agency with an estimated debt load of $130 million.

The death of a newspaper is never a good thing, but the death of a paper that's a legitimate institution feels truly like a death in the family. Yours truly grew up in Denver reading both the Rocky and the Post, and briefly wrote music reviews for the Rocky entertainment section back in the Jurassic day, before the Internet. The Rocky had the populist vibe, from the tabloid shape of the paper on down to the way it was written. You could always curl up with the Rocky in a small place like a car seat or the booth of a diner. If you read the Rocky, you probably bought your booze at Argonaut Liquors instead of a wine shop out in Cherry Creek. You took the bus to work. You was folks.

No more. The Chablis sippers are winning this war, if just barely. Companies are tightening belts that are cinching bone already. As the Rocky gallops into history, you can't help but recall a message from the movies that more than brushes up against reality.

The Hearst Corporation is said to be losing about $1 million per week at The Chronicle. The corporation was started by William Randolph Hearst, the tycoon thought to have been the inspiration for the character Charles Foster Kane, protagonist of the film classic "Citizen Kane."

In one scene, when the young newspaper publisher Kane is confronted by his accountant and interrogated about his profligate spending, Kane speaks — with the smugness of someone certain of his own invincibility, and that of his business model:

"You're right, Mr. Thatcher. I did lose a million dollars last year. I expect to lose a million dollars this year. I expect to lose a million dollars *next* year. You know, Mr. Thatcher, at the rate of a million dollars a year, I'll have to close this place in … sixty years."

The Hearst Corporation in particular, and the newspaper industry in general, have nothing remotely close to that luxury anymore.

3/2/2009

MICHELLE OBAMA, EVERYWOMAN

ARE YOU old school enough to remember Chaka Khan's blazing, bumptious 1978 hit song, "I'm Every Woman"? You could dance to this chart-topper, of course; Chaka Khan wouldn't have had it any other way. But besides its role as a dance-floor staple back in the disco day, its lyrics conveyed the universalist aspects of an anthem. Especially the chorus:

I'm every woman,
It's all in me ...

That sense of typicality, of extraordinariness within the ordinary, was something that eluded black women in the eyes of pop culture, and through no fault of their own. Through the prism of pop culture, black women were always the sassy, plain-spoken, earthy Other -- not so much people as walking stereotypes meant to go no further, to be no more than the relatively narrow and isolationist roles assigned to them by the majority culture.

The walls of that cultural apartheid have been crumbling by degrees for years now. We can thank Michelle Obama for helping to pile-drive a hole through that wall, once and for all.

In little more than seven weeks, Michelle Obama has quietly reinvented the franchise of First Lady. For about as long, the media has obsessed over the bare arms she's displayed on several occasions. We've gotten weekly U.S. Biceps & Triceps Reports about the new First Lady. It's as if Laura Bush had no such physical equipment for the last eight years; that part of the female anatomy apparently didn't exist until Michelle went sleeveless. Without meaning to, she's become a symbol of the national physicality yearning to breathe free.

"Let's face it: The only bracing symbol of American strength right now is the image of Michelle Obama's sculpted biceps," Maureen Dowd wrote March 7 in The New York Times. "Her husband urges bold action, but it is Michelle who looks as though she could easily wind up and punch out Rush

351

Limbaugh, Bernie Madoff and all the corporate creeps who ripped off America."

◊ ◊ ◊

But of course it's more, it's bigger than that. Besides brandishing a refreshingly revisionist sense of fashion -- one in which the lion of haute couture lies down with the lamb of J. Crew -- Michelle Obama has helped revolutionize the national sense of black femininity and motherhood. Her very presence in the White House resets the baseline of expectations when we think of the First Lady.

She's brought a visible, uncompromising sense of protectiveness to the role of Moms-in-Chief, working for a balance of the private and the public for Sasha and Malia, our First Kids. That swing set you can see from the Oval Office? Don't for a minute think that was all the president's idea.

In a mere seven weeks, she's given her quasi-office clout, championing her own causes — including aid to veterans' families, improved nutrition and the plight of working families — in a direct, populist way.

◊ ◊ ◊

Then there's the element of style. We've had issues before with Condé Nast, the monster magazine publisher, but they get credit for realizing what the country has known for awhile: Michelle Obama will be an inescapable presence in the fashion world. The publisher has just featured her on the cover of Vogue, the international style & fashion bible, as well as in a smartly electric illustration on the cover of the current issue of The New Yorker (how different from the New Yorker cover illustration of Barack and Michelle as surrogates for Osama bin Laden and Angela Davis).

Maybe the biggest nod to Michelle Obama as everywoman turns up as an item in an online catalog by Taylor Gifts: A T-shirt bearing a sharp illustration of Michelle Obama assuming the physical posture and dress of the iconic Rosie the Riveter, whose original image appeared on a poster that galvanized the homefront during World War II.

The ballooned caption, "We Can Do It!" is a direct import from the original. With the words arrayed to come from the mouth of the new First Lady, the message goes forth: Despite the panorama of social and economic and personal challenges black women face, along with all women, this shout of the possible is a tonic, a throwdown of uplift that probably couldn't come at a better time, or from a better source.

The wire services have made it a convention of their copy style: The phrase "first lady" is rendered in the lower case — this despite the seemingly obvious titular singularity that comes with use of the word "first." "Not a formal title," says The Associated Press. Fair enough — for them.

But maybe for the rest of us, it's time to break with that convention. Maybe with this First Lady, we can give the title, and the current titleholder, the props they deserve.

3/8/2009

MEETING THE PRESS

POLITICAL capital is a perishable thing. The toothsome political opportunities of a young White House can dissipate quickly, becoming as moldy and unusable as any of the science projects lurking somewhere in your refrigerator right now.

George Bush, who practically crowed about his political capital after the 2004 election, turned into a victim of his own deficit spending. Well before the end of his second term in office, it was clear President Bush was spending political capital he didn't have. The Republican Party paid that bill in November.

Barack Obama doesn't intend to make the same mistake. Tonight, on his 64th day in office, the 44th president and overachiever-in-chief met the press in a prime-time news conference, firing on all hybrid-powered cylinders in making his case to the media and the American public.

With a telling shot at his Republican critics, a call for more authority over some failing non-banking concerns, a thorough breakdown of his first-term priorities, and an appeal to the American people for patience, President Obama clearly recognized that the most valuable political capital is time — and the nation's forbearance.

◊ ◊ ◊

There may be no more electric visual image surrounding the presidency than to see the president walking down the ornate, carpeted hallway leading to the East Room of the White House, on the way to meet the press. It's stagecraft personified. And it's a sign that Obama is growing into the office that both on the way in and all throughout the 58-minute session with the media, the president looks relaxed, animated and completely on point.

He began with prepared, TelePrompptered remarks directed not at the press in the room but the millions watching on TV.

"Now, it's important to remember that this crisis didn't happen overnight and it didn't result from any one action or decision. It took many years and many failures to lead us here. And it will take many months and many different solutions to lead us out. There are no quick fixes, and there are no silver bullets. …

"The budget I submitted to Congress will build our economic recovery on a stronger foundation, so that we do not face another crisis like this ten or twenty years from now. We invest in the renewable sources of energy that will lead to new jobs, new businesses, and less dependence on foreign oil. We invest in our schools and our teachers so that our children have the skills they need to compete with any workers in the world. We invest in reform that will bring down the cost of health care for families, businesses, and our government. And in this budget, we have made the tough choices necessary to cut our deficit in half by the end of my first term - even under the most pessimistic estimates. …

"At the end of the day, the best way to bring our deficit down in the long run is not with a budget that continues the very same policies that have led to a narrow prosperity and massive debt. It's with a budget that leads to broad economic growth by moving from an era of borrow and spend to one where we save and invest. …

"We will recover from this recession. But it will take time, it will take patience, and it will take an understanding that when we all work together; when each of us looks beyond our own short-term interests to the wider set of obligations we have to each other - that's when we succeed. That's when we prosper. And that's what is needed right now. So let us look toward the future with a renewed sense of common purpose, a renewed determination, and most importantly, a renewed confidence that a better day will come."

◊ ◊ ◊

Obama echoed the request of Treasury Secretary Timothy Geithner, made to Congress earlier Tuesday, for unprecedented authority to take over outfits like AIG, performing the same rescue function that the Federal Deposit Insurance Corporation (FDIC) now performs for troubled banks.

"Bankers and executives on Wall Street need to realize that enriching themselves on the taxpayers' dime is inexcusable, that the days of outsized rewards and reckless speculation that puts us all at risk have to be over," he said.

"At the same time, the rest of us can't afford to demonize every investor or entrepreneur who seeks to make a profit. That drive is what has always fueled our prosperity, and it is what will ultimately get these banks lending and our economy moving once more."

◊ ◊ ◊

If Obama's gotten good at anything since he was sworn in, it's in his dealings with the mainstream media. With recent appearances on "The Tonight Show," a weekend interview with "60 Minutes" and an evolving relationship with the maverick media that helped him win the presidency, he's shown no fear in dealing with the White House press corps.

That came across tonight. In the Q&A period, Ed Henry of CNN apparently forgot he was dealing with a brother from Chicago. Henry, trying to look tough and aggressive, kept pursuing a marginal point about how Obama didn't respond immediately, emotionally, reflexively about the AIG bailout bonuses.

"… [O]n AIG, why did you wait — why did you wait days to come out and express that outrage?" Henry asked for the second or third time. "It seems like the action is coming out of New York and the attorney general's office. It took you days to come public with Secretary Geithner and say, 'look, we're outraged.' Why did it take so long?"

With a single sentence, Obama went all street on Henry: "It took us a couple of days because I like to know what I'm talking about before I speak." End of discussion, and maybe the beginning of a new respect from traditional media for Obama's steeliness under fire. Clearly, he won't seek a fight but he won't run from one (especially one he can win hands down).

We're 64 percent of the way through that 100-day expiration date of the earlier manifestation of Obama's political capital, but the president and his team has been making the most of it. Considering that he's had to do as much to undo some of the actions and policies of his predecessor as he has put his own policies in place, the Obama administration has already achieved a great deal in record time.

With his repeated calls for patience — both from a 24/7 media with the appetite and metabolism of a shrew, and from the American people eager for the change he promised — President Obama is calling on the country and the media to awaken to the possibility that our obsession with small ball —the day-to-day, the knee-jerk response, the minuscule and the incremental — can give way to something bigger, more powerful from a leader determined to swing for the fences when it's necessary. And it's necessary now.

3/24/2009

BARBARIANS ON THE TUMBRELS:
AIG'S U.S.A. IOU

C OMES NOW the latest laughable misstep in the fortunes of the American International Group, aka AIG, Inc., the global insurance behemoth whose improvident bets on the future of the housing market — bets made with nothing more substantial than the idea of cash reserves — lit the fuse for the demolition of the national economy, and whose insistence of paying employees bonuses from the public till have made them the symbol of a Wall Street off the rails:

Early this week, undertaking to curb the public relations nightmare associated with the company, AIG announced plans to change the name of the company. The sign at its Water Street headquarters has since come down. Effective more or less immediately, AIG is to be formally known as AIU Holdings — an unfortunate change, for obvious reasons. Bet your mortgage: Some other wiseass in the blogosphere has already conflated the new name with the letters "IOU."

There lies a lesson in how the wrong kind of damage control leads to worse damage than you started with.

Some of the worst injuries inflicted by AIG to this country register on another, different bottom line. Enlightened minds (and a lot that aren't) can debate the wisdom of the managers of AIG in surreptitiously pursuing plans to pay employees with taxpayer money, or the involvement of Treasury Secretary Tim Geithner in those bonuses being approved to begin with; or the wisdom of trying to pry something north of $200 million from the hands of traders until recently more prepared to part ways with their livelihoods and reputations than with their money.

What can't be disputed is the depth of class warfare, the palpable sense of Us Versus Them that the AIG/AIU/IOU imbroglio has awakened in the national heart.

We've always been a stratified nation. The racial divide is the obvious one, of course, but we're also split along lines of gender, religion, sexual preference, political affiliation and income. Those divisions are played out every day in the public square. But it takes a crisis the magnitude of the one we're facing now to awaken the partisanship of our economy, a division that usually stays on the downlow.

Of all the things we don't tell other people, what we earn is probably No. 1. That changes when everybody's business is in the street. Our respective firewalls, our tolerances for risk and pain, our conflicting senses of fair play are all out there now, naked and unavoidable, as the national economy faces its biggest meltdown since the Great Depression.

◊ ◊ ◊

Journalists are no doubt busy burnishing their bottom lines right now, lining up the book deals they'll use to explain How It All Happened, the antecedent events that made the AIG mess possible.

One of the best such writers has already weighed in. In the new issue of Rolling Stone, staff writer and righteous journalistic flamethrower Matt Taibbi offers a thorough, pungent and passionate exegesis of the current crisis, how we got here and how the AIG crisis is really the leading indicator of something larger, more conspiratorial and ominous: "… a kind of revolution, a coup d'état. They cemented and formalized a political trend that has been snowballing for decades: the gradual takeover of the government by a small class of connected insiders, who used money to control elections, buy influence and systematically weaken financial regulations."

◊ ◊ ◊

There are a lot of vantage points from which to look at how we got here. We can thank Hollywood for one in particular. In 1987, 20th Century Fox released "Wall Street," Oliver Stone's muscular, sometimes impressionistic view of one pilgrim's progress through Reagan-era Wall Street.

Stone, never exactly one for subtlety, smartly distilled the go-go spirit of the times in a shareholder-meeting monologue made by Gordon Gekko, a Darth Vader trader of many ethical lapses:

"The point, ladies and gentlemen, is that greed, for lack of a better word, is good. Greed is right. Greed works. Greed clarifies, cuts through and captures the essence of the evolutionary spirit. Greed in all its forms — greed for life, for money, for love and knowledge — has marked the upward surge of mankind, and greed, you mark my words, [will save that] malfunctioning corporation called the USA."

With those words, the masters of the Wall Street universe had finally found a defining phrase short enough to put on the family crest in Latin. Champions of Reagan-era deregulation of the financial markets had their reason for being. Michael Douglas, who played Gekko in the movie, won an Oscar for best actor.

And consider it a certainty: In multiple somewheres around the America of twenty years ago, impressionable teenagers and young adults with a talent for numbers and a passion for money watched that monologue and quietly swore it an allegiance, used that noble perversity of an idea as a spiritual calling — took that ball and ran with it, ethics trailing in their wake, all the way to the derivatives desk at AIG.

◊ ◊ ◊

If Gordon Gekko gave Wall Street a credo, it's fallen to the various business news channels of cable TV to give it an identity, one that's lately revealed how cozy the relationships are between the Wall Street press and the titans they're supposed to cover.

Almost by default, Wall Street media have adopted the raucous plumage of the floor traders they often interview. Programs like CNBC's "Fast Money," "Mad Money" and "Squawk Box" reflect the macho, clubby, red-meat-eating, towel-snapping ethos that powers and animates Wall Street — a boy's-club mentality that, oddly enough, isn't countered in the least by the addition of female analysts featured on TV business news.

It's led to a variety of excesses: "Mad Money," Jim Cramer's Ouija-board casino cavalcade of investment picks and pans, for example, or the meltdowns of such hypercaffeinated chowderheads as CNBC reporter Rick Santelli, who let his emotions get away from him on Feb. 19 in a mad, vein-popping rant on the trading floor of the Chicago Mercantile Exchange, an embarrassing and naked display of just how deeply have vs. have not thinking permeates the money culture.

And those excesses have led to others. You've no doubt seen the reaction to the reaction of the AIG traders to giving up their bonuses. It was probably inevitable: outraged citizens boarding charter buses, rolling the tumbrels next to the gated estates in Fairfield, Conn., where said traders hang their fur-lined hats. It's like a scene from a Frankenstein movie: metaphorical pitchforks and torches aloft, dogs in full cry while the monster huddles behind the moated castle walls.

Indeed, Connecticut has become something of the ground zero for outrage. Witness the content of some of the e-mails sent to the state Attorney General's Office — e-mails that, while morally wrong as wrong can be in what they propose, still express a clear idea of the depth of consumerist rage:

We will hunt you down. Every penny. We will hunt your children and we will hunt your conscience ... Give back the money or kill yourselves.

You motherfucking, cocksucking dicklickers need to be taken out one by one and shot in the head. There's a special place in hell for you pond scum ...

Your blood will run through the streets in the coming months.

Clearly, Mr. Gekko, greed's not good for everybody.

◊ ◊ ◊

What's taking shape is a crisis as much cultural as economic. What the bailouts of AIG, and the rescue packages for other failing institutions do, as much as anything else, is to reveal for Americans of every stripe and W-2 how rigged the game of financial assistance really is in this nation. They show how the culture of money in America has largely become a rapacious exercise favoring the insiders and dismissing everyday people.

Finally, by pretending that ordinary Americans are the outsiders, Wall Street reveals its utter disconnect with Main Street, where John and Jane Q. Public live in an "estate" with a kid's tricycle in the driveway instead of a brand-new BMW; where John & Jane juggle the bills hoping the unemployment check will stretch another week — when they get the next one; where Americans face the decline of their own balance sheets without a bailout in sight.

AIG (or AIU Holdings or IOU Holdups or whatever it calls itself next month) is only the symbol of a deeper disjunction within the American economy. The willingness to ride to the rescue of companies considered too big to fail conceals, just barely, a disdain for a pool of investors too big to ignore: the 100 million everyday Americans who own stock — or who did as of last year ... before the deluge.

Wall Street still looks at those everyday Americans as outsiders, and they will right up until the moment they hear the glass wall between Us and Them start to crash, and they gain that unexpected revelation: that the wall separating our fates, futures and destinies never really existed in the first place.

3/26/2009

SWINGING LONDON

TODAY, the day before the start of the G-20 economic summit, amid a backdrop of the diplomacy and pageantry expected when world leaders meet, London is the scene of a broad range of spirited, sometimes bloody demonstrations that are sending an inescapable signal to those leaders. The have/have not dichotomies of the world's economies have elicited an outrage on the streets of the city. Environmentalists, anarchists, anti-capitalists and others converged, expressing an anger whose breadth and scope you can fairly interpret to be a mirror of populist anger in any of the powerhouse economies represented in London.

"Abolish money!" some demonstrators chanted in marches and protests that led to fires being set at the Bank of England, and windows smashed at the Royal Bank of Scotland.

The ailing Scottish bank faced the vehement protests that stemmed from news reports that its former chief executive, Fred Goodwin, who received an annual pension payout of £700,000 ($1.01 million) when he left in disgrace in October, despite presiding over the bank's record losses of about £20 billion pounds ($28.9 billion) — in this respect no different from any of its wounded American counterparts. (For the Brits, though, it's getting personal: vandals targeted Goodwin's home and car last week).

CNN reported that a flyer for the "G20 Meltdown" event, carries the slogan "Storm the Banks!" and features images of French revolutionaries storming the Bastille in 1789 and a mannequin of a banker hanging from a noose.

London and British authorities — no doubt dismayed at the idea of the phrase "Swinging London" taking on a new meaning; no doubt numbed by the prospect of banker effigies (or the real thing) dangling from Blackfriars Bridge — put the financial district on alert for a week.

◊ ◊ ◊

You can't help but think of the climactic scene in the film "V for Vendetta," in which Big Ben explodes at the stroke of midnight, a pyrotechnic capstone event on a smoldering underground of protest that finally flowers in the destruction of the symbols, and the agents, of the old world order.

But for all the seeming randomness of the protesters' agendas, they collectively work to the advantage of French President Nicholas Sarkozy, already the shit disturber of the G-20 summit. Sarkozy has noisily threatened to walk out of the summit unless it produces tighter global regulations on the financial industry, including tighter policing of hedge funds and tax havens, and more controls over the high-compensation culture of big business.

Precisely the action items that many, if not all, of the demonstrators would surely endorse.

Sarkozy's threat is a hollow one; it wouldn't be good for Franco-American relations to walk out of the summit attended by the president of the United States, then host that same president when he comes to your country to make a major address a few days later. Sarkozy wants desperately for France to be perceived as a major international player, and the G-20 summit is an ideal pulpit from which to make that case. It stands to reason, you can't be a player at a summit if you don't show up.

But Sarkozy's throwdown, and the vast protests in its wake, distill the issues at stake for the G-20; they call the question of how the world's economic titans will begin to address a crisis that began in their houses and infected much of the developing world.

4/1/2009

THE G-20 PRESCRIPTION

EPIDEMIOLOGISTS have for years debated the likelihood of various global nightmare scenarios, usually involving the speed at which a virus could circle the globe on today's modes of transportation. We've heard their fears of some potentially dangerous bug hitchhiking in the nasal mucosa of an airline passenger leaving New Delhi and landing in New York hours later with nothing to declare except the public-health catastrophe he doesn't know about — the disaster that passenger could unleash with one strong productive cough in a warm, crowded place.

The economic epidemiologists who gathered Wednesday and today in London at the G-20 summit — men and women sobered by the impact of the current financial crisis — have offered the first prescription for dealing with something that's gone from being an American problem to a global problem: the virus of fear that girdled the globe at a breathtaking clip.

The G-20 summiteers agreed to a mammoth $1.1 trillion infusion of capital into the International Monetary Fund, loan and guarantees to be used for the hardest-hit developing nations; they also agreed to begin tighter regulation of financial markets, and more stringent standards on executive compensation — a smart concession to summit activists Nicolas Sarkozy of France and Angela Merkel of Germany.

◊ ◊ ◊

"By any measure, the London summit was historic," said President Barack Obama, the junior member of the group and, economically speaking, the biggest stick on the playground. "It was historic because of the size and scope of the challenges that we face, and because of the timeliness and the magnitude of our response."

That response couldn't muffle the impact of two mortar rounds of economic information: the jobs report to be released on Friday will apparently show that 650,000 more jobs were lost in the United States in the month of March, deepening an already dire employment outlook. That report put the exclamation mark on another one: According to the National Economic Council and CBS News, the total global wealth destruction in the current crisis amounts to *$50 trillion* — an estimated $7,385 for every human being on earth — since the recession began at the end of 2007.

Joshua Cooper Ramo, former foreign editor at Time magazine and author of "The Age of the Unthinkable," was therefore probably right in his recent comments to NBC News: "The very nature of the international system is exploding in complexity. The G-20 in that regard is possibly as important a summit as we've had since Yalta at the end of World War II."

That historic parley, at which the Allied powers met to effectively decide the shape and structure of the postwar world, had an impact that endures today; our geopolitical perceptions, our sense of danger and threat, still use the Nazi example as an emotional tripwire.

Today's threats are a different thing. But the economic instability the G-20 summit was meant to address is bound up in a web of global inequities that could be the basis of other, more militaristic manifestations of unrest. Skirmishes over money have a nasty habit of turning into wars. Despite its emotional anti-Semitic inspiration, Adolf Hitler's rise to power had its real roots in a battered hyper-inflated Weimar economy in which a wheelbarrow full of deutschmarks couldn't buy a loaf of bread.

◊ ◊ ◊

Obama, who came to London looking for a global expansion of his domestic stimulus-package concept of direct infusion of capital, put the best possible face on being largely rejected by the summit powers.

"I think we did OK," Obama told reporters Thursday. "We have agreed on a series of unprecedented steps to restore growth and prevent a crisis like this happening again... We have created as fundamental a reworking of resources to these international financial institutions as anything we've done in the last several decades."

Merkel also accentuated the positive, calling the measures "a very, very good, almost historic compromise" that will give the world "a clear financial markets architecture."

"For the first time we have a common approach to cleaning up banks around the world to restructuring of the world financial system. We have maintained our commitment to help the world's poorest," British Prime Minister Gordon Brown said. "This is a collective action of people around the world working at their best."

◊ ◊ ◊

Well, maybe not all people around the world. In a statement, Mary Robinson, former president of Ireland and the honorary president of Oxfam International, voiced concerns that the first focus of all this recovery will be on the G-20 nations themselves — not the poorer countries not represented there.

"I do get the strong sense today that the G20's focus is much closer to home — that this meeting is about reforms through stronger regulation and stimulus packages all designed to move the richer and more powerful countries out of financial crisis," Robinson said.

"The developing world needs its own stimulus package to help ensure better global security and to meet finally the millennium development goals particularly to halve poverty and achieve people's rights to health and education," she said.

In its optics and its reach for solutions, the G-120 summit was a success, but only as far as it goes. You can fairly call it a beginning — the group is to meet again in the fall — and as such the summit deserves to be seen in a positive light. Now comes the trickier part: execution of the ideas. "The proof of the pudding is in the eating," Obama said today, and he's right. What's next is the need to make those ideas concrete, with cash on the barrelhead where it's needed, beyond the borders of those in the G-20.

4/2/2009

REVERSAL OF MISFORTUNE

THE BUSH administration, the gift that keeps on giving more than seventy days after it ceased to exist, left another judicial urine stain on the carpet of the young Obama administration. The new attorney general, Eric Holder, found the source of that stink, and in the process reawakened the confidence of those who believe in the rule of law.

In a statement on Wednesday, Holder requested that the conviction of former Alaska Sen. Ted Stevens be overturned, due to prosecutors withholding evidence vital to Stevens' defense. Claiming there was wide prosecutorial conduct in Stevens being convicted of perjury — for lying on a Senate disclosure form about $250,000 in gifts and home renovations he received —Holder requested the case be thrown out "in the interest of justice."

"After careful review, I have concluded that certain information should have been provided to the defense for use at trial," Holder's statement read in part.

Holder also said that the Justice Department's Office of Professional Responsibility would be dispatched to "conduct a thorough review of the prosecution of this matter."

Stevens defense attorney Brendan Sullivan said "the misconduct of the prosecutors was stunning to me. ... Not only did the government fail to provide evidence to the defense that the law requires hem to provide, but they created false testimony ... and they actually presented false testimony."

International human rights activist Scott Horton hailed the DOJ move in The Daily Beast:

"By walking away from its highest profile public-integrity prosecution of the last several years and directing a probe into the dealings of his own prosecutors, Holder set a new tone in the Justice Department," Horton said. "He also sent a strong signal of what the future may hold for more than a dozen other prosecutions of political figures during the Bush years. The Justice Department is now bracing for a makeover."

◊ ◊ ◊

What's so striking about this isn't necessarily Holder's stand on principle; it's the way in which Stevens, a Rock-Ribbed Republican, was victimized by the Republican-powered Justice Department of the Bush administration — an unlikely example of political misconduct jumping the partisan shark.

It's important not to make too much of Holder's decision exonerating Stevens, whose conviction last year may have cost him re-election in November. At the age of 85, Stevens had political prospects that were declining anyway, and nothing in Holder's action changes in the least the fact of Stevens having done the things he was prosecuted for.

But Holder's announcement puts further distance between his Justice Department and that of his more ethically challenged predecessors.

"He's sent a message to all of his career people that we're gonna play by the rules now," said John Dean, author of "Broken Government" and former Nixon White House counsel, speaking on MSNBC. "I think things had gotten a little loose and slack under prior attorneys general, during the Bush years. This sends a very clear message to his team and his prosecutors as to the conduct of his department."

It's tempting to wax cynical and say that Stevens beat the rap on a technicality, but that technicality is nothing less than the rule of prosecutorial procedure foundational to the law itself. After eight years of the law in relative wilderness, it's refreshing to find that counts for something again.

4/3/2009

THAT WAS THE WEEK THAT WILL BE

WHEN IT goes right, it really goes right: President Obama returns home on Tuesday from Europe with a pocketful of triumph. According to ESPN, the baller-in-chief's picks for the NCAA Basketball Tournament placed him in the 80th percentile of accuracy, with the president correctly choosing North Carolina to win the championship, nailing 14 out of the Sweet 16 correctly, and ending with an overall win-loss record of 40-22. If this presidential thing doesn't work out, there may be a professional place for him in the game somewhere.

But that was just the latest Obama win. The president comes home (Michelle's already back, with the First Kids) with the global wind strongly at his back. The first Obama European residency ends with stellar reviews, Obama oratorically knocking it out of the park with dazzling performances in London, Strasbourg, Prague and Ankara. In speeches that set a new course for American diplomacy, Obama's engaging personal style was wedded to a message of a change in American policy that saw the 44th POTUS embraced by a continent ready for something new from the world's change-agent nation.

But it was more than pure adulation, more than emotionalism. Articulating policy shifts from engagement with Iran over nuclear energy to improving Muslim-American relations, to negotiating a new strategic arms agreement with Russia to setting the United States on a course to "immediately and aggressively pursue U.S. ratification of the Comprehensive Test Ban Treaty" — President Obama set out nothing less than his own agenda for a different, presumably safer planet, a vision of new world order for real.

Barack Obama left Washington for Europe last Tuesday as a new American president, one whose brilliance in the sky remained largely, still, an American phenomenon. He returns home a week later as a statesman, one chastened by the rebuff of some European leaders on his global stimulus plan, but also invigorated by the same message he imparted to millions: The past doesn't have to be prologue to the future.

Years from now, historians may look back at the inaugural Obama World Tour as the period in which his presidency really began — not according to the narrow, procedural calendar of oath-taking and legislation and partisan wrangling, but in the wider context of leadership that the United States has historically presumed to define.

This was a week that Barack Obama spent daring the citizens of Europe, and by extension the world, to envision a seemingly impossible future. If his geopolitical vision is as good as his hoops bracketology, we've got a lot to forward to.

4/6/2009

THE MAN WHO FELL TO EARTH

SOMETIMES bad news travels slow, hanging back like a funeral at the end of a parade. In the wake of much-needed good news, it's sometimes hard to pick up the black crepe that's lurking just behind the confetti.

President Obama had a lot of good news last week and this: domestic poll numbers high, hailed to the skies in Europe and Turkey, and by the troops in Iraq (where he stopped on a surprise visit that was a finely patriotic icing on the cake).

But Obama returns to the United States just as a decision by his Justice Department has begun to resonate in this country, in the fast lanes of talk television and the Internet. Once it achieves critical mass of awareness in the public eye, this Rubicon action by the Justice Department will undo much of the goodwill Obama has cultivated with the American people, and utterly poison the steadily building sense in this nation that Obama was serious about reversing the damage of the Bush years.

◊ ◊ ◊

The Justice Department on Friday submitted to U.S. District Judge Vaughn R. Walker a motion to dismiss a lawsuit alleging that federal agents engaged in illegal e-mail and telephone surveillance of everyday U.S. citizens — perhaps the most cynical hallmark of the Bush administration.

The motion to dismiss the case, *Jewel v. National Security Agency*, claims that disclosing information on the NSA's warrantless wiretapping program would "cause exceptionally grave harm to national security."

In its motion, the Justice Department asserts that litigation over the wiretapping operation would require the government to rival classified "state secrets." It's the same rationale the Bush White House employed in working to protect telecommunications giants from prosecution from spying on American citizens.

The Electronic Frontier Foundation (EFF), the San Francisco-based nonprofit that monitors shifts in communications and Internet law, and a passionate advocate of free speech and consumer rights, lent its support to a 2006 lawsuit by customers of AT&T against AT&T, the Bush administration and the NSA for "illegal and unconstitutional dragnet communications surveillance in concert with major telecommunication companies."

That lawsuit was left unresolved when Congress, last year, passed HR 6304, granting retroactive immunity to telecoms for whatever spying activities they may have performed at the behest of the Bushies — immunity stretching back to 2001.

This unresolved lawsuit is the one the Justice Department, under Barack Obama and Attorney General Eric Holder, is seeking to dismiss.

The motion filed on Friday claims that EFF's assertion that government agencies gathered information on millions of ordinary Americans is false, and that the agencies would need to only violate the First and Fourth Amendments to the Constitution and the separation of powers doctrine if "a participant was reasonably believed to be associated with al Qaeda or an affiliated terrorist organization."

◊ ◊ ◊

It's dismaying to say the least. This is one area, one indisputable point of policy in which President Obama could put daylight — acres of it — between himself and one of the more loathed policies of the Bush administration. What would lead a scholar and a professor of constitutional law to do this, to photocopy the most pernicious clandestine domestic policy of his predecessor and make it his own?

It's dismaying for another reason. Coming at practically the same time as the Justice Department decision to request that the perjury conviction of former Alaska Sen. Ted Stevens be overturned "in the interest of justice," after prosecutorial misdeeds were discovered, the DoJ motion to dismiss fails to build confidence in the idea of the department speaking with one philosophical voice. How can a Justice Department stand fast "in the interest of justice" in one case, and then rationalize condoning warrantless wiretapping — contrary to the Constitution that embodies that justice?

"President Obama promised the American people a new era of transparency, accountability, and respect for civil liberties," EFF Senior Staff Attorney Kevin Bankston said in a statement on the group's Web site. "But with the Obama Justice Department continuing the Bush administration's cover-up of the National Security Agency's dragnet surveillance of millions of Americans, and insisting that the much-publicized warrantless wiretapping program is still a 'secret' that cannot be reviewed by the courts, it feels like deja vu all over again."

◊ ◊ ◊

Even as he triumphs internationally, this DoJ decision, and what it appears to say about the Obama administration's views of the American people, could be his political undoing at home.

The president has drawn fire for this and other inconsistencies of message and intent. He's already blinked, for example, on the matter of whether the Bush cabal should be investigated for war crimes at Guantánamo.

Jonathan Turley, a constitutional law professor at Georgetown University, said Tuesday on MSNBC that President Obama appears to have donned the guise of "constitutional relativists" for whom a foundational national document is apparently subject to contemporizing and annotation, like a college textbook crowded with Post-It notes. "This is the ultimate victory for the Bush officials," Turley said. "They have Barack Obama adopting the same extremist arguments — in fact, *exceeding* the extremist arguments made by President Bush."

Now, with the DoJ motion to dismiss this lawsuit, Obama has suddenly, inexplicably revealed a tone-deafness about the people he was elected to govern; a curious indifference to the potential for damage to the nation's already-fragile psyche; and, ironically, an inability to square the campaign meme of Change with the actions of an administration that change nothing, even when they should.

For months now, people have quietly wondered when Barack Obama's glide path would end, when the curtains of this Oz-wizard would be parted, when the seemingly levitational president would finally come to earth.

Perhaps now we know.

4/7/2009

WAR'S ULTIMATE COST, VISIBLE

ON FRIDAY, a suicide truck driver set off more than 2,000 pounds of explosives near the Iraqi National Police headquarters in the northern Iraqi city of Mosul, killing, among others, five American soldiers. It was the deadliest attack against U.S. forces in more than a year, the Army Times reported.

The process has already started: Five more American families will soon endure the grim visitation of uniformed officers arriving in the driveway with the worst possible news. Five more families will reckon with memories, and thwarted promise, and the need for closure.

Closure. That's the word employed so often to describe the needs of those affected by tragedy, families that seek the resolution of some outstanding issue — a fugitive suspect, a legal technicality, a judicial complication — that prevents them from grieving properly for the dear departed.

◊ ◊ ◊

For 18 years now, military families and the nation they represent have had that emotional finality abridged when it comes to the visible repatriation of American armed forces killed fighting either of two wars in the Middle East. Those families have seen their heroes, our heroes, return to America under cover of an official darkness that has made their homecoming almost invisible. For 18 years, photos of the caskets of slain servicemembers were prohibited.

No more. The United States has reversed its policy of not allowing media coverage of fallen servicemen and women killed in action. Secretary of Defense Robert Gates on April 1 approved a policy change that, under strict conditions, allows the media to record the transfer of the bodies of fallen servicemembers' remains at the Charles C. Carson Center for Mortuary Affairs at Dover Air Force Base in Delaware.

Gates had already announced his intention to change the bitterly debated policy last month, at a March 18 news conference. "We are committed to seeing that America's fallen heroes are received back to their loved ones and their country with the honor, respect and recognition that they and their families have earned," he said.

The Dover transfer ceremonies will be "modified to allow media access, when approved by the immediate families of the individual fallen," Gates said in a March 25 press release.

That fast, with not much more than the stroke of a pen, the policy begun in 1991 by President George H.W. Bush, during the Gulf War is retired. It's scant comfort for many families of the 4,263 other American servicemembers killed in Iraq, or the 677 Americans killed, to this date, in Afghanistan. But Gates' order undoes one of our government's more hotly debated and emotionally disturbing policies.

The Bush #41 policy reinforced the obscenely preposterous idea that war is an antiseptic exercise of political will, one whose devastating personal impact can be mitigated by invisible ceremonies far from public scrutiny. The thanks of a grateful nation recorded secretly and surgically. Bush #43 continued the policy, set it in stone even as the casualties from the Iraq war escalated.

Gates' reversal of policy wisely recognizes the relentless intrusions of a 24/7 media; and perhaps somewhat cannily understands the shift of the American people's attitude toward the war in Iraq, and what it's costing us.

But mostly Gates' change in policy seems to get *who* this war is costing us. The individuals. The people, from cities and small towns on both coasts and everywhere in between. By opening the door of media exposure to this most solemn series of events, it opens the door to letting the nation grieve, openly and properly and with a full acknowledgment of exactly what's at stake when this nation goes to war.

The issue's bigger than the crawl line at the bottom of the TV screen. It's bigger than the ten seconds of reporting from the talking heads at 11 o'clock. It's bigger than these things because when the story is properly told, in images and in words, it sharply distills for our visual culture the bigness of small things, of individual human beings we won't see again, people whose passing diminishes us all.

So many lives have been absented suddenly, lives that in too many cases had hardly begun. They're lives to which we barely had a chance to say hello. The new policy of the United States rightly, finally, gives the nation at least a chance at a proper goodbye.

4/11/2009

PERMANENT MARKER

L ORD ACTON, the famed 19th century British historian, is often quoted (to the exclusion of just about anything else he wrote) that "Power tends to corrupt, and absolute power corrupts absolutely." His 1887 observation, as true today as it was then, is one of those lessons that captains of industry, and leaders of governments, somehow fail to learn.

We hope the elegant simplicity of his most celebrated statement whispers in the inner inner ears of the Obama White House and the Democratic leadership right now, as a new salvo of scholarly studies suggests, with exhaustive statistical evidence, that the Democrats might actually realize what the Republicans can only dream of: a permanent political majority.

Thomas B. Edsall made the case today in The Huffington Post:

"A growing number of political scientists, analysts and strategists are making the case for a realignment of political power in the U.S. to a new Democratic majority based on two trends: 1) the increasing numbers of black and Hispanic voters, and 2) a decisive shift away from the Republican Party by the suburban and well-educated constituencies that once formed the backbone of the GOP."

◊ ◊ ◊

Edsall's persuasive story and analysis distill the recent findings of three political scholars: Ruy Texiera of the Center for American Progress, Emory University political scientist Alan Abramowitz, and John Judis of The New Republic.

Texeira makes his case in his March research paper for the Center:

"[A] new progressive America has emerged with a new demography, a new geography, and a new agenda.

"The new demography refers to the array of growing demographic groups that have aligned themselves with progressives and swelled their ranks. The new geography refers to the close relationship between pro-progressive political shifts

379

and dynamic growth areas across the country, particularly within contested states. The new agenda is the current tilt of the public toward progressive ideas and policy priorities—a tilt that is being accentuated by the strong support for this agenda among growing demographic groups."

Abramowitz, in an April research paper, makes a similarly conclusive case:

"Without question, the most important change in the composition of the American electorate over the past several decades has been a steady increase in the proportion of nonwhite voters. This trend has been evident for at least 50 years but it has accelerated in the last quarter century.

"It is a result of increased immigration from Asia, Africa and Latin America, higher birth rates among minority groups, and increased registration and turnout among African-Americans, Hispanics, and other nonwhite citizens. Moreover, this shift is almost certain to continue for the foreseeable future based on generational differences in the racial and ethnic composition of the current electorate and Census Bureau projections of the racial and ethnic makeup of the American population between now and 2050."

◊ ◊ ◊

The problem for Republicans may not be repaired for awhile. Texiera told Edsall:

"The problem at the moment is they have nothing much to sell at this point that the rising demographic groups and areas are interested in buying. And they still seem pretty far away from recognizing that fact."

Frankly, "nothing much to sell" is a charitable assessment of what's now at the GOP's disposal. Outflanked at every turn by a nimble, responsive, proactive and innovative White House, the Republican Party has entrenched itself in the rigid party ideology that's defined it for generations, retreating to the safe harbor of a reflex to be more opposition than loyal. "Circling the wagons" would be an apt metaphor, if there were any wagons to do it with.

Philosophically scattered to the four winds, the GOP has conceded the philosophical high ground to such incendiary figures as talk-radio windbag Rush Limbaugh and McCarthyite mouthbreathers like Minnesota Rep. Michele Bachmann, and to GOP talking-points photocopiers like Sean Hannity, Bill O'Reilly and Glenn Beck of Fox News. The daily operations of the party are overseen by Michael Steele, the new and largely ineffectual national committee chairman. And national figures like Arizona Sen. John McCain have been reduced to sideshow attractions, with McCain (a frequent guest on Leno and Letterman) apparently seeking to take over where Larry 'Bud' Melman left off.

◊ ◊ ◊

It's high cotton for the Democrats. But the prospect of seemingly endless political prospects can give rise to some dangerous thinking. It was Karl Rove, the Bush chief strategist, who once advanced the idea of a "permanent Republican majority."

Judis told Edsall: "The only circumstances that could bring back the Republicans is Obama's failure to stem the recession. Obama does have to succeed, and so far, he's pretty much on the right track, and the Republicans are definitely not. That suggests to me that he and the Democrats will be able to solidify their majority in 2010 and 2012," Judis said. "But again, I don't fully understand what is going on in the world, and events could defy demography."

The Obama White House gets this. Some have complained that Obama is trying to do too much too soon, missing the need for the urgency. The mess he's been left to clean up is enough for two administrations; its impact is felt widely enough after eight years, across every stratum of American society, that it just makes sense that the Democrats command a strong wind at their backs — the overwhelming support of the American people.

But, same as it ever was: Winds change direction. The unpredictable is the only predictable. If the Democrats are smart, or at least practical, the only permanent majority they're focused on is the one they can reliably count on between now and the next election.

That shouldn't determine their approach to governing, but it must govern their approach to electoral politics. There's an election *next year*, and we're halfway through April already. The Republicans may find the strike zone after all; after generations of relative stasis, the scales might still fall from their eyes about how to reach the people they would govern again, how to evolve as a party.

The Texiera-Judis-Abramowitz studies should be welcome news for the Democratic Party, and a sobering challenge at the same time: While permanence is too much to expect, nothing ensures a lasting political foundation like proven results.

"Republican hegemony is now expected to last for years, maybe decades," the conservative commentator Fred Barnes crowed in 2004. We know how that turned out. There's a lesson there. Absolutely.

4/14/2009

WEAK TEA FROM THE GOP

TODAY across our great land, conservative leaders, their bespoke media and a ragtag core of dead-enders did their best to come up with the launch of a movement renouncing big government and wasteful spending. But today's Tea Bag Tax Day events revealed not much more than the depth of Republican disaffection with anything the Obama administration does, as well as the ways in which that reflexive opposition is the GOP *idée fixe* of the moment, and apparently the future.

It's been planned for weeks now, and today, in demonstrations from Oak Harbor, Wash., to Sag Harbor, N.Y., protesters rallied to express opposition to big government in general, and specifically the multitrillion-dollar Obama budget, a budget made necessary in every way by the profligacies of his predecessor in the White House.

Officials in the nation's capital prevented what could have been a waste-disposal nightmare: the planned dumping of 1 million tea bags on the city — an attempt foiled because some organizers couldn't get the required permits (let's set aside for now the curious fact that you can even *get* a permit to conduct a dumping operation in front of the White House).

But right out of the gate, the big problem for the events was the source for much of the organizational acumen behind them. Lobbyists and business interests were behind the scenes, as well as former House Majority Leader Dick Armey and former House Speaker Newt Gingrich.

News Corporation, the misinformation conglomerate piloted by tireless media buccaneer Rupert Murdoch, did its part as Official Media Mouthpiece to the Tea Bag Games. Continuing the profligate spending that saw News Corp. lose more than $6 billion in the last quarter of 2008, News Corp. tentacle Fox News spent perhaps hundreds of thousands of dollars sending its anchors and staff to various Tea Party locations around the country, capping it all off with a prime-time special from Atlanta. "Thomas Paine," a craggy actor in a powdered wig, made some overbroad connections between the first Tea Party in 1773 and the current event, then introduced

Fox's cavalcade of ideologues: Sean Hannity! Newt Gingrich! Mike Huckabee! Joe the Plumber!

This clearly orchestrated, top-down, big-budget promotion put the lie to the idea, advanced by conservatives, that Tea Bag Day was some explosive expression of pent-up American frustration and rage. (We just had one of those on Nov. 4; it turned out rather well.) With such heavy hitters aboard, Tea Bag Day was weakened at the start by the intimate involvement of the very government and corporate insiders the event was intended to protest against.

There *was* a populist element to all this; you can't ignore it when American citizens gather to peacefully air their grievances in a unified chain of protests across the country. But there was a deep partisanship to it, some of it ugly and personal and even disturbing (OBAMA = HITLER, read one sign at the rally in Washington). The mix of lobbyists and insiders responsible for the Tea Bag protest, as well as anti-immigrationists, nativists and even white supremacists in Arizona made for one hell of a cocktail: tea mixed with the bile of agendaless conservatives bent on derailing a corrective to the mess their leadership created. And a hearty dash of snake oil.

◊ ◊ ◊

The protesters' boilerplate complaint seemed to be a philosophical platform you could write in big letters on a 3x5 index card: *Taxes are bad, the budget is too big, we can't afford it, Obama has no clue, and we're taking our country back!* You don't have to drill down terribly far to see the Tea Party protests as another transparent example of the GOP's current bankruptcy of ideas beyond the reflex of just saying No.

But the people who attended these anti-tax rallies, and the monied interests who lashed all this together, have to contend with some inconvenient facts that undercut the emotional, populist, quasi-hysterical rationale for the Tea Parties in the first place:

Effective April 1, the tax rate for 95 percent of all American wage earners went down, increasing their take-home pay. For the remaining 5 percent of American workers — those probable Tea Bag Day no-shows who earn $250,000 or more — taxes went up slightly, to previous levels of the Reagan administration.

All across America today, people protested that their taxes were too high two weeks to the day after their taxes went down. And this earnest attempt to dovetail the angst of Tax Day with a protest against those taxes didn't take something else into account: About 70 percent of Americans already get tax refunds from the IRS.

Then there was President Obama's well-timed announcement today of his plans to provide a tax credit of $2,500 for students to get college educations, and his plans to simplify the "monstrous" tax code itself.

Let's see, now … tax refunds, a new tax cut and, just maybe, aid to cash-strapped families of college students … Question to protesters: what the hell's wrong with that?

Clearly, what's driving this thing is politics. It's elder statesmen like Gingrich and Armey, along with party climbers like Indiana Rep. Mike Pence, who characterized the Tea Parties as "a building movement in this country … a growing tidal wave of discontent." It's built into the rhetoric of those farthest on the Republican right, some of them congressmen unalterably committed to both opposing President Obama's initiatives for repairing the economy, and opposing attempts at bipartisan outreach on that and other issues that urgently need attention.

The facts are as simple as a chronology of events: the Bush administration preceded the Obama administration. The problems with the economy didn't begin eighty days ago when Obama took office. The actions of the Obama White House are, for all the astronomical numbers in the budget, nothing more or less than a sober, measured attempt at correcting the policies and practices of the past eight years — a bid at correction that emphasizes the importance of the middle class.

But it's hard to hear that or anything else when your ears are stuffed with tea bags.

We'll see if this tea-lovers event actually is the first burst of the kind of truly viral, grassroots movement the Republicans need to revive their flagging political fortunes. We'll wait to find out if the one-issue identity of this protest develops into the principled, dedicated opposition that makes our democracy not just functional, but possible.

For now, though, Tea Bag Day was a sound and fury signifying nothing but Republican desperation, fodder for late-night comedians, and a buying opportunity for investors in Unilever, the parent concern of the Thomas J. Lipton Company.

4/15/2009

BARRY AND THE PIRATES

Leon, somewhere in Libya right now there's a janitor working the night shift at the Libyan Intelligence Headquarters. He's going about his job 'cause he has no idea that in about an hour he's gonna die in a massive explosion. He's just going about his job 'cause he has no idea that an hour ago I gave an order to have him killed. You just saw me do the least presidential thing I do.

— From "The American President," screenplay by Aaron Sorkin

◊ ◊ ◊

INTELLECTUALLY, we know it's true, of course, but emotionally it still stuns us a little when we see it actually happen: for all the pomp and majesty of his office, despite his ability to impart small-d democratic benevolence and values around the globe, the President of the United States of America has a frighteningly awesome power to get people killed.

We saw this play out over the last week, in one of the too-often repeated acts of piracy off the coast of Somalia, after Richard Phillips, the captain of the 17,000-ton container ship Maersk Alabama, was kidnapped by four Somali pirates who held him in one of the Alabama's lifeboats. As the drama played out over three days, it captured the world's attention, and that of President Obama, and that of the United States Navy, which sent the destroyer USS Bainbridge to the region to rescue the captain and bring the situation to a close.

Shortly after tying up with the drifting lifeboat to stop its drift toward the Somali coastline, the Bainbridge dispatched three Navy snipers to its deck. There, in the dark and on the deck of a rolling ship, said snipers calmly aimed high-powered rifles at the lifeboat, fired and killed three of the pirates with apparently simultaneous shots to the head. (The fourth pirate was captured by the Navy after jumping off the lifeboat earlier.)

Numerous news reports made the point of mentioning that President Obama "personally approved" the operation, and the administration gained generally high marks for the surgical performance of a mission that could have gone horribly wrong.

◊ ◊ ◊

But for this president, an entirely necessary demonstration of presidential authority may have had an especially barbed resonance attached.

There's no escaping the fact that the Navy snipers, doing the job they were trained to do, nonetheless killed three Somalis who were apparently only teenagers, three people who took a desperately criminal path to acquiring food, self-respect and economic self-sufficiency. Three young black men executed by the United States, on the authority of the black man who runs the United States.

Yes, there's no getting around the fact that when Barack Obama took the oath of office 89 days ago, he swore to preserve, protect and defend the Constitution — and by extension, to do the same for his country and the people living under the Constitution.

Word is bond: "We must continue to work with our partners to prevent future attacks, be prepared to interdict acts of piracy, and ensure that those who commit acts of piracy are held accountable for their crimes," the president said April 13.

But for this first African American president, even if he never said as much, there's bound to have been at least one hot pang of deep regret at having to kill three Africans, people whose lives had barely begun. People with a common ancestral heritage. The authorization of sudden and impersonal death shouldn't be an easy, rote thing to do, even when legally justified; we can be sure it was not for President Obama, as vulnerable and empathic and human as any of his 43 predecessors, and more so than many of them.

◊ ◊ ◊

Leave it to conservative malcontents of the moment to put an ugly spin on things. GOP voice box Rush Limbuagh took crassness to a whole new level on Tuesday, when the former recreational pharmaceutical enthusiast offered the following analysis on his talk-radio show:

"You know what we have learned about the Somali pirates, the merchant marine organizers that were wiped out at the order of Barack Obama, you know what we learned about them? They were teenagers. The Somali pirates, the merchant marine organizers who took a U.S. merchant captain hostage for five days were inexperienced youths, the defense secretary, Robert Gates, said yesterday, adding that the hijackers were between 17 and 19 years old. Now, just imagine the hue and cry had a Republican president ordered the shooting of black teenagers on the high seas. ..."

Thus, by playing a race card of his own invention, Jabba the Rush racialized the issue of protecting American citizens abroad; laughably rebranded the Somali pirates as "merchant marine organizers"; and actually dared to align the killing of these freelance buccaneers with the killing of African Americans here at home.

"If only President Obama had known that the three Somali community organizers were actually young black Muslim teenagers, I'm sure he wouldn't have given the order to shoot," Limbaugh said. "That's the correct way to look at it. If only Obama had known."

Rush the Hutt's perverted calculus of course fails to pass the muster of reality at many levels. The U.S. military isn't in the habit of checking IDs before conducting a military operation; nor do they vet the targets of such operations for their race or socioeconomic status. When necessary, U.S. armed forces are an equal opportunity destroyer. Often, tragically so.

It's a tribute to Obama's deliberate style of conducting business that this event was resolved in an orderly fashion, and conducted with such deft surgical use of military resources that, to this point, conservative thought leaders and the reflexively-opposed Republicans in Congress haven't had that much to say negatively about the Phillips rescue.

◊ ◊ ◊

In his first emergency international crisis occasioning the use of armed force to save American lives, President Obama has an unqualified success, if a tragic one. The rescue of Captain Phillips shows that Obama means to chart a new course in America's relationship with the world, even as he intends to continue the defense of American interests — like American citizens — with force, if required.

This grim, low-key triumph puts the lie to statements by obstreperous, duplicitous French President Nicolas Sarkozy, who said privately that Obama was "weak" and "inexperienced." France had a similar hostage rescue situation days before the Maersk Alabama was seized, one that ended with the death of one of the hostages.

But this wasn't a Bring It On moment for Obama; while the mission was accomplished, you won't see a banner screaming those words on the USS Bainbridge. The Obama administration has shown itself to be that rarity, something we haven't had in the White House in far too long: a team that respects the use of force, uses it reluctantly, and uses it precisely, with a response tailored to the threat.

Of all the three o' clock mornings he's had since Jan. 20 (and count on it, he's had at least a few), Obama no doubt had a singular one on Easter Sunday, that special date in the Christian calendar. By the time he and the First Family had finished attending church, it was all over. The crisis was done, American interests had been defended, emergency food relief meant for Africa's impoverished millions got to its destination … and somewhere in Somalia three families mourned three lives they would never see again.

It may have been the least presidential thing a president does. In other equally compelling ways, it's also the most presidential thing a president is forced to do.

4/18/2009

AND A CHILD SHALL LEAD THEM: MEGHAN MCCAIN ROCKS THE HOUSE

THE REPUBLICAN Party, eager if not straight-up desperate to find someone to fill its existential vacuum and speak truth to power in the Age of Twitter, may have found its salvation in an apple who didn't fall far from the tree.

Meghan McCain? You go girl.

With a steadily escalating profile in interviews and online, the 24-year-old daughter of Arizona Sen. John McCain is proving to be that rarity in Republican politics: someone with the ovarian fortitude to stand up and dismiss the old guard, saying things about the GOP the GOP leadership wouldn't dare volunteer. With no promises to keep or fears of excommunication from the rock-ribbed right, she's been speaking with a candor that spans generational lines — just what the Republicans need. If only they'll listen.

Hurricane Meghan most recently surfaced at a weekend address before the Log Cabin Republicans in Washington, McCain squarely confronted the generational divide the GOP has failed to either acknowledge or work to correct. The high point of the address was a three-point *cri de coeur*, one the party elders can't sweep under the rug.

"Number one, most of our nation wants our nation to succeed. Number two, most people are ready to move on to the future, not live in the past. Number three, most of the old-school Republicans are scared shitless of that future."

It doesn't get much plainer than that, folks. All the GOP position papers and think-tank studies, all the surveys and talking points and speculations about the Future of the Party come down to those forty-one words.

With that succinct call to arms, McCain issued a firm slap upside the head of conservative voice box Rush Limbaugh, presented a sketch (if not a blueprint) for the party's future, and put the graybeards of the GOP on notice that anything less than openly embracing that American future would court more of the disasters the party's endured since 2006.

Some party water carriers get the point. "Some of the things she articulated are really emblematic of the issues the party's facing right now," said Republican strategist Doug Heye, today on MSNBC. "What she said should give Republicans something to think about."

Meghan McCain has taken rhetorical 2x4s to the heads of conservative darlings before. In interviews and in her writing on The Daily Beast and other appearances, she's taken on conservative pit-bull apologists Ann Coulter and Laura Ingraham, and the rigidity of Republican thinking generally.

She made many of the same Log Cabin address points in a March 23 interview with Larry King on CNN. "I think that's the problem right now, is that the party is without a leader and sort of without a vision."

Clearly, outspokenness isn't specific to the Y chromosome of the McCain family DNA. Sen. McCain has long developed a reputation as something of a too-plain-spoken battler in Congress; the halls of the Senate ring with stories of McCain's mercurial temper showing itself, the senator involved in one rhetorical or physical scrap or another. As we know.

But with the younger McCain, that scrappiness is wrapped in a package of smoothly delivered political pragmatism that belies the youth of the one expressing it. And maybe that's the point — that someone so young *gets it*, understands intuitively what the Republicans need to be contenders again, makes this viewpoint exactly what they need. This is more than reaching across the proverbial aisle; Meghan McCain's throwdown is a dare to the GOP to rethink what it is, from the ground up. If she decides to go that way, she may be a better politician than her father ever was.

Hey Boehner, Kantor, Gingrich, Rush the Hutt! Want a vision for the possible future of the GOP? Meghan McCain may have laid one out in the King interview, when the Venerable One on CNN asked her how she defined herself politically. "I consider myself a progressive Republican. I am liberal on social issues, and I think the party is at a place where social issues shouldn't be the issues that define the party."

Want another blueprint to the future? Listen to what Meghan McCain told the Log Cabin Republicans on Saturday — the way she blends party orthodoxy with the individuality of the electorate:

"I am proud to join you in challenging this mold and the notions of what being what a Republican means. I am concerned about the environment. I wear a lot of black. I think that government is best when it stays out of people's lives and businesses as much as possible. I love punk rock music. I believe in a strong national defense. I have a tattoo. I believe government should always be efficient and accountable. I have lots and lots of gay friends, and yes, I am a Republican."

Proposed to Republicans: a tweak of the Bible, something straight outta Isaiah, more or less:

If thou seekest to depart from thy wilderness, yea, take ye the hand of the fair maiden who cometh from the desert, and the child shall lead ye out. And the lion shall dwell with the lamb, and the elephant shall find common cause with the donkey — for thy party's sake.

4/20/2009

DAYS OF HAIR ON FIRE:
THE BUSH WHITE HOUSE
RATIONALE FOR TORTURE

THERE'S a kind of longed-for red meat journalists scarcely seem to get in the Internet era: a scandal with vast political and constitutional implications. That's the multicourse feast that journos are apparently just beginning now, in the wake of a widening gyre of disclosures about the rationalization and use of torture methods by the Bush White House.

It was about a week ago when Attorney General Eric Holder released four of the Justice Department torture memos dating to August 2002, documents thought to be the blueprint for a legal rationale for torturing terrorist suspects under the grand pretext of national security.

These followed the infamous John Yoo memo of March 2003, up until recently the rhetorical smoking gun of the Bush White House reasoning for the torture of terrorist suspects.

But now, into the past: Today's Washington Post reports that the timeline for this panoramic criminality reaches back even further. The Post is reporting that the Joint Personnel Recovery Agency, the government agency responsible for training military interrogators, advised William J. Haynes, lawyer for then-Secretary of Defense Donald Rumsfeld in July 2002 that using methods of torture such as sleep deprivation, exploitation of phobias, forced nudity and waterboarding were "unreliable" as a way of getting information.

"The requirement to obtain information from an uncooperative source as quickly as possible — in time to prevent, for example, an impending terrorist attack that could result in loss of life — has been forwarded as a compelling argument for the use of torture," the document said.

"In essence, physical and/or psychological duress are viewed as an alternative to the more time-consuming conventional interrogation process. The error inherent in this line of thinking is the assumption that, through torture, the interrogator can extract reliable and accurate information.

History and a consideration of human behavior would appear to refute this assumption."

The JPRA recommendation was disregarded. That same month, Rumsfeld and national security adviser Condoleezza Rice, later secretary of state, gave their blessing to CIA operatives' use of so-called "alternative interrogation methods" when interrogating Zubaydah. Methods that included waterboarding.

◊ ◊ ◊

But that just gets you to July 2002. Turns out you can wind the clock back even further than that. The blogger Invictus did. In a blog entry from last Dec. 12, detailing his own personal coverage of Senate Armed Services Committee hearings in September, Invictus noted:

one document produced from the December 2001 contact — a fax cover sheet from the Pentagon's Joint Personnel Recovery Agency (JPRA), sent from "Lt. Col. Dan Baumgartner" to "Mr. Richard Shiffrin," who worked for Haynes in Rumsfeld's DoD General Counsel office — introduces a theme of aggressive courting by [JPRA] personnel to take on the interrogations/exploitation task.

Baumgartner was a training expert with JPRA. Shiffrin was a deputy general counsel in the Defense Department.

Invictus quotes from Baumgartner's opening statement before the Senate committee in June 2008:

"My recollection of my first communication with [Defense Department Office of General Counsel] relative to [interrogation] techniques was with Mr. Richard Shiffrin in July 2002. However, during my two interviews with Committee staff members last year, I was shown documents that indicated I had some communication with Mr. Shiffrin related to this matter in approximately December 2001. Although I do not specifically recall Mr. Shiffrin's request to the JPRA for information in late 2001, my previous interviews with Committee staff members and review of documents connected with Mr. Shiffrin's December 2001 request have confirmed to me the JPRA, at that time, provided Mr. Shiffrin information related to this Committee's inquiry."

Baumgartner's recall was pretty good. Borrowing from the Senate Committee report, The New York Times reported on April 22 that in December 2001, Baumgartner warned in a memo that physical pressure (read: torture) was "less reliable" than other interrogation approaches, could backfire by raising prisoner resistance, and would have an "intolerable public and political backlash when discovered." But his memo somehow got routed to the Defense Department, Haynes' domain, instead of the C.I.A.

◊ ◊ ◊

For those of you keeping score at home, trying to make sense of things, this is what this means:

Just months after the horrors of Sept. 11, 2001 — well before our military invasion of Iraq, before the high-value terrorist suspects were captured, before torture could have been used on those suspects, before torture could possibly have been a last-ditch way to extract information *from* those suspects — the Bush administration, in the anguished hair-on-fire days after the worst attack on American soil, had already begun to build a rationale for torture as part of the American arsenal.

This puts the lie to the notion that the notorious abuses at Abu Ghraib prison that seared the conscience of the world were the work of a few bad military actors, a handful of soldier xenophobes with a mean streak and blood in their eyes, avenging 9/11.

This puts the lie to the idea that Khalid Sheikh Mohammed and Abu Zubaydah were subject to waterboarding only when CIA and military personnel were at their teeth-gnashing wit's end to extract intelligence.

Torture was in the cards as a weapon for the Bush White House well before the bombs started falling in March 2003, before Mohammed or Zubaydah were captured. The plans for that shock & awe by invasion were long preceded by plans to induce shock and the fear of death by drowning — one of the methods of torturing prisoners the Bush White House quietly

embraced in the name of national security, and in violation
of the Uniform Code of Military Justice, the United Nations
Convention Against Torture, Common Article 3 of the 1949
Geneva Conventions, and the basic decency that binds us
together as human beings.

◊ ◊ ◊

The unraveling of that great lie takes place in the midst of
the overwhelming opinion of analysts, psychiatrists and
intelligence-gathering experts that torture almost always fails
to elicit the results intended.

Mohammed was waterboarded 183 times; Zubaydah
83 times. You don't have to be an intel specialist to see the
unpromising inverse proportionality of such a practice; it's the
law of diminishing returns according to Gitmo: the more one
tortures, the less likely the torturer gets anything meaningful
— or even anything real.

"The reliability and accuracy of this information is in
doubt" if it's obtained through "physical or psychological
duress," the JPRA warned in July 2002. "In other words, a
subject in extreme pain may provide an answer, any answer, or
many answers in order to get the pain to stop."

It's of course anyone's guess as to how far back this
evolving reverse chronology of Bush-era torture techniques
really goes. Vice President Dick Cheney's been on board with
the practice since at least October 2006. "It's a no-brainer for
me," he said on a conservative talk radio program from Fargo
N.D., "but for a while there, I was criticized as being the vice
president 'for torture.'"

Watergate, among many other celebrated political scandals
here and abroad, showed us how such flagrant excesses of
constitutional authority are never spasmodic exercises in
freelancing; they're really planned, systematic strategeries
devised by the guy in the grey suit who looks out the window
all day. The fish stinks from the head down.

As the Senate committee report reverberates around
Washington, as dominoes fall and smart, hungry journalists
fill in the gaps, the former Vice President for Torture and the

figures in the administration he once worked for will find there's no reverse-engineering the history that reveals itself one document, one backtrack, one revelation at a time. A clock that runs backwards can tell time very well.

4/25/2009

ARLEN SPECTER'S
GREAT MIGRATION

THE NATION'S capital rarely experiences earthquakes of any detectable magnitude. The last one in the area occurred on May 6, 2008. According to the U.S. Geological Survey, that temblor measured 1.8 on the Richter scale. The epicenter was maybe a mile west-southwest of Annandale, Va. (38.828°N, 77.234°W). That quake jostled Northern Virginia. Some people in nearby Silver Spring and Bethesda, Md., felt it too.

That seismological event pales in comparison with the earthquake that occurred early this afternoon East Coast time. The epicenter was in one of the meeting rooms on Capitol Hill, where Arlen Specter, for 29 years a Senator and until now the ranking Republican on the Senate Judiciary Committee, announced his switch to the Democratic Party. The USGS didn't record anything, but on the Richter scale of politics, the shock waves of this event may just be beginning.

"I found myself increasingly at odds with the Republican philosophy and more with the philosophy of the Democratic Party," Specter said at a press conference.

"I have traveled the state and surveyed the sentiments of the Republican Party in Pennsylvania and public opinion polls ... and have found that the prospects for winning the Republican primary are bleak. I am not prepared to have my 29-year record in the United States Senate decided by the Pennsylvania Republican primary electorate. ... I'm prepared to take on all comers in the general election."

◊ ◊ ◊

There's no denying that Specter's decision was politically pragmatic. Specter was looking down the barrel of a serious primary challenge from former GOP Rep. Pat Twoomey. "Former Pennsylvania Congressman Patrick Toomey was seen as a strong candidate who could possibly have defeated Specter in the Republican primary. Additionally, Toomey is widely acknowledged as the more conservative candidate," Talk Radio News Service reported today.

But there was apparently more than a little principle behind his decision. Specter's prepared statement said: "I have been a Republican since 1966. I have been working extremely hard for the Party, for its candidates and for the ideals of a Republican Party whose tent is big enough to welcome diverse points of view. While I have been comfortable being a Republican, my Party has not defined who I am. I have taken each issue one at a time and have exercised independent judgment to do what I thought was best for Pennsylvania and the nation. ...

"I have decided to run for re-election in 2010 in the Democratic primary."

If Al Franken wins his never-ending court case in Minnesota against Norm Coleman, as is fully expected, Democrats would have achieved the numerical Holy Grail of congressional politics: the filibuster-proof level of 60 votes, and thus the ability to advance the agenda of the Obama administration in a period of national urgency that screams for action, not gridlock, in the Congress.

It's not clear when Specter would start formally caucusing with Democrats, but since Specter has reportedly been talking to a number of high party officials — Vice President Biden, among them — for weeks now, it's safe to say that as a political matter, caucusing has already begun.

◊ ◊ ◊

As you might expect, the Republican long knives have been drawn, the usual mouthpieces of the party weighing in against Arlen the Apostate.

Talk-radio Doberman and former recreational pharmaceutical enthusiast Rush Limbaugh jumped in early. "A lot of people said, 'well, Specter, take McCain with you, and his daughter with you," he fumed this morning.

"Senator Specter didn't leave the GOP based on principles of any kind," said RNC Chairman and erstwhile GOP ambassador to hiphop America Michael Steele. "He left to further his personal political interests because he knew that he was going to lose a Republican primary due to his left-wing voting record."

Steele, jabbering in hip-argot mode again, told CNN later that Specter would definitely be in the crosshairs. "[I]f Senator Specter survives into the fall, get ready to go to the mat, baby, because we're coming after you and we're taking you out."

The Hill reported Tuesday that Senate Republican Leader Mitch McConnell of Kentucky said Specter's decision was a "threat to the country."

McConnell accused Specter of having practiced naked politics (imagine that).

"I think the threat to the country presented by this defection really relates to the issue of whether or not in the United States of America our people want the majority to have whatever it wants without restraint, without a check or a balance," McConnell said at a press availability attended by The Hill.

◊ ◊ ◊

But some on the right were more practical.

"This is a sad day for the GOP," Michael Smerconish, a conservative Philadelphia radio host, told Sam Stein of The Huffington Post. "He is what the party needed to be. They need to cultivate more Specters instead of deriding him as a RINO [Republican In Name Only]."

"On the national level of the Republican Party, we haven't certainly heard warm, encouraging words about how they view moderates, 'either you are with us or against us,'" said Sen. Olympia Snowe of Maine, one of the few remaining so-called moderates left standing.

Snowe told The New York Times that Republican leaders didn't get the idea that "political diversity makes a party stronger, and ultimately we are heading to having the smallest political tent in history for any political party the way things are unfolding."

Specter said as much himself. "Well, the party has shifted very far to the right. It was pretty far to the right in 2004."

"This is a painful decision," he said. But "[d]isappointment runs in both directions."

◊ ◊ ◊

Burnishing his reputation as an iconoclast willing to break with party orthodoxy, Specter said he wouldn't be sitting in the Democrats' amen corner on every piece of their legislation. "I will not be an automatic 60th vote," he said at the press conference. "I will not hesitate to disagree and vote my individual thinking." To reinforce this, Specter mentioned that he would continue to oppose the Employee Free Choice Act, a darling bill of the Democrats — the so-called "card check" proposal that would make it easier for workers to form unions.

At least one other Democrat played down the idea of lockstep party-line votes.

"Sixty members doesn't translate to 60 votes, so it doesn't really change anything for me," said conservative Democratic Sen. Ben Nelson of Nebraska to Ryan Grim of The Huffington Post. "The automatic assumption that people will take from this is, 'Ah, things are changing.' And maybe they will, but it's not automatic."

But there's no denying the impact this top-shelf defection will have on the Republicans, already in deep existential crisis, and on an Obama administration, which today, a day early, realized perhaps the perfect political capstone on a breakthrough first 100 days.

And there's no way the Republican party can overlook the story that's bigger than Specter's flight to the Democrats: the fact that 200,000 Pennsylvania Republicans made the same migration before the presidential election last year.

There's your aftershock. What matters isn't what Arlen Specter did, it's the seismic shift in political thinking that Arlen Specter now represents.

4/28/2009

DAY 1(00)

THE ROADS and turnpikes of the state of Pennsylvania will probably be a joy to drive on very soon. Besides receiving its part of the stimulus money devoted to the national infrastructure, the Keystone State can be expected to eventually gain other benefits from the party in power, the Democrats, whose ranks swelled by one on Tuesday, when PennsylvaniaRepublican Senator Arlen Specter walked across the aisle, apparently for good.

Specter's reverberant action on Tuesday conveyed unto the Democrats the numerical bragging right, the legislative tipping point of a 60th seat in the United States Senate. In ways we've yet to see, that lever of a decided majority may be the most powerful weapon at the disposal of President Barack Obama.

Today — the 100th day of an Obama administration poised for action on a number of vital fronts — can also mark the first day of a truly productive phase of an administration suddenly liberated from the prospect of indefinite senatorial gridlock.

It took him a hundred days, but now, today, Barack Obama may well have achieved his first chance to truly, fully govern this nation.

◊ ◊ ◊

We've been waiting for today — the 100-Day Milestone Benchmark Touchstone — almost as long as we had to wait for Bo, the first dog. Both wings of the punditburo will cough up bulletized hairballs, "report cards" and subjective checklists of promises kept and promises shunted, for now, to the back or the side of the first-term agenda.

Even by the twisted, elastic, utterly partisan yardstick of the Republicans who oppose him as a conditioned reflex, President Obama has so far been more than game to the challenge of the presidency, a thoroughbred whose biggest shortcoming may be an outsize sense of what's possible in a nation whose largest institutions — the ones right now most in need of various rescues — are the ones that move the slowest.

Michael E. Ross

He's advanced on several fronts: repealing restrictions on stem-cell research; rolling back destructive Bush White House initiatives on energy and the environment; closing the Guantánamo Bay prison and torture facility; and endeavoring to impose a finality — an end time if not an end date — on the tragic, costly and unnecessary war in Iraq.

But what's important isn't so much what Obama has achieved legislatively or by executive order; what predominates in these 100 days has to do with what he represents to the American people: a sense of the possible, that indelible embrace of the future we haven't had in quite a while. It's not tangible, it doesn't lower your mortgage interest rate, and it sure as hell isn't folding money.

But that *feeling* of things improving, the ability to impart that intrinsically American sense of Yes is as central to the presidency as the nuclear launch codes. That appeal reflects not the cult of personality, as the conservatives insist, but the *power* of personality. And there's a profound difference between the two.

◊ ◊ ◊

The American people are able to make that distinction. The latest Associated Press poll finds public approval of Obama in the 60 percent range, up there with heavy hitters like Roosevelt, Reagan and Clinton at similar points in their presidencies. And the new NBC News/Wall Street Journal poll, sampling Americans' feelings towards Obama, found that 51 percent approve of him and his policies, while another 30 percent approve of him personally even though they disagree with those policies.

That's why the end of the "honeymoon" predicted by the punditburo and ardently desired by the Republicans may not come to pass in the usual way. Americans understand that the listing ship of our economy didn't take on water overnight, and couldn't possibly be righted in a hundred days, or two hundred or maybe even three.

That doesn't mean President Obama gets a pass. Style points get you just so far. Some of his most important campaign

404

pledges — an insistence on the rule of law; a refusal to turn a blind eye to lawbreakers — have yet to fully materialize. As Obama's taken up the baton of leadership, he's found himself squaring the circle between the rhetoric of the campaign and the reality of governing.

Sen. Specter's defection will make that reconciling of principle and practice an easier thing to accomplish. But President Obama must going forward continue to stay out in front of the American experience, holding himself accountable for the nation's policies, staying in touch with the country he leads and doing it with the visible accessibility we associate with the nation's best leaders.

◊ ◊ ◊

It's like when you're riding the New York City subway or the BART train in San Francisco, and midway through your journey, the train … slows … to a stop somewhere under the heaving bowels of Manhattan or some point under the cold water of San Francisco Bay.

You don't know why you've stopped. You're sure it's for a good reason. But it's reassuring to hear the voice of the engineer, telling you: *Everybody chill, we have a technical difficulty, we'll be moving soon.* You can't do anything about it, but it's just good to hear someone's on the case doing his level best to get things moving again. Somebody's at the helm. Someone's in charge.

Whatever happens over the next 1,363 days, President Obama will do himself a lot of good by maintaining and building on the visceral connection he has with the American people. No doubt, his legislative agenda will advance in fits and starts; setbacks and missteps are coming that he won't be able to do anything about; we can count on coming global upheavals that Obama can neither predict nor prevent.

But as long as Obama maintains his dialogue with the American people, and continues working to pursue the agenda that won him election, he'll be able to make withdrawals from the tranche of national goodwill he now enjoys.

Michael E. Ross

There's no challenge he'll face in the future that can't be first addressed by his being the communicator-in-chief, the kind of communicator he's been for the last hundred days, the kind this Bushed nation has desperately needed for the last eight years.

4/29/2009

406

PLANET MICHAEL

OVER forty years, Michael Jackson proved he knew how to take center stage. On Thursday he showed he knew how to exit the stage, too. Jackson's joyous, macabre hold on the popular imagination was so total that when he passed on Thursday afternoon in Los Angeles, hundreds danced under the marquee of the Apollo Theater in Harlem; hundreds of people, black or white, laughing and in tears, singing the songs that made him the most influential figure in pop-music history.

He jacked up cell-phone traffic and damn near crashed the Internet; AT&T reported that it was sending text messages at a rate of 65,000 per second in the hours after the news broke. Google went into "self-protective mode" after being flooded with searches related to nothing more complex than the singer's name.

Now comes the postmortem. Less than 24 hours after the word went out that he was dead, the speculation's begun on what brought on the demise of a man at the heartbreaking age of 50. Jackson's long known to have abused prescription drugs; some are darkly invoking the idea of a departure like Elvis, with narcotics prescribed by, if not administered by, an unknown doctor feelgood.

MJ's passing leaves a number of questions about his three children, the oldest an impressionable 12 years old. The wrangling over their custody, and ugly insinuations about their biological provenance, has already started.

And Michael's death effectively creates a California Estate Lawyers' Full Employment Act; resolving his financial condition — a farrago of suits, countersuits, unpaid bills and obligations — could tie up attorneys for months or years to come.

◊ ◊ ◊

So now he belongs to the fans and, absolutely, the lawyers. But Michael's early departure also cements him to the ages. Like Louis, Miles, Bing, Sinatra, Trane and Elvis, Michael is now in the hall of the immortals and, on the basis of commercial impact, may be the first among equals. History knows Michael Jackson on a first-name basis from now on.

The lucrative value of his image, its merchandising potential, will make him more marketable now than he was before. It's been said: death can be a brilliant career move; witness the still-thriving catalogs of some of those in the rock pantheon of untimely departures: Buddy, Jimi, Janis, Elvis, Bob and Kurt.

Amazon.com reported Thursday having exhausted its presumably large cache of Michael Jackson albums and DVDs; eBay saw a big spike in its traffic, caused largely by items of Jackson memorabilia, their worth ghoulishly escalated in an instant. That $500 million debtload Michael was facing may be more easily retired now than when Michael was alive.

And eventually, Hollywood loves an icon: Sure as night follows day, right now, a scriptwriter there is sketching out the first outlines of what will become a Major Motion Picture.

◊ ◊ ◊

But ultimately, it's bigger than iconography and marketing and royalties and the images we associate with them. Like Louis and Ray and Miles and James, Michael changed the sound of our sound.

As you'd expect, the immediate vacuum of his absence was filled by the media, in a clamor for clicks, viewers and readers that goes on today.

But with his suddenly inescapable ubiquity in the mediascape — All Michael All the Time — Michael Jackson became visibly again what he's always been (more surreptitiously) for years: not just a component of popular culture but one of its central, indispensable molecules whose absence would change the sound we hear, dull the beats we move to, dilute the spectacles we've become accustomed to.

Sir Mix-a-Lot said it Friday from Seattle, put the Michael Jackson phenomenon in a context that has less to do with adoration of a public figure and more to do with participation in that figure's vision: "He was that planet we all wanted to land on."

◊ ◊ ◊

And ultimately we *did* land on that planet, or we discovered, on Thursday afternoon, that Michael's planet is the one we're already on. The one that Michael's sound unified. The one that Michael's music proves we share. The one whose spiritual oxygen is permanently juiced by a voice and musical talent the likes of which we will never see again — but which will be with us every day, everywhere, forever.

That'll do for a snapshot definition of timelessness. Need another one? There may be no better proof of Michael Jackson's impact in the world of music and culture, the irrepressible joy of his sound amid the horrors of our modern life, than what's happening in world capitals from London to Berlin to Beijing in his honor, and what happened in flashmobs in London and Liverpool ...

And what happened spontaneously and boisterously in New York City, where it all began.

Three hours after he was dead, Michael Jackson was live at the Apollo.

You want timeless? Top that.

6/27/09

INDEX

Symbols

414

417

W

Y

Z

SOURCES & SELECT BIBLIOGRAPHY

Over the four years and five months these blog posts and essays were written (http://culchavox.blogspot.com), the author borrowed and attributed numerous quotes from several news sources, including The Associated Press, The New York Times, The Washington Post, the Los Angeles Times, The Wall Street Journal, Newsweek, The Huffington Post, MSNBC, CNN, ABC News, CBS News, NBC News, National Public Radio, Time, Radar, The Nation, The Atlantic, BBC News, The Politico, Salon, the Gallup Poll and the Pew Research Center for People and the Press. The sources have been attributed to the best of my ability.

The author gratefully acknowledges use of the following:

"Norman Whitfield: Just His Imagination" © 2008 Washingtonpost Newsweek Interactive, reprinted by permission.

"The All-American Family Crisis" © 2008 Washingtonpost Newsweek Interactive, reprinted by permission.

"Comic Relief in the Obama Age" © 2009 Washingtonpost Newsweek Interactive, reprinted by permission.

"Movement Music" © 2009 Washingtonpost Newsweek Interactive, reprinted by permission.

"August Wilson's Century in Blacks and Blues" © 2005 MSNBC Interactive News LLC, reprinted by permission.

"Cavemen 'R' Us," © 2007 PopMatters Media LLC, reprinted by permission.

"The Movers Are Here," "'Slumdog Millionaire' and the New American Movie" © 2009 The Loop21 LLC, reprinted by permission.

¶ Excerpts of fewer than 150 words were made from the following:

ABOUT THE AUTHOR

*M*ichael E. Ross writes frequently on the arts, race matters, politics and American culture. He was born in Washington, D.C. and has lived in Germany, Chicago, Colorado, northern California, New York City and Washington state. A graduate of the University of Colorado, with a bachelor's degree in journalism, he has been a reporter, critic and editor at various news outlets, including The New York Times, the San Francisco Chronicle, the San Jose Mercury News and msnbc.com; and an adjunct professor at the Columbia University School of Journalism. His reviews, fiction, essays and criticism have appeared in The New York Times, The Times Book Review, Essence, Wired, Emerge, Mother Jones, Entertainment Weekly, the San Jose Mercury News, Konch, Salon, the San Francisco Chronicle, Quarterly Black Review, The Loop21, PopMatters, The Root and other publications. Author of the novel Flagpole Days (2003) and the essay collection Interesting Times (2004), he contributed to the anthologies MultiAmerica (1997), edited by Ishmael Reed; and Soul Food (2000), edited by Eric Copage. He blogs frequently at culchavox.blogspot.com, and lives in Seattle.

www.ingramcontent.com/pod-product-compliance
Lightning Source LLC
Chambersburg PA
CBHW051221050326
40689CB00007B/745